Media & Culture Series

城市与城市文化

Cities and Urban Cultures

〔澳〕德波拉·史蒂文森
Deborah Stevenson

著作权合同登记　图字:01-2005-6607 号

Cities and Urban Cultures
Copyright © Deborah Stevenson, 2003
ISBN: 0 335 20844 4

Original language published by The McGraw-Hill Companies, Inc. All rights reserved. No part of this publication may be reproduced or distributed by any means, or stored in a database or retrieval system, without the prior written permission of the publisher.
Authorized English language reprint edition jointly published by McGraw-Hill Education (Asia) Co. and Peking University Press. This edition is authorized for sale in the People's Republic of China only, excluding Hong Kong, Macao SARs and Taiwan. Unauthorized export of this edition is a violation of the Copyright Act. Violation of this Law is subject to Civil and Criminal Penalties.

本书英文影印版由北京大学出版社和美国麦格劳-希尔教育出版(亚洲)公司合作出版。此版本仅限在中华人民共和国境内(不包括香港、澳门特别行政区及台湾地区)销售。未经许可之出口,视为违反著作权法,将受法律之制裁。

未经出版者预先书面许可,不得以任何方式复制或抄袭本书的任何部分。

本书封面贴有 McGraw-Hill 公司防伪标签,无标签者不得销售。

图书在版编目(CIP)数据

城市与城市文化/(澳)史蒂文森(Stevenson,D.)著. —影印本. —北京:北京大学出版社,2007.6
(媒介与文化书系)
ISBN 978-7-301-12395-9

Ⅰ.城⋯　Ⅱ.史⋯　Ⅲ.城市-文化-研究-英文　Ⅳ.C912.81

中国版本图书馆 CIP 数据核字(2007)第 083337 号

书　　　名:城市与城市文化
著作责任者:〔澳〕Deborah Stevenson　著
责 任 编 辑:周丽锦
标 准 书 号:ISBN 978-7-301-12395-9/G · 2111
出 版 发 行:北京大学出版社
地　　　址:北京市海淀区成府路 205 号　100871
网　　　址:http://www.pup.cn　电子邮箱:ss@pup.pku.edu.cn
电　　　话:邮购部 62752015　发行部 62750672　编辑部 62765016　出版部 62754962
印　刷　者:北京飞达印刷有限责任公司
经　销　者:新华书店
　　　　　　730 毫米×980 毫米　16 开本　11.25 印张　235 千字
　　　　　　2007 年 6 月第 1 版　2008 年 11 月第 2 次印刷
定　　　价:20.00 元

未经许可,不得以任何方式复制或抄袭本书之部分或全部内容。
版权所有,侵权必究
举报电话:010-62752024　电子邮箱:fd@pup.pku.edu.cn

媒介与文化书系编委会

主　编：龚文庠

副主编：李琨

编委会成员（按拼音顺序）：

　　陈韬文　龚文庠　李　彬
　　李金铨　李　琨　潘忠党
　　邱林川　吴　靖　许　静
　　杨伯溆

出版声明

  本套丛书是对国外原版图书的直接影印，由于各个国家政治、经济和文化背景不同，对于原作者所持观点，还请广大读者在阅读过程中加以分析和鉴别。书中的观点均不代表出版社观点。

  我们希望本套丛书的出版能够让读者有更多的机会了解、学习和借鉴国外先进的研究成果。我们欢迎业内专家和学者对我们的工作进行指导，欢迎读者给我们提出宝贵的意见和建议。

北京大学出版社社会科学编辑室
2008 年 11 月

总　　序

　　传播学是 20 世纪诞生于美国和欧洲的一门新兴学科,引进中国只有二三十年。1998 年国家教育部才将它列入正式学科目录。中国经济持续高速发展,带动了媒体产业的大改革、大发展,传播学就成了顺应时代潮流的热门学科。

　　然而由于这是一门年轻的"舶来"学科,按照一些学者的说法,尚处在从"译介"到"本土化"的初级阶段。在教学、研究的过程中,我们常感到对一些术语、概念、理论难以把握,往往是众说纷纭、莫衷一是。有时在激烈争论之后才发觉问题出现在翻译上。例如将"communication"译为"传播",有人就方便地将"传播"误解为"宣传＋广播"。既然新闻是宣传,传播也是宣传,就可以用"新闻传播学"来涵容,甚至取代传播学。有人说,新闻学研究新闻媒体,新闻媒体就是大众媒体,所以新闻学与传播学没有多大区别,因为新闻学研究的就是大众传播。于是出现了将传播学视为新闻学之分支的怪现状。究其原因,一些模糊或错误概念的产生,根子还在对原义的理解。仍以英文"communication"为例,这个词在中文里没有对等词,译为"传播"是很勉强的。"Communication"含有双向的意思,如:"to share or exchange opinions"(*Longman Dictionary of Contemporary English*),而中文的"传播"有明显的从一方传往另一方的倾向。如果直接阅读英文词典或原著中对"communication"的界定和解释,就很容易把握原义,在讨论中也可以避免因译文歧义而白费口舌。

　　以本人阅读译文的亲身体验为例。在读亚里士多德的《修辞学》时我查看了几种英文译本,其中最令我受益的是 1926 年的译本,它采用希腊文原文与英译文逐页对照的版式。其他英译本多将书名译为"*Rhetoric*"(中国人民大学出版社的最新中文译本也译为《修辞学》),而 1926 年英译本却译为"*Aristotle's 'Art' of Rhetoric*"。这是按照希腊文原版本直译出来的,中文对应译文为《亚里士多德的讲演"读本"》。希—英对照译本传达了其他译本中"损失"掉的一个重要的意义:"art"在希腊文中是多义词,此处的"art"意为"handbook"(读本、手册),也就是讲演手册。亚氏写此书的背景是,他不满于当时"智者"(Sophists)们撰写的多种"读本"(art),于是自己写一部读本来正本清源,因而书名为《亚里士多德的讲演"读本"》。如果不是读到 1926 年的希—英对照译本,笔者就无法了解原著书名所含有的如此重要而丰富的信息。

　　我们当然不能一概否定甚至取消翻译,因为没有翻译,不同文化之间就无法交流,艺术家、科学家、思想家的智慧就不可能为全世界共享,人类文明也不可能像今天这样灿烂。然而目前我们的翻译作品,尤其是学术著作的翻译,反映出浮躁、不负责任的态度。

我们需要大力提倡认真、严谨的译风,像严复那样,"一名之立,旬月踟蹰"。对于学术译作,如果有条件,我们还应当尽量提供方便,至少让读者在遇到疑问时能够查对原文。

基于以上理由,北京大学新闻与传播学院与北京大学出版社共同编辑出版了《世界传播学经典教材》书系,分为英文版和中文版两类。英文版为原著影印本,加上我们的导读或部分译文;中文版为全文翻译,而每部英文中译本都有原作可以对照。书系中所有影印本和中译本都将依据我们获得版权的原著最新版本。

《世界传播学经典教材》书系共14部,包括下列类型的著作:(1)传播学中有影响的名著,如曾10次再版的《说服:接受与责任》(*Persuasion: Reception and Responsibility*)。(2)传播学的重要分支学科,如《组织传播:方法与过程》(*Organizational Communication: Approaches and Processes*)、《跨文化交流》(*Communication Between Cultures*)、《媒介法原理》(*Major Principles of Media Law*)、《电子媒介经营管理》(*Management of Electronic Media*)等。(3)综合性研究,如《媒介研究:文本、机构与受众》(*Media Studies: Texts, Institutions and Audiences*)和《影响的互动:新闻、广告、政治与大众媒介》(*The Interplay of Influence: News, Advertising, Politics, and the Mass Media*)等。

我们即将推出的第二个书系是《媒介与文化》,包括《媒介文化中的罪与法》(*Crime and Law in Media Culture*)和《电影与文化的现代性》(*Cinema and Cultural Modernity*)等。

《媒介与文化》书系有三个特点:(1)主要是从文化批评的视角来剖析媒介、文化、社会的三角关系。(2)作者多为英国和澳大利亚学者,作品代表美国以外的学术观点。(3)这是一批研究性著作,但作者多数在大学任教或从事研究,他们既有深厚的学术功底,又善于将文章写得深入浅出,所以这些学术著作也多被推荐为大学相关课程的基础教材或必读参考书。

传播学理论的译介是一项庞大的工程,我们欢迎并希望更多同行、专家和有志者参与其事,互相切磋,共同推进传播学在中国的发展。

书籍的前言中经常流行一句套话:由于时间仓促,水平有限,错误在所难免,请读者见谅。有人批评说,时间仓促就不要急着出书,水平有限就应当等水平够格再发表,怎么反过来要求读者原谅呢? 这话说得真好。我们将以严肃负责的态度,尽力把好本书系的质量关。读者诸君如发现问题,恳请不吝赐教。

龚文庠 于北京大学

2006年2月

目录

最后一班有轨电车（诗二首）（肯尼斯·斯莱瑟）   iv
丛书编者前言   v
致谢   vii

1 城市文化   1
   引言：想象中的城市   1
   本书章节结构   6

2 阴影和烟雾构成的风景：工业城市的出现   12
   引言：乡村与城市   12
   工业化与城市发展   13
   城市主义产生的背景   15
   重新审视乌托邦   19
   自由、孤独与现代大都市   23
   对城市的民族志研究及城市生活的模式   26
   结论：梦想家、规划者和改革家   29
   深入阅读书目   31

3 充满差异的城市：不平等、边缘化与恐惧   32
   引言：从共识到冲突   32
   社会公正与"城市问题"   33
   城市里的性别问题   37
   城市差异的政治   40
   新的分裂的城市？   44

	全球趋势与地区多样性	48
	结论：微观视角与宏观视角	51
	深入阅读书目	53
4	**意义与记忆：解读城市的文本**	**54**
	引言：城市的文化	54
	对城市的体验	55
	文本和语境	58
	走入"迷宫"	62
	行走与日常生活的策略	67
	结论：表面与深层	70
	深入阅读书目	72
5	**城市设计：从城市美化运动到现代主义的"终结"**	**73**
	引言：林荫大道、摩天大楼和杂乱建筑	73
	权力的风景	74
	"街边的芭蕾"	78
	垂直的城市	82
	后现代景观	87
	结论：从空间到场所	91
	深入阅读书目	92
6	**作为风景的城市：文化与城市形象的再塑造**	**93**
	引言：让城市妙趣横生	93
	城市的衰落与全球化	94
	出售城市	98
	"全球同一的城市主义"	100
	文化规划与"有创造力的城市"	104
	规划文化公民权	107
	结论：幻想中的城市	111
	深入阅读书目	112
7	**想象城市：电影、地图与赛博空间**	**113**
	引言：内城	113
	描绘城市景观	115
	关于城市的艺术	119

虚构的城市郊区 123
虚拟社区 128
结论：文字与图像 132
深入阅读书目 133

8 | 结论：超越城市主义？ 134
术语表 141
参考文献 144
索引 159

(本书目录、作者简介及内容提要的编译者为李东航)

CONTENTS

'LAST TRAMS I' AND 'II' BY KENNETH SLESSOR   iv

SERIES EDITOR'S FOREWORD   v

ACKNOWLEDGEMENTS   vii

1 | CITY CULTURES   1
Introduction: a city imagined   1
The structure of *Cities and Urban Cultures*   6

2 | LANDSCAPES OF SHADOW AND SMOG: THE EMERGENCE OF THE INDUSTRIAL CITY   12
Introduction: the rural and the urban   12
Industrialization and urban growth   13
Background to urbanism   15
Reimagining Utopia   19
Freedom, loneliness and the modern metropolis   23
Ethnography and the patterning of urban life   26
Conclusion: dreamers, planners and reformers   29
Further reading   31

3 | CITIES OF DIFFERENCE: INEQUALITY, MARGINALIZATION AND FEAR   32
Introduction: from consensus to conflict   32
Social justice and the 'urban question'   33
Gender in the city   37
The politics of urban difference   40

	New divided city?	44
	Global trends and local diversity	48
	Conclusion: the micro and the macro	51
	Further reading	53
4	**MEANING AND MEMORY: READING THE URBAN TEXT**	**54**
	Introduction: the culture of cities	54
	The city experienced	55
	Texts and contexts	58
	Into the 'labyrinth'	62
	Walking and the tactics of everyday life	67
	Conclusion: surfaces and depths	70
	Further reading	72
5	**DESIGNING THE URBAN: FROM THE CITY BEAUTIFUL TO THE 'END' OF MODERNISM**	**73**
	Introduction: boulevards, skyscrapers and pastiche	73
	Landscapes of power	74
	A 'sidewalk ballet'	78
	The vertical city	82
	Postmodern landscapes	87
	Conclusion: from space to place	91
	Further reading	92
6	**THE CITY AS SPECTACLE: CULTURE AND THE REIMAGING OF CITIES**	**93**
	Introduction: making cities fun	93
	Urban decline and the global	94
	Selling the city	98
	'An urbanism of universal equivalence'	100
	Cultural planning and the 'creative city'	104
	Planning cultural citizenship	107
	Conclusion: fantasy cities	111
	Further reading	112
7	**IMAGINING THE CITY: MOVIES, MAPS AND CYBERSPACE**	**113**
	Introduction: inner cities	113
	Mapping the landscape	115
	The art of the city	119
	The imaginary suburb	123
	Virtual *gemeinschaft*	128
	Conclusion: words and pictures	132
	Further reading	133

8 | CONCLUSION: BEYOND URBANISM? 134

GLOSSARY 141

REFERENCES 144

INDEX 159

Last Trams

I

That street washed with violet
Writes like a tablet
Of living here; that pavement
Is the metal embodiment
Of living here; those terraces
Filled with dumb presences
Lobbed over mattresses,
Lusts and repentances,
Ardours and solaces,
Passions and hatreds
And love in brass bedsteads . . .
Lost now in emptiness
Nothing but nakedness,
Rails like a ribbon
And sickness of carbon
Dying in distances.

II

Then, from the skeletons of trams,
Gazing at lighted rooms, you'll find
The black and Röntgen diagrams
Of window-plants across the blind

That print their knuckleduster sticks,
Their buds of gum, against the light
Like negatives of candlesticks
Whose wicks are lit by fluorite;

And shapes look out, or bodies pass,
Between the darkness and the flare,
Between the curtain and the glass,
Of men and women moving there.

So through the moment's needle-eye,
Like phantoms in the window-chink,
Their faces brush you as they fly,
Fixed in the shutters of a blink;

But whose they are, intent on what,
Who knows? They rattle into void,
Stars of a film without a plot,
Snippings of idiot celluloid.

Kenneth Slessor (1988)

SERIES EDITOR'S FOREWORD

'The subtlest change in New York is something people don't speak much about but that is in everyone's mind. The city, for the first time in its long history, is destructible.' These words were written by E.B. White in his essay 'Here is New York', published in April 1949. He continues: 'A single flight of planes no bigger than a wedge of geese can quickly end this island fantasy, burn the towers, crumble the bridges, turn the underground passages into lethal chambers, cremate the millions. The intimation of mortality is part of New York now: in the sounds of jets overhead, in the black headlines of the latest edition.' Evidently White had spent part of the previous summer reacquainting himself with the city, reminiscing about his life there as a younger person, and thinking about how the atomic bomb had changed much of what he had come to take for granted.

These words assume a new resonance today. Their prophetic quality has been much remarked upon by those who have returned to them after 11 September 2001. Several media commentaries have invoked them to chilling effect, contrasting the images they call to mind with the realities of that day's tragic loss of life. The deliberate crashing of the passenger airliners has ended once and for all the 'island fantasy', to use White's evocative phrase, that such catastrophes do not happen in places like the United States. Central to Deborah Stevenson's *Cities and Urban Cultures* are pressing questions about the cultural imaginings of cities as lived spaces. In the case of New York on that fateful Tuesday, she offers the important insight that the destruction of the World Trade Center towers 'was considerably more than a personal or local tragedy. It was imbued with a range of national, global, cultural, urban and symbolic significances. Indeed, it went to the core of what it meant to be "modern".'

Cities and Urban Cultures is a timely and richly perceptive exploration of a fascinating subject. Deborah Stevenson begins the discussion by highlighting the historical and intellectual foundations of the study of cities and urban culture. An array of approaches to understanding contemporary urban experiences, both lived and imagined, are evaluated with care. Her description of life in the emerging industrial city of the nineteenth century succeeds in pinpointing the formative basis of its current mythology, not least with regard to the tensions between urban and rural cultures. Similarly thrown into sharp relief are the structural factors which underpin the political economy of today's cities, where hierarchical relations of class, gender and ethnicity are of particular significance. She proceeds to show how people's everyday experiences of urban life can be deeply contradictory, being simultaneously sources of exhilaration, fear and apprehension. Under close scrutiny here is the articulation of these experiences in the cultural representation of cities – from the norms and values embedded in urban landscapes, buildings and monuments, to their inscription in art, literature and film, among other types of texts. Such representations, Stevenson argues, are pivotal in shaping the ways in which we know and imagine the city, framing its past but also the prospects for its future renewal. The city of tangible surfaces, she adds, is inseparable from the city of popular culture, anecdote and memory.

The Issues in Cultural and Media Studies series aims to facilitate a diverse range of critical investigations into pressing questions considered to be central to current thinking and research. In light of the remarkable speed at which the conceptual agendas of cultural and media studies are changing, the authors are committed to contributing to what is an ongoing process of re-evaluation and critique. Each of the books is intended to provide a lively, innovative and comprehensive introduction to a specific topical issue from a fresh perspective. The reader is offered a thorough grounding in the most salient debates indicative of the book's subject, as well as important insights into how new modes of enquiry may be established for future explorations. Taken as a whole, then, the series is designed to cover the core components of cultural and media studies courses in an imaginatively distinctive and engaging manner.

Stuart Allan

ACKNOWLEDGEMENTS

My fascination with cities goes back at least to the 1970s and the evocative poetry of Kenneth Slessor, which I read while at school in a small town in rural New South Wales, Australia. When I was growing up, the city was always 'other', a place to visit, a place of endless possibilities, of dreams and fantasies, a place of the future. For me, Slessor's poetry captured the intrigue of this imagined city. It still does. I am extremely grateful to Justin Vaughan at Open University Press, and Stuart Allan, editor of the Issues in Cultural and Media Studies series, for giving me the opportunity to write this book about the city. I thank them, too, for their confidence and enthusiasm throughout.

The list of people who have provided friendship and support over the last year is long and includes colleagues, friends and family. A few must be signalled out for special mention. In particular, the assistance and encouragement I received from my colleagues at the Cultural Industries and Practices Research Centre at the University of Newcastle was invaluable. I am extremely grateful to David Rowe for giving up his Easter to read and comment on the draft manuscript. As ever his comments were thoughtful and encouraging. I also thank (for various reasons and in alphabetical order), Lee Artis, Jo Hanley, Gaynor Heading, Ellen Jordan, Terry Lovat, Shelagh Lummis, Kevin Markwell, Colin Mercer, Toby Miller, Georgia Paton and Peter Wejbora. My thanks go, too, to Donna Russo for her work on the bibliography, Richard Lever for compiling the index, and Christine Firth at Open University Press for her careful editing. This book was written while I was on Outside Study Leave from the University and much of the research was supported by a grant from its Research Management Committee. I thank the University for providing this assistance. I also thank Harper-Collins Publishers for granting me permission to reproduce Slessor's poem *Last Trams*.

Finally, I acknowledge the unwavering support of my family. I especially thank my parents Nancy and Bob, my siblings and their partners, and my sons Rohan and Cameron. Maybe one day they will understand the curious madness that compels me to sit at a computer all day long.

Deborah Stevenson

1 | CITY CULTURES

Seeing Manhattan from the 110th floor of the World Trade Center. Beneath the haze stirred up by the winds, the urban island, a sea in the middle of the sea, lifts up the skyscrapers over Wall Street, sinks down at Greenwich, then rises again to the crest of Midtown, quietly passes over Central Park and finally undulates off into the distance beyond Harlem. A wave of verticals. Its agitation is momentarily arrested by vision. A gigantic mass is immobilized before our eyes.

(de Certeau 1988: 91)

Who built it? Anon, that's who. Nobody built the New York skyline. Nobody by the thousands.

(Helene Hanff, *Apple of My Eye*, 1984: 35)

Introduction: a city imagined

On 11 September 2001, graphic images of the destruction of two of the world's tallest buildings – the north and south towers of the World Trade Center in New York City – unfolded on television sets around the world. The enormity and complexity of this tragedy, while manifest, were, nevertheless, compounded by the fact that most people witnessed it as a media spectacle. Thus, it was within established media interpretative frames (including the plots and images of countless Hollywood movies) that their initial reactions were formed. But then in many respects New York is a media construction – the skyline of Manhattan is instantly and globally familiar even though the majority of the world's population has never been there and will never go. Indeed, Manhattan emerged as a landscape of towers at the same time as film technology and the movie industry were developing in the United States. It was largely as a result of this coincidence that the Manhattan backdrop became one of the most significant and defining images not just of architectural **modernism**, but also of the values and achievements of the twentieth century. Manhattan equals New York and New York is perhaps the world's greatest city. It was within this set of imaginings that in the early 1970s the 'twin towers' assumed their place both as potent symbols of late modernity and testimonies to the global economic power of New York and the United States. Rising 411 metres above ground level, the towers dominated the city's skyline and provided some of the most sought-after postcard views and establishing shots of New York. The destruction of the towers, therefore, was considerably more than a personal or local tragedy. It was imbued with a range of national, global, cultural, urban and symbolic significances. Indeed, it went to the core of what it meant to be 'modern'.

Those who are old enough can remember when the twin towers passed the Empire State building (also in New York City) as the world's tallest buildings. Even in the 1970s, such 'facts' were still regarded as important markers of 'man's' ability to 'conquer' nature and nowhere was evidence of this supremacy more visible and irrefutable than in the great cities of the world and their architectural and engineering triumphs – in particular, their bridges and skyscrapers. The metropolis was the antithesis of nature and the symbol of its defeat. In order to appreciate the depth of this sentiment and the cultural significances that the New York skyline came to assume, it is necessary first to understand the social and economic contexts within which its early skyscrapers were constructed and the skyscraper building frenzy that gripped New York between the First World War and the great depression of the 1930s.

Robert Hughes (1997: 404ff) suggests in his book *American Visions* about the history of American art that it was during this period that the New York skyscraper emerged both as a cultural icon and artform. He argues that from 1926 in particular, the building boom in New York was dominated by a 'race to the sky' – a race ultimately won by the Empire State building on its completion in 1930. Skyscrapers were seen as heroic not only because of their breathtaking height. The entire process of building them was regarded with fascination and awe, while speculation abounded regarding how high these buildings might eventually go. In addition, key milestones reached during the construction of many skyscrapers became the focus of public celebrations which often featured such attractions as 'girl dancers [being] hired to perform on . . . bare girders, hundreds of feet up in the dizzying air, for the avid media' (Hughes 1997: 405). Needless to say, it was opportunistic local politicians and the commercial enterprises responsible for building the towers who staged such promotional stunts. Until the early 1930s, the construction, completion, official opening and final form of each new skyscraper were events – central elements of the spectacle of

New York City. What developed, according to Hughes (1997: 405) was a 'romance' between New Yorkers, their skyscrapers and their city. Although all Americans 'were dazed by the force of their new imagery' (Hughes 1997: 405) to such an extent that, Hughes goes on to assert:

> No American painting or sculpture . . . was able to accumulate, at least in the ordinary public's eyes, the kind of cultural power that the skyscrapers had. Nor indeed, could it have done so – most Americans didn't care about art, especially modern art . . . Big buildings were always before you; mere paintings were not.
> (Hughes 1997: 419)

And courtesy of film, art and photography the 'big buildings' were also 'before' the rest of the world, and it too was mesmerized. The landscape of New York looked vastly different from those of European cities:

> In Paris, only monumental buildings devoted to sacred or governmental institutions were allowed to exceed the height limit; in London, only purely ornamental towers could rise above the roofscape. In New York, however, the soaring commercial tower had already become the salient ornament of the city-scape and the inalienable right of realtors.
> (Stern et al. 1987: 508)

One visits New York first and foremost to see and experience its landscape. In the passage quoted at the start of this chapter cultural theorist Michel de Certeau describes the elation he felt at seeing (from the observation deck of the World Trade Center) the city of New York laid out and 'immobilized' before him. Similarly, Philip Kasinitz (1995), echoing de Certeau, celebrates the world's 'great' cities (and the significant structures we gaze on them from) in the following way:

> The exhilaration we feel when we view a great city from one of those rare vantage points where one can 'take it all in' – Paris from the Eiffel Tower, Lower Manhattan from the Brooklyn Bridge – is the thrill of seeing in one moment the enormity of . . . human work.
> (Kasinitz 1995: 3)

Despite the 'exhilaration' that might be felt when viewing a 'great' city from the top of a 'great' built structure, our feelings towards the city and its skyscrapers are also deeply contradictory, being simultaneously sources of exhilaration, fear and apprehension – 'cities are great as well as fearsome' (Zukin 1997: vii). They also 'represent the basest instincts of human society' (Zukin 1997: 1). We are aware of this ambiguity even as we celebrate them – we are both attracted and repelled. Viewing a city from a great height is a way of taming it. However, the observer is also rendered vulnerable by the experience. In order to journey to the top of a skyscraper one must trust in the knowledge and skills of countless faceless 'experts' – builders, engineers, labourers, maintenance workers and architects. This trusting is, as Anthony Giddens (1990) explains, a core feature of late modernity. The helplessness felt when watching the wounded towers of the World Trade Center crumble onto the streets of lower Manhattan revealed the ambivalence with which we regard the skyscraper and the fragility of our trust in the expert knowledge systems on which we rely.

In art, too, the 'darker side' of our relationship with the city and the skyscraper has also been explored/exposed. The city's looming shapes frequently have been compelling symbols of danger and the unknown even as they speak of progress, modernity and the future. For instance, the plays of light and shade featured in Hugh Ferriss's (1929, 1953) architectural renderings of New York in the 1920s create brooding landscapes that capture the conflicting emotions stimulated by cityspace and the skyscraper. In many of Ferriss's drawings the tops of skyscrapers are shrouded in shadow while their bottoms – those edges encountered on the street – are luminous. The result evokes notions of the known and the unknown. What is known is what can be seen at street level, while what is unknown looms in the twilight above. In representing the ideas and urban imaginings of those architects who were at the forefront of reshaping the Manhattan skyline, Ferriss's work was as much about the city as its future was being imagined during this period of skyscraper-building as it was about the city at the time. His representations were of an urban and architectural utopia that was inspired by the present and made possible by contemporary technology but which was yet to take shape.

Many key themes in the study, interpretation and experience of cities coalesced around the events of 11 September and, thus, this moment points to a host of issues that underpin the concerns of this book – in particular, the nature of (post)modern **urbanism**, the ambivalent relationship that exists between people and their cities, and the various ways in which this relationship is shaped through experience, imagination and power. The academic study of the city is an endeavour that can be traced back to the nineteenth century and the work of the 'founding fathers' of sociology, including Karl Marx, Friedrich Engels and Max Weber. Sociology was concerned with industrialization and modernity – and as cities were the places where the consequences and contradictions of both were most evident and most profoundly experienced, they became the almost accidental objects of their attention. During the twentieth century, however, a specific urban subdiscipline developed within sociology and continues to be a major field of enquiry. The concerns of urban sociologists have been varied, though, not just in terms of their particular urban object of study but also methodologically and theoretically. Research has focused variously on such issues as defining and quantifying urbanism, exploring the relationship between the city and society, and investigating the role of the state in framing urban development. Thus urban sociology has connected with and informed the work of many within other disciplines, including human geography, urban planning, economics and urban history.

Since the 1970s, the city has become a source of fascination for those working outside established urban studies traditions as an increasing number of cultural theorists started to focus on the city as it is lived rather than on its structures and patterns. At the same time sociology and its established methods and interpretative frames were (paradoxically) both being challenged and augmented by the insights of cultural theory. The result of these differing influences has been the opening of a number of potentially fruitful pathways for urban research and analysis, as Rosalyn Deutsche (1996) explains:

> Now there is growing interest in interdisciplinary mergers of critical urban and cultural discourses. On the one hand, aesthetic practitioners – architects, urban planners, artists – have used the contributions of urban theory to examine how their work functions in urban social contexts. Urban scholars, on the other hand, have turned to cultural theory to study the city as a signifying object. Both groups hope that encounters between the two fields – themselves composed of several disciplines – will expand our ability to understand and intervene in what urban theorists call the politics of place.
>
> (Deutsche 1996: 206)

Too often, though, dialogue between the cultural studies and more sociological approaches to the urban has not been easy and attempts to bring the considerable insights of each together have often been strained (Morris 1992; Deutsche 1996). Thus, as academics seek to understand the fabric of the urban environment and the cultures of everyday urban life, there are those more sociologically informed analyses which continue to emphasize the role of the city in fostering social and cultural inequality, arguing that the urban landscape is implicated in structural oppression and marginalization, in particular those based on class, gender, race and ethnicity. While, on the other hand, many cultural studies approaches to urbanism regard the city as a significant site of empowerment and resistance, with academics working within this broad tradition often seeking to celebrate lived urban rhythms, anonymity and difference.

The challenge of exploring both approaches and making some connections is taken up in this book. *Cities and Urban Cultures* seeks to make sense of a range of culturally informed theories of the city by considering them alongside broader (established) urban studies traditions. A central underpinning assumption of the book is that these seemingly contradictory approaches can, in shifting combinations, provide rich complementary conceptual and empirical insights into the complex cultures of urbanism. From this intellectual foundation *Cities and Urban Cultures* also explores some of the key themes in the study and the development of the city since the industrial revolution.

The structure of *Cities and Urban Cultures*

Cities and Urban Cultures considers important issues in the academic analysis of cities and the urban condition from their nineteenth-century origins through to the representation of urban life and cityscapes in popular contemporary texts, such as film and real estate advertisements. It also considers a number of major city-building trends and discourses that have shaped urban landscape. Along the way, the book introduces readers to a range of significant themes within urban studies, including the city as spectacle, the postmodern city, and the significance of difference, inequality and resistance to the urban experience and its analysis. It also explores such practices as urban redevelopment, the vertical city and the role of the arts in city reimaging. Although each chapter is self-contained and can be read in isolation, significant links are made throughout between issues and debates that are addressed in different chapters. This endeavour commenced in this introductory chapter in pointing to the historical and intellectual foundations of the study of cities and urban culture and the implicit tensions between different approaches. These issues are developed in subsequent chapters. This chapter has also highlighted the central role which the city of New York has played in framing the contemporary urban experience both as it is lived and imagined.

Chapter 2 attempts to describe and explain life in the emerging industrial city of the nineteenth century. In particular, the chapter introduces ideas and concepts, such as **gemeinschaft** and **gesellschaft** which, I argue, implicitly underpin the study of urbanism whether from cultural or more sociologically informed perspectives. The emergence of industrial capitalism spurred the growth of the modern city and with this growth came an academic concern with the nature and experience of urban life. Initially, cities were regarded as unpleasant and unnatural places, which were either to be destroyed or rebuilt in the image of the country, and in this, early theorizing directly compared the quality of life in the city to that of the (imagined) country. City life (as *gesellschaft*) was regarded as superficial and impersonal while life in the country (*gemeinschaft*) was celebrated as fostering positive and enduring relationships between close friends and kinship groups. Significantly, this work and the blueprints for utopian urban societies they fostered regarded both urban and rural cultures as the direct result of environmental features, such as size, density and heterogeneity and not of structural or cultural factors. One early sociologist who was concerned with the lived dimensions of the urban and who also (intriguingly) regarded city life positively was the German Georg Simmel. As the chapter details, Simmel believed that the modern city, although a site of rationality and calculation, was also a site of liberation that freed people from the constraints and obligations that are a feature of communal country life. The chapter goes on to investigate the influential work of urban sociologists associated with the University of Chicago who both undertook the first detailed ethnographic studies of urban life and pioneered quantitative methods of urban research. The influence of the **Chicago School** pervaded urban sociology for most of the twentieth century.

Chapter 3 considers key academic approaches to the analysis of the relationship between the city and socially marginal groups through a discussion of the theoretical and empirical insights from various perspectives, including Marxist **political economy** and Feminism. It was theorists working within structural traditions informed by the sociological theories of Marx and Weber, who were the first to challenge the dominant Chicago School-inspired approaches to urbanism. Indeed, Marxist urban political economy was regarded in the late 1970s and early 1980s as the 'new urban sociology' (Zukin 1980). Marxists saw the city as being central to the reproduction of capitalism and class inequality and thus subjected the idea of urbanism that lay at the core of traditional urban studies to sustained critical scrutiny. According to the Marxist critique, key features of the urban experience could not be seen as outcomes of environmental factors (such as the size of the city) but were the cultural expressions of the capitalist mode of production.

As the role played by the city in the structuring of oppression was being acknowledged, there were those working from more culturally informed perspectives who, following Simmel and others, argued that the city and attachment to its places can provide opportunities for the tolerance of difference that are not possible elsewhere. These arguments came from theorists who wanted to move away from a rigid concern with social structures and the forces of oppression and explore the importance of identity, difference and the 'micro' to the urban experience. The chapter then goes on to examine the trend towards increased urban surveillance and the social and spatial implications of a fear of crime and of difference. The ways in which these factors are being inscribed in the contemporary urban landscape are examined in the chapter. Far from facilitating diversity and encounters with strangers, there is evidence to suggest that a new divided city is emerging where the middle and upper classes actively seek to control their environments and to insulate themselves from the urban 'other'.

The foundations of cultural studies approaches to the city are further explored in Chapter 4. In particular, the chapter introduces and evaluates ideas about the relationship between the city, urbanism and the construction and negotiation of meaning. The insights of Roland Barthes and his use of semiotics have been pivotal in this respect. When conceptualized as a text, it is possible to uncover the range of cultural values embedded in urban landscapes, buildings and monuments as well as in the many ways in which the city is represented. The chapter moves on to discuss the rich legacy of Walter Benjamin which with Barthes's work underpins many cultural studies approaches to the study of the city and urban cultures. In particular, the chapter considers Benjamin's writings on nineteenth-century Paris which explored how the work of artists, and the experiences and strollings of the urban *flâneur* provided an almost forensic way of knowing the city. With reference to the work of both Elizabeth Wilson and Janet Wolff, the chapter also situates women in the discursive and theoretical spaces of the urban *flâneur* and the negotiation of place. The third major theoretical framework considered in the chapter is that of Michel de Certeau, who provides a way of analysing how, by using cityspace in a myriad of idiosyncratic ways, people subvert the meanings and values of the powerful, including resisting totalizing notions of the urban. Through the act of walking, cartographic space is transformed into a place of meaning and memory. Thus, within a single urban landscape will exist multiple places defined through use, imagination and a range of cultural practices.

In Chapter 5 the relationship between urban culture – as theory and lived experience – and the aesthetic practices of design and architecture is investigated. The chapter begins with a consideration of the influential **City Beautiful** movement, which was inspired by the reconstruction of Paris in the nineteenth century and reached maturity in the twentieth century in the design and redevelopment of numerous city centres worldwide. The chapter suggests that the wide boulevards and monumental urban landscapes that were a central feature of the City Beautiful were the direct result of political, military, gender and economic power, and the spaces frequently were used for overt displays of such power. At the same time, these places can also facilitate public engagement and association, a role which connects with that of the urban marketplace. As community gathering places and sites of commercial exchange, the marketplace has long played a significant role in framing and facilitating urban culture and politics.

Also discussed in the chapter is the immense influence on city form and urban life that modernist architecture has had, including such central notions as 'less is more', 'form should follow function' and houses are 'machines for living'. These principles underpinned a range of interventions in the urban landscape from the construction of tower residential developments for the poor and the building of networks of roadways, through to the wholesale clearance of urban areas deemed to be slums and the destruction of neighbourhood communities. The chapter suggests that within these late modernist trends germinated the seeds of the development of architectural **postmodernism**. Postmodernism as a reaction to the totalizing logic of modernism emphasized the 'local' and the contingent. In architecture and urban design, postmodernism has led to attempts to create built environments that are 'relevant' to local communities and their histories. The result, however, is frequently little more than a pastiche of ornamentation and form – strangely superficial and serial although justified in terms of the idiosyncrasies of place. Nowhere has this 'sameness' been more evident than in the redevelopment of abandoned waterfront sites into the spectacular landscapes of middle-class leisure and consumption. It is these and other related redevelopment trends which are the focus of Chapter 6.

Chapter 6 investigates the city reimaging and urban renewal projects that, since the 1980s, have been undertaken in cities around the world in an effort to compete with other cities on the basis of amenity, lifestyle and spectacle. The chapter argues that it is possible to see these city reimaging approaches as comprising something of a spectrum. At one end being those developments that emphasize pleasure and entertainment through the integrative use of thematic architecture and 'event' shopping experiences. At the other end are more low-key **cultural planning** approaches with their focus on the development of local cultural identity and the idea of the creative city. In this context, the **festival marketplace** approach involves the constructions of spectacular themed urban precincts usually on abandoned waterfront or industrial land. These redevelopments are intended to be centres of recreation and tourism and the impetus for local economic rejuvenation. High-profile festival marketplaces include South Street Seaport in New York and Harbor Place in Baltimore, Maryland. Elsewhere, such as in the Scottish city of Glasgow, different city reimaging strategies have been adopted. These more low-key approaches emphasize the potential of the creative arts and cultural industries to animate the city and express local identity, history and difference, as well as attract tourists. The advocates of cultural planning also argue that such strategies should foster the development of inner city public gathering spaces, such as parks, cultural precincts and town squares. They regard these places as being fundamental to the urban public sphere and to a locally based democratic citizenship. However, as the chapter argues, not only are many such pronouncements deeply nostalgic but frequently they are grounded in an idealized conception of the **public realm** and romantic notions of a lost rural past.

Representations are pivotal in shaping the ways in which we know and imagine the city. We encounter images of cities in all forms of popular culture, including films, magazines and newspapers, as well as in literature, art and in maps. In addition, city life is frequently both celebrated and berated in the lyrics of popular songs from Gershwin to Rap. Such concerns are the focus of Chapter 7. As argued, popular culture provides people who have never been to many of the 'great' cities of the world, like New York, with strong impressions of their physical and symbolic form. Cultural texts define the symbolic parameters of what is meant by the term 'urban' and frame imagined urbanism. As is argued in the chapter, frequently this defining has involved denoting a powerful anti-urbanism in opposition to a celebration of the rural. The chapter also considers the ways in which the suburbs and suburban life are imagined and represented in this context as liminal spaces that are neither rural nor urban and yet are constructed in text in terms of both discourses.

The chapter goes on to consider claims that new forms of 'community' and collective identity are being forged in cyberspace often as a specific reaction to contemporary urban life. The argument is that these emerging forms of 'virtual *gemeinschaft*' are rearranging and transforming 'maps of meaning' and changing the fundamental nature of urbanism. It is suggested in the chapter that many of these claims disregard the social, political and urban contexts within which new technologies are developing and fail to engage with the theories and findings of traditional urban studies. In essence, we are witnessing a re-emergence of the utopian, but fundamentally anti-urban, views of the early urban theorists. The concluding chapter brings together the themes of the book and highlights significant trends in the way the city and urban culture have been analysed and represented. The chapter closes with a discussion of the centrality of the city to contemporary life and its cultural expression and speculates on what moving 'beyond urbanism' might mean.

It is important to note that, as with any book of this sort, the grouping of topics into particular chapters is somewhat arbitrary – the book and its ideas could easily have been organized differently. No matter which divisions were adopted, however, there would inevitably be problems of flow and continuity; for instance, the discussion of architecture and design undertaken in Chapter 5 is clearly important to the issues considered in Chapter 4; likewise the discussion in Chapter 7 about representation and the city needs to be read alongside the discussion of the city as text and urban semiotics undertaken in Chapter 4. To help deal with this complexity and to highlight conceptual and analytical paths that could have been taken I have directed readers to relevant chapters and flagged various links throughout. In addition, the book, like much academic thinking about cities and urban cultures, has a western bias which, while a shortcoming, is unavoidable. The combination of very different demographic, social and political histories along with a breathtaking diversity of cultures (urban and otherwise), and the limitations of urban cultural theory, make it extremely difficult to consider the non-western city and life therein in any depth in a book such as this. Thus 'the city' that is the object of this book is the city of the 'west', the city of privilege.

2 LANDSCAPES OF SHADOW AND SMOG: THE EMERGENCE OF THE INDUSTRIAL CITY

> The bourgeoisie has subjected the country to the rule of the towns. It has created enormous cities, has greatly increased the urban population as compared with the rural, and has thus rescued a considerable part of the population from the idiocy of rural life.
>
> (Marx and Engels [1848] 1972: 84)

Introduction: the rural and the urban

There is an Aesop's fable about a town mouse and his friend, a field mouse, in which the security, predictability and banality of life in the country is contrasted favourably with the chaos, diversity and danger that is supposedly the lived experience of the urban dweller. Variations of this tale have been told and retold for generations, and the fable has informed the plots of numerous contemporary novels, television programmes and films. Although having its roots in antiquity, the story of the town mouse and the country mouse developed a compelling resonance with the coming of industrialism and the rapid growth of the complex modern city that industrialization prompted. Indeed, ideas grounded in the comparison between the city and the country have become central to the mythologies of modernity, and the concerns of Aesop have troubled many, including sociologists, moralists, philosophers, novelists and artists since the industrial revolution. Of particular import has been the question of whether the quality of life in the city is intrinsically different from that experienced in the country and, if there is a difference, to discern whether or not one is fundamentally better than the other, and why. These concerns frame the discussion of this chapter, which begins by exploring academic and popular descriptions and explanations of the emerging cities of industrial modernity.

The chapter argues that, initially, the cities of industrialism were derided as dirty and alienating places, which were to be endured and/or rehabilitated. Moreover, while the culture of urbanism was seen as anonymous, unfriendly and superficial, the culture of the country was regarded as involving positive, intimate and enduring relationships between family members and close friends. There were some early urban analysts, however, who argued that the anonymity of the modern city was a source not only of loneliness but also of freedom because the city liberated its residents from the constraints of traditional community obligation that are integral to life in rural settlements. This view of urban culture is explored before the chapter goes on to discuss the link between the emerging academic interest in modern urbanism and the application of ethnographic methods to the study of urban life and, in particular, of urban subcultures. This research initially was centred on the University of Chicago. Throughout, the chapter introduces influential ideas, methods and concepts which continue to underpin (often implicitly) the academic study of urbanism, and which also contribute to the potency of the urban in popular discourse and imagination.

Industrialization and urban growth

The industrial (and associated agricultural) revolution which occurred in Europe during the eighteenth and nineteenth centuries not only changed the nature of work, but also dramatically transformed the organization of society, gender and kinship relationships, and the dominant form of human settlement. In particular, the composition of, and link between, the rural and the urban was completely overturned as a result of the large-scale migration of potential industrial workers from the countryside to the cities where the factories of the emerging manufacturing bourgeoisie were located. The scope of the demographic change that occurred at this time is underlined by research showing that at the beginning of the nineteenth century only 15 British towns had populations of more than 20,000 but by its end there were 185 (Kasinitz 1995: 8). Indeed, it has been estimated that in 1800 only 2.2 per cent of the population of Europe lived in cities of more than 100,000 – today that geopolitical space is predominantly urbanized and highly industrialized.

Kingsley Davis ([1965] 2000) makes an interesting analytical distinction between the process of **urbanization** and that of urban growth, which is worth considering in this context. It is Davis's contention that 'the term "urbanization" refers to . . . the proportion of the total population concentrated in urban settlements, or else to a rise in this proportion . . . cities can grow without any urbanization, provided that the rural population grows at an equal or greater rate' (Davis [1965] 2000: 5). In other words, it is possible (even quite common) to have urban growth without urbanization – the issue is the balance between the two and the proportion of the population living in the country as compared with that living in the city at the time of urban expansion. Following Davis, the demographic changes that occurred with industrialism, first in Britain and then more generally in Europe, clearly involved urbanization on a scale never before experienced. This urbanization led to a dramatic reversal of the 'rough balance' (Mumford 1961: 446) that had existed relatively unchallenged between the proportion of the population living in the towns and the proportion residing in the countryside.

With the industrial revolution, predominantly agrarian societies (comprised of a rural peasantry living in small settlements) were transformed into societies that were overwhelmingly urban, and urbanism became the core residential experience and way of life of the majority of the population. This urbanism involved the advent of new forms of sociality, changed power relations and, in the view of some commentators, the development of a distinctly urban sensibility (Simmel [1903] 1995; Wirth [1938] 1995). Anthony Giddens (1990: 6) makes the following point about the emerging cities of industrialism: 'Modern urban settlements often incorporate the sites of traditional cities, and may look as though they have merely grown out of them. In fact, modern urbanism is ordered according to quite different principles from those which set off the pre-modern city from the countryside in prior periods.'

In the developing nations of Asia, Africa and South America, urban centres also dominate the landscape and frame the ways of life of a high proportion of the population. This is the case even though industrialism and urban expansion occurred much later in these regions than it did in 'the west'. In fact, Davis ([1965] 2000) contends that the high global rates of urbanization evident since the 1940s largely reflect the timing of industrialization and urban change in these areas. Unlike nineteenth-century Europe, however, the rapid expansion of cities in the so-called 'Third World' has not solely been the outcome of the mass migration of rural dwellers to the cities in search of industrial work. Although this movement has been significant it has occurred alongside exponential natural population increases within the cities themselves which suggests, first, that many of these cities would have grown substantially without any sizeable rural migration (Davis [1965] 2000). And, second, that in spite of the phenomenal urban growth that these nations have experienced, they may not necessarily have 'urbanized' in Davis's terms because the natural population increases in rural areas similarly have been considerable. In spite of different histories and urban development trajectories, however, the reality is that today most of the nations of the world are urbanized and in some industrialized countries, such as Australia, Britain and the United States, more than 50 per cent of the population live in cities of 100,000 or more. Indeed, in Australia, the proportion of the population who are urban dwellers is approximately 85 per cent.

The technological basis for the industrial revolution in Europe was the application of steam power to machinery first for the purposes of manufacturing and production and, then for transportation. Along with underground mining for the coal that was required to fuel the steam engines and factories, these factors and the need for a high concentration of industrial workers to live in close proximity to their places of work, provided the impetus for the rapid, unprecedented urbanization that was experienced at this time and which led to the development of the modern city (Mumford 1961: 446). The significant and, indeed, continuing link between industrialization, economic growth and urbanization has been noted by numerous urban scholars (such as Mumford 1961; Davis [1965] 2000).

The subsequent development of new modes of transport (in particular, the steam train) was also a major stimulus for urbanization. For instance, although constructed initially for trade and the transportation of raw materials and finished products between cities, the building of railways also made it possible for people to move relatively easily across large distances (Mumford 1961; Frost 1991). The result was the emergence of dormitory suburbs along transport corridors that radiated from the city centre and the industrial areas. The amenity and environmental quality of these suburbs varied sharply between the spaces of the rich and those of the poor. Likewise, divisions emerged between life in the inner city and in the suburbs. Rapidly changing urban environments, the quality of life found in many industrial cities, the potential for new forms of transport to shape the urban landscape, and the development of residential suburbs all, in different ways, contributed to the imagining of new – planned – urban futures or utopias, such as the **Garden City** (discussed on pp. 22–3). What is clear, however, is that neither urbanization nor urbanism can be regarded simply as matters of demography.

Background to urbanism

With industrialism, archaic towns of nineteenth-century Europe were forcibly expanded – villages became towns, towns became cities, and ultimately, many cities grew into metropolises. None of these places, however, was equipped to cope with this dramatic growth. The result was haphazard urban development often involving the speedy erection of cramped makeshift dwellings along squalid narrow alleyways where industrial workers lived with their families in the shadows of the factories. At the same time, many properties that had formerly housed single families became 'rent barracks' where an entire working-class family lived in a single room – often with their livestock (Mumford 1961: 460). Friedrich Engels in his sweeping documentary account of the 'great' nineteenth-century industrial 'town' of Manchester draws the following conclusion about living conditions in its working-class districts:

> In a word, we must confess that in the working-men's dwellings of Manchester, no cleanliness, no convenience, and consequently no comfortable family life is possible; that in such dwellings only a physically degenerate race robbed of all humanity, degraded, reduced morally and physically to bestiality, could feel comfortable and at home.
>
> (Engels [1892] 1969: 96)

While the renowned urban historian Lewis Mumford (1961) has the following to say about the life in the cities of industrialism:

> the change from organised urban handicraft to large scale factory production transformed the industrial towns into dark hives, busily puffing, clanking, screeching, smoking for twelve to fourteen hours a day, sometimes going around the clock . . . The new industrial city had many lessons to teach; but for the urbanist its chief lesson was in what to avoid.
>
> (Mumford 1961: 446)

Following Davison (1983), James Donald (1992) argues that among the first to document the bleak conditions of nineteenth-century urban life were researchers concerned with the emerging problem of urban governance. These researchers regarded the city as an organic or natural system, which, like a living organism, functioned as an interrelated unit according to objective knowable rules. In particular, they adopted the metaphor of the human body and the explanatory frames of illness and medical diagnosis to describe and explain the problems of the city. They argued that in order to heal the sick urban body, the source of the disease needed to be identified and removed. To this end, it was necessary first to undertake a statistical rendering of the city-body to discover and understand the universal rules that governed its functions. They went on to call for greater surveillance and policing of the urban environment. In these pronouncements, claims Donald (1992), lay the genesis of the social welfare argument that the well-being of the poor was essential to the healthy functioning of the city. These arguments provided the foundations for the public health and sanitation movements which gained considerable momentum and moral force during the nineteenth century and early twentieth century and informed a number of prescriptions for urban reform.

Much has been written both at the time and since about the wretched quality of life that the working class endured in the burgeoning industrial cities. Most notably, in fiction, the works of Charles Dickens (such as *Oliver Twist*, *Nicholas Nickleby* and *Hard Times*) graphically describe the squalid conditions that existed in many British cities; for instance, his rendering of the city of 'Coketown' in the novel *Hard Times* remains compelling. Similarly, William Blake's (1970) poetic description of an urban landscape of 'dark satanic mills' is now firmly fixed in contemporary imaginations. These, along with such works as Gustave Doré's poignant images of London's East End slums (in Blanchard 1872), provided the middle class with a view of living conditions in parts of the city that few had been forced to confront before. The subsequent emergence of popular journalism along with the widespread use of photography from the nineteenth century onward contributed, and gave undeniable visual expression, to critical urban commentary (Stout 2000). Frederic Stout (2000: 146) explains the creative relationship between the visual artist and the city as follows: 'The great themes of the city – its kinetic activity, its juxtapositions and ironies, its massive forms and tiny details – provided the artist with a subject matter that could not be ignored and pioneered modes of visual perception and communication that were to fundamentally transform the nature of social life.' Despite the descriptions, images and recommendations of urban reformers, and the contributions that came also from literature and popular journalism, it was some time before national governments passed legislation intended to regulate the living and, indeed, the working conditions of the urban poor. It was even longer before formal town planning became a concern of governments (Hall 1989), and several generations before these legislative changes and improvements in public hygiene and sanitation enhanced environmental conditions in areas other than those inhabited by the wealthy and the middle class (Mumford 1961: 462).

As the squalid neighbourhoods of workers' housing and the places of their leisure were burgeoning, many of the rich and, more significantly, the up-and-coming middle class or bourgeoisie (whose wealth was built on trade, manufacturing and finance) started to retreat from the city to the homes they were building in the emerging suburbs and the countryside (Girouard 1986, 1990). In the following passage Graeme Davison (1994) explains the impetus for suburbanization in England at this time:

In its original British context, the suburb was . . . a zone of exclusively bourgeois residence. In the pre-industrial city the elite and the plebs had lived in much the same neighbourhoods, the elite in the grand houses facing the squares and parks; the plebs in the cramped lanes and back-streets. From the early nineteenth century, however, the middle class began to show a growing fear and fastidiousness towards their working-class neighbours. They sought to insulate themselves, and especially their wives and children, from the uncouth and possibly dangerous life of the streets. Thus began the slow process of class segregation that eventually brought about the distinctive concentric-zones of middle-class and working-class residence that we associate with the late nineteenth century [English] city.

(Davison 1994: 101)

Differences and inequalities of class were inscribed on the landscapes of the cities of industrial capitalism from the early days of their development. This segregation does not mean, however, that middle- and upper-class areas necessarily exhibited high standards of cleanliness. Mumford (1961: 462) contends that the physical conditions of entire nineteenth-century and early-twentieth-century cities and not only the working-class areas were degenerate. He argues that in the city-building frenzy that followed industrialism, there was a noticeable decline in collective standards of sanitation and an abandonment of many hygienic practices that had been widespread prior to industrialization. For instance, he notes that in many English towns in the sixteenth century it was an offence to throw rubbish onto the streets; however, in the industrial cities of the nineteenth century this was a common practice. He goes on to describe how city-wide many of these practices and substandard conditions were, saying that upper-class residential areas were frequently little more than 'intolerable super-slums' (Mumford 1961: 464–5), and that overcrowding was as common in the emerging middle-class areas as it was in those inhabited by the poor. Mumford, though, is not suggesting that all areas were as bad as each other. Rather, what he is saying is that differences between areas were a matter of degrees not absolutes. It is important to marry the conditions he describes with the considerable differences in streetscapes and urban environments found in the different zones of the city. No matter what hygienic conditions prevailed (and mindful of the dreadful living conditions of domestic workers 'below stairs'), the conditions in the affluent areas cannot meaningfully be compared directly to those found in working-class areas. To start with, even if some areas were crowded by today's standards, the affluent had larger housing, a greater number of parks and gardens, wider streets and, of course, access to carriages, which meant they did not have to walk through the dirty streets if they chose not to. The towns and cities of the nineteenth century may have had generally low standards of public and private hygiene but it was most certainly easier to be a rich inhabitant of these cities than a poor one.

Industrialization revolutionized the way people live. It also prompted a revolution in the way people think about society. Significantly, the academic discipline of sociology developed in tandem with urbanization and industrialization. Sociology is at its core a discipline of urban society and, thus, cities and the variety of experiences associated with living in them have been objects of research and debate since the nineteenth century. And it was in part the conditions endured by the urban industrial working class that prompted early attempts to explain industrial society. Albeit often indirectly, the themes of urbanization and the effects and consequences of urban living are evident in many of the works by the intellectual founders of sociology, including Karl Marx, Max Weber and Emile Durkheim. And, as mentioned previously, at least one of the most influential explanations of life in the industrial cities of the nineteenth century came from Marx's friend and collaborator Friedrich Engels. Engels's works *The Condition of the Working Class in England* ([1892] 1969) and *The Housing Question* ([1872] 1942) are powerful, relentless descriptions and analyses of life in the urban slums. In many respects, the general theories of the early social thinkers, in different ways, informed almost all the urban research conducted within the discipline of sociology throughout the twentieth century (Saunders 1981). Significantly, too, many foundational sociological ideas about the city and urbanism were formed in opposition to ideas about the country. Urban analyses, although grounded in empirical observation, were pervaded by a keen awareness of what had supposedly been lost, destroyed or surpassed by urbanization – these were the positive communal relationships and quality of life believed to exist in the country. As is argued throughout this book, the opposition between the city and the country continues to frame analyses and assessments of city life. It found its most potent expression, however, in the urban utopian discourses and visions of the nineteenth and early twentieth centuries.

Reimagining Utopia

Urbanization prompted a belief in the existence of an identifiable urban culture and a specifically urban way of life (or sensibility), along with the emergence of pervasive ideas and value judgements about this urbanism.

These ways of seeing and explaining urban life were outcomes of a coincidence of many factors but, in particular, the visual, the literary, the lived and the imagined were influential (see Chapter 7). Such discrete factors combined to describe the urban way of life largely in terms of its opposition to a romanticized rural existence. The rural became 'the natural', the wholesome and the safe – the ideal against which all other forms of settlement were judged. In contrast, the city was thought of as a place of impoverished landscapes, degradation and dispossession, as well as the site of potentially dangerous (even revolutionary) forces (Short 1991). It was also regarded as a place of powerlessness and, in the eyes of many commentators, of social breakdown and *anomie* (Durkheim [1893] 1960). In his book *The Country and the City*, Raymond Williams (1973a) suggests that the popular view that a causal relationship exists between settlement types and the quality of life within these settlements has a tradition that can be traced to classical times. In the everyday imagination, Williams argues, life in the country is always pictured as a secure, even innocent existence of community and solidarity. As other commentators have also noted, this picture of ruralism is routinely contrasted with its antithesis – life in the cities – which is represented as the 'unnatural setting for the anonymous interaction of an alienated population' (Short 1991: 44). However, with the industrial revolution of the eighteenth and nineteenth centuries and the rapid urbanization it prompted, the **rural–urban dichotomy** gained even greater mythological force. It has become so pervasive that, according to Williams (1973b: 426), 'the contrast of country and city is one of the major forms in which we become conscious of a central part of our experience and the crises of our society'.

This dichotomous view of the country and the city was incorporated into the early academic discourses of urban sociology in two ways. First, through the application of Ferdinand Tonnies's ([1887] 1957) concepts *gemeinschaft* and *gesellschaft* to classify and describe the social relations found in the city and the country, that is ruralism and urbanism. Second, these quality of life assessments were linked with the idea of a rural–urban continuum (Saunders 1981: 94). According to Tonnies's original formulation, social relationships can be categorized as either *gemeinschaft*, meaning that they are intimate and enduring and exist between people with kinship, friendship and neighbourhood ties (in other words 'community' relationships), or they can be classified as *gesellschaft*, which are impersonal and often contractual, that is 'association'.

In 1938, Louis Wirth, a human ecologist of the Chicago School of urban sociology, drew on Tonnies's typology in order to explain and categorize relationships within different types of settlements. In particular, Wirth was interested in providing a systematic definition of 'urbanism' as a 'way of life' unique to cities and a direct outcome of the heterogeneity, size and density of the urban environment. Thus he classified rural relationships as 'primary' (*gemeinschaft*) in that they involved homogeneous populations and entrenched group solidarity. He claimed that these relationships were fundamentally better than the 'secondary' (*gesellschaft*) relationships of the heterogeneous people who lived in the anonymous, densely populated spaces of the modern industrial city. Wirth further suggested that settlements and the quality of life therein could be ranked on a continuum with simple rural societies at one extreme and complex urban settlements at the other. This idea was later developed and refined by others, such as Sjoberg (1960), Redfield (1965) and Frankenberg (1965). The recurring assumption, though, was that the growth of the modern city had somehow annihilated the *gemeinschaft* of ruralism (or was in the process of doing so). At its core, this discourse is a nostalgic one, grounded in the belief that a golden age of small-scale settlements and enriching community life has been lost or destroyed. The challenge that emerged was – could this positive way of life be regained and was it necessary to destroy the city in the process or could it be rehabilitated?

Mark Girouard (1986) draws on a mythical tradition associated with the biblical city to identify two contrasting viewpoints of the nineteenth-century industrial city that, he argues, emerged in literature, art and other popular discourse at the time – the city as Babylon and the city as Jerusalem. Both these urban imaginings pivot on the idea of community lost and, starting from the pervasive somewhat depressing view of the contemporary urban landscape, position the city and urban life as being in opposition to the country. These views did not differ fundamentally from each other in their assessment of the modern urban condition. But, where one view (the city as Babylon) regarded the city as a place from which to escape, the other saw it as being (like Jerusalem) a place to be rebuilt and remade into a better place – an urban utopia. 'The degree of reaction varied . . . between those who accepted great cities as agents of civilization, but tried to transform them by liberal injections of "the advantages of the countryside", and those who rejected them altogether' (Girouard 1986: 348).

Ideas about how to rebuild the industrial city in a way that would ameliorate the urban (usually by making them more like the country) developed apace in the late nineteenth century. These urban reform views pivoted on utopian visions that can be traced back at least to the work of Thomas More ([1516] 1996) in the early sixteenth century. However, the linking of a utopian society with the urban has a much longer tradition; as David Harvey (2000: 156) points out, the 'figure of "the city" and of "Utopia" have long been intertwined'. For instance, in his vision for an ideal republic, Plato fused citizenship with a prescription for the optimal city as a place limited in size by 'the number of citizens who might be addressed by a single voice' (Mumford 1961: 65). What is possibly more significant than any historical link between Utopia and the city, however, is that utopias (including Judaeo-Christian visions of Heaven) invariably have a spatial form. Indeed, many of the Utopias imagined prior to the industrial revolution occupied real space on real maps (Bruce 1996: xii). And, even when their spatial form is urban, it is always contained, clearly demarcated, and draws heavily on the discourses and imagery of the rural and the fostering of a (lost) *gemeinschaft*.

Geographical separation and the existence of physical boundaries or barriers have traditionally also been of great importance in utopian discourse. These boundaries can be both natural and constructed – variously taking the form of agricultural 'green' belts, rivers, oceans and/or walls. What is striking about Thomas More's ([1516] 1996: 52–4) description of Amaurote – the 'chief' city of Utopia – is the centrality of nature to the built form of the place. Most notable being the dominance of water imagery, with the relationship between waterways – rivers, oceans, brooks and springs – and the fabric of the city being a significant expressive theme. More's descriptions of urban housing and streetscapes are framed in terms of an imagery of gardens and of there being a permeability between the inside and the outside. Although written before industrialization, this view is one that is deeply embedded in nostalgia for the imagined settlements and communities of an earlier time. More's utopian city is one of order, cleanliness and the bountiful abundance of nature. He also specifies that the 54 cities of Utopia are small in scale, uniformly laid out, and separated by a prescribed minimum tract of rural land ([1516] 1996: 50). This imagined urbanism is tranquil and conforms to set rules. It is not chaotic or haphazard.

When, in response to the prevailing conditions of the emerging industrial city, utopian blueprints for the ideal city began to be formulated, the anti-urban utopia was already an existing discourse. In addition, it was, following More's vision, prescriptions for cities of orderly spaces grounded in a discourse that celebrated an idealized bucolic rural idyll that had salience – the Jerusalem of Blake's poetry with its 'dark satanic mills' was to be (re)built in the image of 'England's green and pleasant land[s]'. The utopian dream of the 'Garden City' or 'new towns' movement was perhaps the most famous and influential example of such an 'anti-urban' (Appleby 1990) or pro-rural urban philosophy. And, inspired in part by Edward Bellamy's tale of political utopianism entitled *Looking Backwards* (1888), the most significant blueprint for (re)building the city was that detailed by Ebenezer Howard in his seminal book *Garden Cities of Tomorrow* ([1902] 1965).

Howard's vision of a model urban community went beyond the rural–urban dichotomy and advocated the possibility of a third type of settlement that combined the attractions of the city (jobs, high wages and social opportunity) with the sunshine, fresh air and 'natural' environments of the country. In other words, Howard's was a model that combined the 'best' of the city (civilization) and the 'best' of country (nature). His 'three magnets' vision for the ideal city comprised decentralized, self-contained urban villages ringed by farmlands and gardens. Like Thomas More he, too, prescribed the population densities of these communal villages. He proposed that they would have populations of approximately 30,000 people, most of whom would live in zoned, homogeneous neighbourhood units that housed about 2000 residents (Howard [1902] 1965). In addition, the collective ownership of property was fundamental to the idea of the Garden City – a prescription that was soon abandoned, however, in the *realpolitik* of urban reform (Short 1991: 87–8). While neither Howard, nor the Garden City movement that his ideas fostered, 'invented' the popular planning notions of 'green belts', 'garden suburbs' or 'urban villages', there can be no doubt that this work was influential, if not in popularizing these ideals, then, in providing the intellectual terrain on which they were later to develop.

Underlying utopian views of the planned reimagined city – the city as Jerusalem – including the idea of the Garden City, is the theme that the modern city, in spite of or when freed from its physical horrors, has the potential to be a liberating place. This view of the city is certainly foundational in the work of Howard, who saw the town as the 'symbol of society' ([1902] 1965: 48), a place of sophistication, civilization, creativity and uplifting cultural pursuits, as well as a place of crime and squalor. In particular, the idea that in the city individuality is tolerated (even promoted) emerged as a recurring theme of the 'city as Jerusalem' discourse. This is a theme that found its most potent expression in the sociology of Georg Simmel.

Freedom, loneliness and the modern metropolis

With the publication of his essay 'The metropolis and mental life', German sociologist Georg Simmel ([1903] 1995) became the first scholar seriously to problematize the idea and lived experience of modern urban culture and the urban condition. Unlike other urban theorists and sociologists of his time, Simmel's analysis of urbanism was not grounded in nostalgia for a lost rural existence (some imagined *gemeinschaft*) or a deep distaste for city life. Indeed, his paper was in many respects a celebration of the urban in spite, or because, of its 'limitations'. Nor was Simmel interested in asserting that the culture of urbanism was somehow caused by settlement patterns or types (in particular, by size, density and heterogeneity), or that making changes to the way cities were designed and built would result in a quantifiable improvement in behaviour and social life (a belief that underpinned many of his contemporaries' proposals for urban utopias, discussed above). Rather, Simmel was interested in analysing 'the specifically modern aspects of contemporary life' or culture and, as modernity had found its most obvious expression in the metropolises of industrialism, these spaces and the urban condition became the almost accidental objects of his attention.

As he was a sociologist Simmel also had an overarching concern with the question of social order and both his primary objects of analysis and his conclusions reflect this preoccupation. Hence Simmel set out to explore the relationship between 'metropolitan individuality' and the internal and external factors by which this relationship had been shaped. He contends that the mental life – or culture – of those living in the metropolis has largely been framed by people's responses to a series of 'violent stimuli' which accompany 'every crossing of the street' (Simmel [1903] 1995: 31). The result is a society organized according to the principle of difference – and, in particular, coping with difference. Significantly, Simmel regards this city of difference as simultaneously the site of freedom and of isolation. In his view, both these contradictory conditions are deeply embedded in the social structures and circumstances of the modern metropolis. Thus, the factors which separate people from each other are, he argues, the very factors that make freedom possible. This analysis pivots on the identification of a number of key elements of urban culture, which require further elaboration before an appreciation of Simmel's understanding of the link between freedom, modernity and the metropolis is possible.

In Simmel's assessment, modern urban dwellers are instrumental, blasé and reserved. These three characteristics, he suggests, are the result of people's intellectualized responses to the sensory confusion of the modern metropolis. They are also the individualized outcomes of the imperatives of the money economy (which Simmel views as being inseparable from the metropolis and from modernity). Simmel contends that, in contrast to the emotional relationships and reactions of small town and rural dwellers, people living in the modern city necessarily approach life in a highly intellectualized and somewhat detached way. He argues that this 'intellectualistic character' has developed not because people living in the city are fundamentally different from those living in the country, but as a protective (cultural) response to the relentless bombardment of stimuli that one experiences in the modern city. If city dwellers responded to all stimuli in the same highly emotional way that the small town dweller did, he asserts, the result would be instability, confusion and disorder, 'one would be completely atomized internally and would fall into an unthinkable mental condition' (Simmel [1903] 1995: 37). However, this is rarely the case because the urban dweller has developed an effective way of coping – a protective armour against the confusion of the metropolis. 'Instead of reacting emotionally, the metropolitan type reacts primarily in a rational manner ... Thus the reaction of the metropolitan person to ... events is moved to a sphere of mental activity which is least sensitive and which is furthest from the depths of the personality' (Simmel [1903] 1995: 32).

In order to protect themselves from potential instability and chaos, Simmel argues that people living in the metropolis are rational in their responses to life and to other people, and are more blasé and reserved (the two other elements of the protective shield) than are rural dwellers. In addition, he contends that people in the city frequently approach life and their social relationships in instrumental and increasingly calculating ways – dealing with people with detachment and an eye to a set of predetermined or desired outcomes. Simmel's belief in the indivisibility of the metropolis and the money economy is clearly evident here. He thinks that the market and the interpersonal relationships, individuality and systems of exchange required and structured by the imperatives of the market, have reduced all social interactions within the city to the level of rationality and calculation. As Simmel rather colourfully notes, 'London has never acted as the heart of England but often as its intellect and always as its money bag' ([1903] 1995: 33). In the metropolis where social experiences are framed by calculability, detachment and reserve inevitably are found the conditions for loneliness and isolation. In this negative appraisal of the urban condition, Simmel does not seem to be significantly at odds with the views of his contemporaries. However, it is at this point and grounded in this analysis that his views diverge dramatically from those of others. Simmel goes on to argue that the very social, economic and psychological conditions that he has described as features of life in the metropolis and as the foundations of personal loneliness and isolation, are simultaneously the sources of freedoms that are unimaginable (indeed impossible) in the country or the close-knit village.

According to Simmel ([1903] 1995: 38), the most basic stage of social life is the

> relatively small circle almost entirely closed against neighbouring foreign or otherwise antagonistic groups but which has however within itself such a narrow cohesion that the individual member has only a

very slight area for the development of his own qualities and for free activity for which he himself is responsible.

(Simmel [1903] 1995: 38)

The emotional attachments that are central aspects of life in small bounded settlements fostered the development of the limiting, indeed, stifling bonds and boundaries of community solidarity and surveillance. However, a broadening of the conditions of the organization of society – a situation that reaches maturity in the metropolises of modernity – results in a weakening of the constraints imposed by the unified, delineated group or community. In other words, an increase in number, spatiality and 'the meaningful content of life' has, in Simmel's assessment, made it possible for individuals to experience a freedom of movement, association and ideas not otherwise possible. In this respect, his celebration of the urban is uncompromising:

> the citizen of the metropolis is 'free' in contrast with the trivialities and prejudices which bind the small town person. The mutual reserve and indifference, and the intellectual conditions of life in large social units are never more sharply appreciated in their significance for the independence of the individual than in the dense crowds of the metropolis.
>
> (Simmel [1903] 1995: 40)

Although Simmel was not an urban sociologist *per se* his ideas and theories of the metropolis and urban culture continue to be of consequence for the study of the city. Indeed, his work influenced Walter Benjamin's writing on urban culture (see Chapter 3) and many of his ideas found very direct expression in the work of sociologists associated with the University of Chicago. For instance, Robert E. Park, one of the founders of the Chicago School of urban sociology, studied under Simmel in Berlin. The Chicago School was arguably the most influential school in urban sociology for most of the twentieth century and its contributions to understanding **city cultures** were many. In particular, the scholars of the Chicago School undertook pioneering research into urban subcultures and introduced ethnographic methodologies to urban studies.

Ethnography and the patterning of urban life

In the inter-war period sociologists associated with the University of Chicago, including Robert Park, Roderick McKenzie, Louis Wirth and Ernest Burgess, set out methodically to study life in the city (Park 1936, 1952; Park et al. [1925] 1967; Wirth [1938] 1995). Their work, in turn, was influential in establishing urban studies as a specific subfield of research within the discipline of sociology. The Chicago School sociologists saw the city as being like an ecological organism or unity which, in response to the dictates of the physical environment and the pressures of population change, was evolving and adapting systematically and coherently. The task of the researcher was to uncover the patterns and rules governing these urban processes. Cities, they argued, spontaneously were acquiring and modifying their form and structure in an effort to establish a level of harmony and equilibrium between urban dwellers and urban space. For example, it was suggested that as one group of city dwellers moved out of a particular area or neighbourhood (such as the inner city) another group automatically moved in to replace them, 'Once set up a city is, it seems, a great sorting mechanism which . . . infallibly selects out of the population as a whole the individuals best suited to live in a particular region or a particular milieu' (Park 1952: 79).

One outcome of this 'sorting' process seemingly was the creation of cities that were partitioned or divided into 'natural areas' which, the Chicago scholars argued, were 'characterised both by a physical individuality and by the cultural characteristics of the people who live in [them]' (Zorbaugh 1926: 223). Such places included neighbourhoods with a high concentration of residents from a single ethnic or racial background (such as a 'Chinatown' or a 'Little Sicily'), as well as areas inhabited by people at the same life cycle stage or with similar income levels. Natural areas (zones) developed, it was argued, not as a result of the rational interventions of planners, but as outcomes of people's adaptive responses to urban life and the processes or forces of urban development. The focus was very much at the neighbourhood level and on identifying homogeneity within neighbourhoods and the differences between them. Assessments of zones were usually made with reference to a single descriptive demographic indicator, such as race or ethnicity, although they also argued that a feature of every city was a dominant central business zone ringed by a transitional zone of urban decay and heterogeneity.

According to the Chicago School theorists the major principles underpinning the ordering of cities into natural areas are the ecological processes of competition, dominance, invasion and succession. For instance, they argued that the dominant area of the modern city was the central business district (CBD), which was always in competition with the zone that surrounded it (Park 1936). As a result of this competition and the pressure of the 'invading' CBD, the residents of the adjoining area eventually are forced to move out and settle in homogeneous residential zones further away from the centre. The abandoned area then becomes a 'transitional zone' and its physical environment soon falls into disrepair. Before long, drug dealers, alcoholics, the homeless and other heterogeneous 'deviant' populations move into the transition zone. Ultimately, though, as 'invasion' gives way to 'succession', the transition area is rezoned from residential to business – and then the process will begin all over again. The Chicago School scholars argued that this process of competition, dominance, invasion and succession is played out in predictable ways in cities across the United States.

The Chicago sociologists set out first to identify the 'natural areas' of the city and then either to 'map' the social profiles of many of these areas or perhaps undertake an in-depth analysis of everyday life there. Researchers did this by employing either (or occasionally both) the methods of quantitative statistical analysis, (in particular of census data), or qualitative participant observation. One outcome of their dual approach to studying the city was to foster the development of two rather discrete methodological traditions within urban sociology. The first of these traditions involved the 'ecological mapping' of whole cities and individual neighbourhoods whereby census and other official statistics were used to produce locality profiles. From these statistics researchers could chart the degree of residential homogeneity, diversity, social disorganization, the concentration of different ethnic, racial or social groups, or the distribution of social 'pathologies' and 'deviant behaviour', such as divorce, delinquency, mental illness, criminal activity and non-nuclear families. The human ecology view held that the foundations of many so-called urban pathologies and anti-social behaviour could be traced directly to the morphology of the city. From a perspective that owed much to a Social Darwinist 'survival of the fittest' philosophy (Alonso 1963), it was subsequently argued that careful manipulation of the physical landscape, for example slum clearance, could be employed as an effective strategy for dealing with deviance in urban neighbourhoods, such as the transitional zone.

The second part of the urban research agenda developed by members of the Chicago School did not necessarily involve ecological mapping, although this information and data were often used as a starting point. Rather, the Chicago theorists advocated applying the ethnographic technique of participant observation to the study of urban life. In fact, one of the School's founders, Robert Park, reportedly told his students to 'Go and sit in the lounges of the luxury hotels and on the doorsteps of the flophouses; sit in the Orchestra Hall and the Star and Garter Burlesque. In short, gentlemen, go get the seat of your pants dirty in real research' (quoted in Kasinitz 1995: 17). The ethnographic method of urban research that Park advocated required researchers to immerse themselves in the cultural life of the group being studied so thoroughly that the subtle and complex rules, values, norms and everyday cultural practices of the group would be exposed. The result was a proliferation of detailed in-depth studies of a diverse range of urban subcultures and compelling descriptive accounts of the rich tapestry of life in the 'natural areas' first of Chicago, then of cities around the world. The focus of research, frequently, was on the lives and social relations of those regarded as being on the margins of society – such as gangs (Thrasher 1927) or transients (Anderson 1923) – or on life in the so-called slum areas of the city (Zorbaugh 1929). However, the ethnographies of the Chicago School were also influential in prompting the development of the 'community studies' tradition of sociology which usually involved in-depth analyses of life in small towns (Bell and Newby 1974, 1982; Wild 1981). Such ethnographies are so rich in descriptive detailed they have been labelled the sociological version of the novel (Bell and Newby 1982).

Although looking for trends and patterns and advocating uniform explanations for the distribution of urban life, this work was at the same time an acknowledgement of the diversity of urban cultures and of the need to get in touch with them. As a result, these detailed studies of life in different parts of the city and in rural communities soon undermined any belief in a uniform urban experience or way of being (urbanism), and highlighted the variety of urban life. Ethnographic research provided evidence that people living in areas that to outsiders looked dysfunctional or boring (for instance slums, or homogeneous residential neighbourhoods) might actually enjoy interactions and social relations which are every bit as positive as those supposedly enjoyed by people living in the country. A colourful and influential study of community and family relationships in a local area was undertaken by British researchers, Michael Young and Peter Willmott, and published in [1957] 1962 as *Family and Kinship in East London*. While not an ethnography in the strict (anthropological) sense of the term, Young and Willmott conducted a survey of residents in the working-class East London suburb of Bethnal Green and a series of in-depth interviews over a two-year period; they found that people identified strongly with their neighbourhoods and had extremely close ties with their neighbours, many of whom where their relatives. Herbert Gans (1962a, 1962b) subsequently built on Wirth's work to argue that urbanism could not be explained in terms of the differences between rural and urban environments but in terms of people's social class, life cycle stage and social mobility.

Conclusion: dreamers, planners and reformers

The discussion of this chapter provides a frame for understanding the emergence of the modern city and the specific ways of life (or cultures) that supposedly developed therein. The industrial revolution of the eighteenth and nineteenth centuries, first in Britain and then elsewhere, prompted urbanization on a scale so great that the traditional demographic and environmental balance between the rural and the urban was overturned and previously agrarian societies were transformed into highly urbanized ones. As a result of the speed and extent of this demographic change, and of the squalid nature of the emerging urban environments, urban life, initially, was compared with life in the country. The outcome was that the urban was regarded in every way as being the antithesis of the idealized rural. For instance, where the country was thought to foster enriching *gemeinschaft* relationships between kinship and community groups, the city was seen as a place of moral degradation, family breakdown, and the erosion of humanity – *gesellschaft*. While the city was a place of pollution, vermin and squalor, the country was idealized as a place of sunshine and gardens. This rural–urban dichotomy may have overstated the differences between the country and the city, and certainly ignored the close communal relationships to be found within cities, but it was definitely the case that the environments of the burgeoning cities were degenerate – especially the areas inhabited by the industrial working class. It was fiction writers, moralists and social reformers who first drew attention to the living conditions of the urban poor. And the question which emerged from their revelations centred on whether the city was to be condemned and abandoned (as the bourgeoisie did in retreating to the suburbs) or if it, like the mythical Jerusalem, could be rebuilt in the image of the country? This problem found expression in a number of proposals for urban utopias with the Garden City being perhaps the most famous and influential.

The city and its cultures soon became the concerns of academics, in particular those associated with the emerging discipline of sociology. The explanations of urban life of these academic analyses also pivoted on the rural–urban dichotomy. Two important sociological perspectives on the city which emerged in the early years of the modern city were discussed in the chapter. First, the ideas of Georg Simmel were introduced as someone who, although working implicitly within the rural–urban dichotomy, saw the city as being a liberating environment. Simmel's ideas, however, while initially influential, were somewhat idiosyncratic and it was not until recently that they have again seriously been considered within mainstream urban studies. Far more influential was the human ecology perspective of the Chicago School of sociology who introduced both ethnographic methods and the practice of social mapping to the study of the city. In addition, Chicago researcher Louis Wirth was the first systematically to define the nature of urbanism, arguing that it was a way of life common to all cities that resulted from the size, density and homogeneity of the urban environment.

Despite theoretical insights and empirical investigation that showed *gemeinschaft* relationships were as likely to be a feature of the everyday interactions of residents living in towns and cities as they were of those who live in the country, the rural–urban dichotomy remains pervasive in the popular imagination and continues, often insidiously, to colour many academic debates about quality-of-life and settlement types. Similarly, the Chicago School influenced the emergence of a number of associated academic traditions and methodological practices associated with the study of the city, such as social mapping, network analysis and community studies research. Most of these were uncritical and highly descriptive ways of documenting city life. Although undergoing substantial empirical fragmentation combined with the significant theoretical modifications of later researchers, the human ecology of the Chicago School dominated urban studies until the late 1960s when an emerging body of Weberian and Marxist informed analyses challenged its hegemony. These theoretical frameworks rejected the idea of an urban system and associated definitions of urbanism, in favour of explanations grounded in a concern with inequality and social justice. These theories of the urban are explored in the next chapter.

Further reading

Mumford, L. (1961) *The City in History: Its Origins, its Transformations and its Prospects*. London: Secker and Warburg.

Simmel, G. ([1903] 1995) The metropolis and mental life, in P. Kasinitz (ed.) *Metropolis: Centre and Symbol of our Times*. London: Macmillan.

Wirth, L. ([1938] 1995) Urbanism as a way of life, in P. Kasinitz (ed.) *Metropolis: Centre and Symbol of our Times*. London: Macmillan.

3 | CITIES OF DIFFERENCE: INEQUALITY, MARGINALIZATION AND FEAR

> The carefully manicured lawns of Los Angeles's Westside sprout forests of ominous little signs warning: 'Armed Response!' Even richer neighborhoods in the canyons and hillsides isolate themselves behind walls guarded by gun-toting private police and state-of-the-art electronic surveillance. Down-town, a publicly-subsidized 'urban renaissance' has raised the nation's largest corporate citadel, segregated from the poor neighbourhoods around it by a monumental architectural glacis.
>
> (Davis 1990: 225)

Introduction: from consensus to conflict

Along with size and density, the overarching characteristic of a city is, as Louis Wirth ([1938] 1995) suggested, heterogeneity. Heterogeneity or diversity are inscribed on the urban landscape in a range of ways, including in the appearance and location of housing, restaurants, signage, parks and other facilities and forms of infrastructure. In addition, the diversity of the population is a defining demographic marker of the city – people look different, have different relationships to the means of production, different racial and ethnic backgrounds, genders and lifestyles (including sexuality). But difference has implications beyond the descriptive; indeed, difference also structures the experiences and lives of urban dwellers and is both cause and manifestation of inequality and disadvantage. A concern with the expression of difference has a long history in the study of the city; for instance the researchers of the Chicago School (discussed in Chapter 2) were interested in identifying and then mapping differences in behaviour, status, race, class and ethnicity. Since the 1970s Feminist and Marxist theorists have explored the reasons and implications of social difference/inequality beyond its appearance and distribution. More recently, cultural theorists have imbued the idea of difference with a more nuanced relevance, moving the focus away from social structures to consider the array of identity-forming affiliations and processes that are embedded in everyday urban life.

This chapter reviews some of the major theoretical and empirical insights on the relationship between socially marginal groups and urbanism. At the same time as recognizing the centrality of the city to the structuring of oppression, it is also suggested in the chapter that the city and attachment to its places have been shown to provide opportunities for the tolerance of difference not possible elsewhere. The chapter begins by undertaking an overview of influential critiques of the human ecology approach to urbanism. These theoretical challenges came initially in the 1960s and 1970s from an emerging body of Weberian and Marxist urban sociology but were followed soon after by Feminism. For the first time, the idea and experience of urbanism that lay at the core of traditional urban studies were subjected to sustained critical scrutiny. The Paris-based sociologist Manuel Castells was one who argued that those social relations which had previously been described (both positively and negatively) as 'urbanism' were, in fact, the cultural expressions of the capitalist mode of production and thus, part of the ideological superstructure.

While Marxist urban studies placed a concern with urban inequality and social justice at the forefront of their analyses of the city, there have also been efforts to consider the lived dimensions of urbanism. To this end, many theorists have sought to focus on the role of the city in constructing identity and facilitating the celebration/expression of difference rather than on social structures. After discussing how difference has been conceptualized within more culturally focused urban studies, the chapter goes on to suggest that manifestations of social difference/division are now appearing in the urban landscape in new and disturbing ways. In particular, there has been an increase in surveillance and segregation which works against the acceptance and fostering of diversity. Finally, themes of local difference and identity are investigated in relation to processes of **globalization** and the tensions between the particular and the general. Considered, in this context, are the ways in which such tensions are being investigated within specific localities in terms of a politics of consumption.

Social justice and the 'urban question'

During the 1960s, British and French urban research began to emerge that was concerned, not with ideals of consensus and harmony and their role in determining the shape of the built environment, but with urban conflict and social tension. This was research that did not focus on the city *per se* but on the ways in which expressions of power, politics and economics were being enacted in the context of the city. In other words, the emphasis was on urban processes rather than urban patterns (Williams 1983: 2). Informed by the theoretical insights of Max Weber and Karl Marx, what came to be known as the urban managerial (Weberian) and the urban political economy (Marxist) views soon undermined and, subsequently, replaced the influential functionalist academic analyses of the city derived, in particular, from the Chicago School (see Chapter 2). Initially significant in changing the urban studies agenda was the work of British sociologists John Rex and Robert Moore (1967), who developed the notion of 'housing classes'. Inspired by Weber, this paradigm argued that the city was divided into differentially advantaged and disadvantaged 'classes' which were in conflict or competition with each other over the scarce resources of the city, such as housing. These classes were based on differences other than economic factors. It was another British sociologist, Ray Pahl (1970, 1975), who coined the term 'urban managers', the name by which the whole tradition of Weberian urban sociology came to be known. According to Pahl, urban managers, such as real estate agents, social workers, urban planners and local bureaucrats controlled access to the city's scarce resources and facilities. He argued that it was the decisions these urban managers made regarding access to, and the distribution of, resources which privileged some groups and disadvantaged others giving rise to, or reinforcing urban inequality.

In Weberian urban sociology, institutional or professional position is conceptualized as being the source of power and inequality, while the state is viewed as a distinct 'dimension of stratification' (Pickvance 1984: 37), which like power that is derived from institutional position, is separate from the economic sphere. However, before long it was acknowledged, even by Pahl (1978) himself, that rarely do urban managers act as independent agents or autonomous decision makers. Rather, they operate within a system that is structured by the private ownership of the means of production, thus the role of the urban manager is one of mediator or agent for the urban interests of private capital (Halligan and Paris 1984: 5). The state, too, came also to be seen as serving the interest of capitalism and not as an independent realm.

The release of the English translation of Manuel Castells's book *The Urban Question* (1972) was influential in crystallizing the critical challenge to both Weberian urban managerialism and the human ecology of the Chicago School. Castells's work also engendered an ongoing, often abstruse academic debate about what is urban sociology and what should be its specific object of study (Saunders 1981, 1983, 1985; Kirby 1983; Paris 1983). Responding to widespread urban protest and student unrest in cities, such as Paris in the late 1960s, Castells was at the forefront of a burgeoning French Marxist urban sociology which had been influenced specifically by the structuralism of Louis Althusser. Although focused on the city, *The Urban Question* was an important contribution to an intellectual debate between French socialists about appropriate responses to the changing character of the French state (Gottdiener 1984). Castells's main academic targets, therefore, were not so much the Weberian urban sociology of British theorists or the human ecology of the Chicago School (see Castells 1976a) but the humanist Marxism of influential French thinkers, such as Henri Lefebvre ([1974] 1991). Lefebvre and others were exploring the liberating potential of everyday urban life and the consequences of political struggle over the production of urban space. A crucial issue in Lefebvre's work (which was not published in English until the 1990s) was the way in which the social relations of the capitalist mode of production are reproduced and organized through the production of space. This process is one in which, he claims, 'spatial practices', 'representations of space' and 'spaces of representations' are fused in a dialectic.

Castells, on the other hand, was not interested in the 'lived' but in the structural and the objective. In particular, he sought to assert the scientific basis of urban sociology and to identify which function(s) of the capitalist mode of production was specific to the city and, thus, should be the principal object of study for urban sociology. He argued that, since the social organization of **collective consumption** (education, health service provision, town planning and transport), including its function in reproducing labour-power, occurred in cities then collective consumption should be urban sociologists' object of investigation (Castells 1972, 1976a, 1976b). In this context, Castells (1976b: 75) defines collective consumption as 'consumption processes whose organization and management cannot be other than collective given the nature and size of the problems'. His point, too, was that the provision of collective consumption was often the source of considerable tensions and urban protest. He argued that if these struggles over collective consumption were linked to working-class movements/politics they could be the impetus for social revolution and the overthrow of capitalism. The outcome would be the creation of a 'better' society (including better cities). In this respect, Marxist-informed urban studies must be seen in the tradition of utopian writings on the city discussed in Chapter 2. Although not providing a prescription for a 'better city' as such, Marxism was underpinned by the belief that equitable cities and a fairer distribution of urban resources would inevitably result from the defeat of capitalism.

Marxist political economy was grounded in the understanding that capital is 'the principal architect of spatial structures' (Badcock 1984: 53) and thus the fundamental cause of social inequality. Marxists also explored the role that the city plays in the reproduction of labour and capitalism. While it was the structural Marxism of Castells that, initially, was influential and informed the writings of theorists, such as Chris Pickvance (1976), Michael Harloe (1977) and Patrick Dunleavy (1980), before long Marxist urban studies was broadened by the economic geography of David Harvey (1973) and the historical perspective of Enzo Mingione (1977) among others. Harvey's early work emphasized macro-economic conditions, such as over-accumulation and over-production, more than social and political factors. Mingione's work stressed the importance of considering the intersection between regional development and historical conditions. In spite of differences in emphasis, Marxists shared a core concern with structural urban inequality and a belief that capitalism was the cause of this inequality. Marxism became so influential in urban studies during the 1970s that Sharon Zukin (1980) confidently claimed that urban sociology was no longer a fragmented and disorganized minority field of research focused on 'social problems'. In its place a 'new' urban sociology had emerged that was not only rigorous but also 'part of a unified intellectual world view ... focus[ed] on linkages and structures that are readily related to empirical observations of urban blight, the flight of capital, redlining (ie the discriminatory mortgage policies of banks), government subsidies and the dual labour market' (Zukin 1980: 583).

Almost as these words were being written, however, many both within and outside urban studies could have challenged the certainty with which Zukin expressed her view. The underpinning theoretical and philosophical 'truths' which justify claims, such as those of Zukin's, were already being called into question by exponents of the emerging interdisciplinary field of social research and explanation that has come to be known as cultural studies. Despite having significant points of difference, both Weberian urban managerialism and Marxist political economy explore the urban landscape from the standpoint of structural (that is social, economic and political) inequality. In other words, city form and the development of cities are regarded as outcomes of factors such as 'market forces' and 'modes of production' and not as the result of complex human actions and systems of meaning. In addition, neither the Weberian nor the Marxist urban paradigms recognized that gender relations and inequality are fundamental constraints on access to urban resources. The significant neglect of gender in the study of cities and urban cultures was also a central element contributing (with cultural studies) to the 'crisis' of urban sociology that beset the subdiscipline in the 1980s. So before exploring the cultural studies challenge and the assertion of the notion of 'difference', it is important first to consider the foundations of Feminist contributions to the study of the city.

Gender in the city

An interest in women's relationship to the city and the view that their experiences of its spaces might in fact be very different from those of men developed from the 'second wave' Feminist challenges to dominant theoretical models of sociological thought in the 1970s (Firestone 1970; Millett 1970; Mitchell 1971). Critics highlighted the failure of social theory and research to take into account issues of gender difference and the pervasiveness of structural gender inequality. The insights of Feminism challenged the traditional foundations of urban thought in a number of ways. These are well summarized in the following extract from the editorial of the supplement of the Feminist journal *Signs* (1980: S1) dedicated to women and the city: 'Three hypotheses underlie this special issue of *Signs:* The . . . city has both enhanced and constricted women's lives; the experience of men and women in American cities is quite significantly different; and, finally, studies of such divergences and their effects are original and provocative.' The contributions to the supplement scrutinized dominant theories of the urban, and their underpinning gender stereotypes. A specific challenge was directed at Marxist political economy for being concerned only with the effects of the capitalist mode of production and for neglecting the relations of the sphere of reproduction (Markusen 1980).

A cursory glance at the urban landscape, however, is unlikely to reveal any obvious gender differences. As Janice Monk (1992) suggests, it is easy to see expressions of class, status, race and ethnicity in cityspace, it is also easy to map them as the Chicago School did. We know we are in a working-class area without being told because we recognize (and understand) the spatial codes – the form of the gardens; the size and quality of the housing; perhaps the material from which they are built; the leafiness of **public space**; the proximity of parks and gardens; the absence or presence of polluting industries, and so on. Likewise, there are a raft of clichés associated with the housing and decorating styles of different ethnic and racial groups with which we are familiar and which can mark the ethnic composition of a neighbourhood. Gender, though, is much less evident – men and women inhabit the same areas. Working-class neighbourhoods are home to both men and women just as surely as middle-class men and women live in the same places. Research has shown, however, that in spite of this spatial co-presence, men and women not only use cityspace in different ways but also experience it differently.

Because gender roles and relationships are largely taken for granted in our society the gendered nature of the urban experience was ignored until relatively recently. So, too, was the extent to which cities and suburbs reinforce gender differences and inequalities. Following the logic of the rural–urban dichotomy – and the romanticization of the rural – there was a pervasive view within early Feminism that women had been disadvantaged by urban life and that the form of the modern city (in particular, the separation of work and home) reflected and reinforced this disadvantage. This view was, in part, predicated on another dichotomy – the distinction between the public and the private realms with the public being linked to the city and the private to the home and the suburbs (Wilson 2001). Thus the starting point for attempts to insert a concern with gender into urban studies was that even though men and women live in the same houses, neighbourhoods and suburbs, they occupy different spaces for work and leisure. Underpinning this argument is the recognition that men and women traditionally have performed very different roles in society – with men travelling to work each day and women remaining at home to take charge of the household, and care for children and elderly relatives. This segregation is often called the 'gender division of labour'. The spatial implication of the gender division of labour was that the suburbs had come to be seen as the 'natural' spaces for women and children and the city as a place for working men. In other words, the city could be divided (at least at the level of ideology) into discrete male and female zones (Saegert 1980; McDowell 1983; Matrix 1984).

Feminists have explored how urban policy, the structure of cities, as well as urban studies have in some way marginalized or ignored the needs and priorities of women. Of significance have been studies of the impact of suburbanization on the lives of women. For instance, Sophie Watson (1988) provides a systematic account of the role played by housing location and tenure in reproducing patriarchal structures of injustice. Watson claims, in particular, that both the promotion of home ownership as the dominant form of housing tenure and of the suburb as the premier residential site reinforce the disadvantage of women. The 'suburbanisation of home ownership', says Watson (1988: 42), continues to reproduce social and spatial relations which limit women's access to resources, facilities, labour markets and finance capital while, at the same time, it reinforces domestic relationships that are often detrimental to women. Delores Hayden's (1980) utopian prescription for a 'non-sexist city' was one attempt to find new ways of planning and living in cities that were not predicated on the public/private–city/suburban split and, thus, would not disadvantage women.

The vexed issue of urban safety has been another preoccupation of Feminist scholars who have highlighted the ways in which the fear of being physically attacked in public (and increasingly private) space insidiously shapes how women use and relate to the city. It is argued that women divide the city into places that are 'safe' and those that are not, identifying such features as streets that can be walked alone and those that must be traversed with others or by private car. Of particular significance, therefore, are the strategies of avoidance many women adopt almost reflexively in their use of the city, especially after dark. In this regard, Dora Epstein (1997) provides a most compelling account of the ways women negotiate their fear when imagining the city:

> There is a story to this fearing, this fearing that maps the cityscapes into places I will go and places I will not. As speaking subjects, sentient members of urban terrains, we can narrate our cartographies of avoidance, our fearing, far better than we can narrate how the fearing came to be. We know, can articulate, what we have deemed 'unsafe' – the strange, the unfamiliar, the supposedly violent 'other' against which we have insulated and barricaded ourselves – and what we have deemed as 'safe' – the lit, the populated, the orderly, or seemingly controlled to which we have clung. We felt justified when violence occurred in the realm of our 'unsafe'; felt shock when it occurred in our 'safe'.
> (Epstein 1997: 134)

The issue of women's safety in, and fear of, public space connects with the contemporary trend towards increased urban security and attempts to control what groups use which parts of the city and how, that are discussed on pp. 44–7. It is also relevant to cultural planning prescriptions for the development of public space and the (re)creation of citizenship (see Chapter 6). Clearly, too, there other factors besides gender, such as class, race and ethnicity which also structure/influence how women use the urban environment and for what purposes.

Many Feminist-informed urban studies have argued that the position of women within society and the city is perhaps best explained with reference to both the capitalist mode of production and the structures of patriarchy (Winchester 1992; Bondi and Christie 2000). However, as already suggested, there has in recent years been something of a move away from overly structural approaches focused on sameness and equality to arguing that women's difference (including their varying uses and experiences of space) should be acknowledged and celebrated, and that their lives and priorities should be valued in their own terms (Morris 1988). The realization was that not only were the interests and urban experiences of women frequently not the same as those of men but also they were not necessarily the same as those of other women.

The view that analyses of urban life that are grounded solely in structural conceptions of class and patriarchy fail to acknowledge women's diversity, coalesced with a more widespread challenging of traditional explanatory frames and the totalizing narratives of social theory that came from cultural studies. The result was an upsurge of interest within social and urban theory in the relationship between cities, urbanism, identity and difference. In particular, theorists employed qualitative research methods to explore urban experiences and to listen to the voices of those (including women) who had been overlooked when the focus was on 'big' economic or structural issues. In practice, this has involved trying to understand the meanings that these groups actively derive from their urban environments as well as considering how urban space accommodates their diversity rather than how it facilitates inequality and oppression.

The politics of urban difference

The idea of difference entered the vocabulary of cultural urbanism as a result of the same disparate intellectual influences that reoriented social science generally, including poststructuralism, psychoanalytical theory, postcolonial theory and Feminism. This emerging concern with diversity focused on how 'empowerment, oppression, and exclusion work through regimes of difference' (Jacobs and Fincher 1998: 2) – in other words, on the dynamic relationship between identity and power. One outcome of this focus was a move away from thinking about identity and subjectivity as static, essential categories, to seeing them as shifting, decentred and 'multiply located' (Jacobs and Fincher 1998: 4). To recognize that people engage with the world through a range of (perhaps oppositional) subject positions and that each of these should be considered and celebrated in and on its own terms. This meant acknowledging that people are not solely (or primarily) 'women', or 'working class', or 'white' (to name but three) but simultaneously racialized, gendered and classed. They are also occupants of particular geographical spaces and imagined communities. In Liz Bondi's (1993) view, identity is most often formed and expressed through 'hyphenation' in the sense that people routinely relate to a number of categories of self-identity, such as 'black-American-woman' or 'white-Jewish-woman'; rarely do they describe themselves just as 'woman'.

Hence it is argued that the political and social interests of any individual subject are multiple – those of a black-working-class-lesbian-woman-living-in-the-inner-city are likely to be very different from those of a white-middle-class-heterosexual-woman-living-in-the-outer-suburbs. While they may have some interests (both positive and negative) in common as an outcome of their shared gender and biology, there will be vast interests that they do not share and social and cultural differences which may override those associated with sex and gender. As a result, it has become unsustainable or at least contestable to speak with a single voice for 'all women' or 'all workers' or 'all people of colour' as theories like those traditionally associated with Feminism and Marxism have done. Urban culture has come to be conceptualized by many as 'a diversity of sub-cultures' (Miles 1997: 27). This outcome is one that has had considerable implications for the practice of urban politics and the analysis of power relations (for instance, see contributions to Keith and Pile 1993), as well as for strategic interventions and processes such as urban planning and development.

The point, too, is that identity or subjectivity, increasingly, are conceptualized as being fluid. For instance, one may choose to emphasize one's gender today and race tomorrow, or race may always be privileged. Likewise, one may choose to be a man or a woman, or to deny those socially ascribed categories completely by adopting a hybrid gender position. These are all actions, choices and performances which, when viewed as part of a politics of difference, are accepted as valid. Identity can no longer be seen as having an 'essence'. For those concerned with the urban it is clear that it is in the city that difference is most evident. It is also where, as Simmel argued (see Chapter 2), the freedom to be different is possible. Cities are places where difference is both created and most likely to be tolerated.

The focus on diversity and identity has made it conceptually possible to see that different groups may use, experience and relate to the same urban spaces in a range of ways often at the same time. And that these spaces have a relationship to any number of often-competing identities and subject positions. The same urban park may be a place for stay-at-home mothers to take their children to play; the toilet block in the park might be an active beat for gay men; its footpaths might be skateboard tracks for local teenagers; its benches 'home' to the homeless; its lawns places for lovers to meet or city office workers to eat their lunch; and its gardens places of work for council labourers and gardeners. One space, different uses and different meanings, all of which are framing a range of identities, including being markers of belonging. Following de Certeau (1988), it can be argued that these uses of space may, in turn, be contrary to the ways in which planners expected the space to be used (see Chapter 4). In addition, an individual may use the same space differently at different times according to their changing situation and in line with their own shifting subjectivity. As they derive various (frequently contradictory) meanings from their relationships with this space, they are not necessarily the passive victims or recipients of dominant ideologies and oppressive power relations.

A cultural approach to the idea of difference makes it possible to appreciate that, at the level of lived experience, spaces such as the home and suburbia which, when seen in structural terms are said to contribute to the subordination of certain groups, may at the level of the micro be sites of empowerment for those groups. Such insights emerge most sharply from qualitative research that involves actually listening to the experiences and priorities of the people who use particular spaces, rather than focusing on overarching objective structures, such as class or patriarchy. For instance, Susan Thompson (1994) undertook an in-depth qualitative study of migrant women's experiences of their suburban homes and neighbourhoods in an Australian city. Her findings highlight that these women use, and identify with, these spaces in ways that contribute not to their subordination, but to the expression of their personal power.

In opposition to the dominant Feminist view, they regard their homes and neighbourhood communities as central to their positive sense of self and to the construction of their personal and cultural identities. Their homes are also 'symbol[s] of success in the adopted country and a means of maintaining cultural, religious and personal links with the past' (Thompson 1994: 41). Thompson argues that the homes and neighbourhoods of the migrant women in her study were spaces of 'opportunity' rather than of oppression. Similarly, my own research investigating women's relationship to their suburban neighbourhoods found that the suburbs are places of considerable diversity and play an important role in the construction and expression of women's identity and experience of 'community' (Stevenson 1999a). In the neighbourhoods that were studied, it was the priorities, interests and actions of women which were pivotal in shaping and maintaining highly significant quasi-primary neighbourhood-based networks. These networks were defined in terms of geographical space and cut across a range of interests, including class, age, ethnicity and race.

Clearly, the issue of power remains central to any analysis of the cultural politics of difference, and much of the work exploring empowerment draws on the theories of Michel Foucault. Instead of conceptualizing power as an entity to be possessed and wielded, or as being embedded in social structures, such as class or gender, Foucault (1980) focused on micro-situations and the negotiated nature of power, including the importance of discourse. However, there are dangers in focusing exclusively on micro-situations, and the celebration of difference and diversity. The rejection of frameworks for understanding systematic structural inequality and for conceptualizing social justice can lead to an idealization of city life. This can provide an alibi for ignoring the sharp social polarization evident within cityspace. If everything is to be explained and appreciated in its own terms then it is impossible to consider the bigger urban issues of access, equity and 'social justice' (Harvey 1992). As Marshall Berman (1988: 35) explains, there is no place in Foucault's view of the world for freedom – large-scale political struggle is futile. However, it is extremely difficult to acknowledge the significance of the micro and the validity of the voices of the 'other' while at the same time supporting the possibility of collective identity and an agenda for reform through collective action. This is the fundamental tension between universalism and individualism (McGuigan 1999: 88), which Iris Marion Young (1990, 1995) sets out to resolve.

Young argues that in the city 'social justice . . . requires the realization of a politics of difference' that does not involve reflexive exclusion (1995: 268). One of her goals is to find a mid-point between the individualism of liberal political theory and the idealized conceptions of community invoked by its (Leftist) critics. She argues that both positions are actually grounded in a denial of difference – either in the sense of celebrating individualism or in fostering the obliteration of difference by requiring conformity and universality. The existence of community is predicated on sameness and the delineation and maintenance of boundaries. It is, she argues, an ideal that has led to racism, sexism and homophobia, fostering exclusion within and between groups. In contrast, an acceptance of difference and the mingling with strangers is a fundamental part of urban life and this understanding provides her with the key material for her blueprint for a politics of difference:

> The ideal of community denies and represses social difference . . . as an alternative to the ideal of community, I propose an ideal of city life as a vision of social relations affirming group difference . . . Different groups dwell in the city alongside one another, of necessity interacting in city spaces.
>
> (Young 1995: 251)

Young argues that people in the city do not expect those they encounter to be 'like' them in the sense of comprising some homogeneous predictable community. And that even though they may feel a strong sense of belonging to certain groups and spaces this belonging is not the result of homogeneity or shared values. In fact, she claims that in the city people actively seek out social situations and spaces that bring them into contact with large numbers of strangers. Young's politics of difference works from this understanding to argue for ways of recognizing difference within social institutions and political processes. The provision of public space and places that are accessible to everyone and can be used in a range of ways (like the uses of the park discussed earlier) is central to the process she describes (see also the discussion of cultural planning in Chapter 6).

Young's idealization of city life notwithstanding, recent research suggests, however, that our cities are becoming even more sharply divided into ghettoes of homogeneity than, previously, was the case. Rather than seeking heterogeneity in their urban lives, people actively seek to avoid contact with difference. The result is the adoption by middle- and upper-class urban dwellers of increasingly elaborate strategies to control their environments and to avoid unexpected encounters with the 'other'.

New divided city?

There is overwhelming empirical evidence showing that rather than facilitating difference, contemporary cities are actually fostering, and giving visual expression to, greater social, cultural and economic inequality, leading, in particular, to the development of enclaves of homogeneity (Marcuse 2000). Peter Marcuse (2000) claims that cities have become 'quartered', suggesting that although they have always been divided the origins and form of contemporary urban division are different and more alarming than those of the past. According to Marcuse (2000: 271) 'Some divisions arise of economic functionality, some are cultural, and some reflect and reinforce relationships of power; some are combinations of all three.' His thesis is that while zoning to separate economic/industrial activities from others is fairly understandable, it is less easy to accept the stark urban segregation that results from power and cultural differentials. These divisions, he argues, are according to class, race, ethnicity and lifestyle, with each having very marked effects on the 'life' of the city, including on its form and democracy. For instance, he suggests, that while ethnicity and lifestyle separations tend to be the result of largely voluntary actions and thus can be 'consistent with a democratic city life' (Marcuse 2000: 272), class and racial divisions are not. In Marcuse's view, this urban partitioning is the outcome of structural inequality and imbalances of power that go against the ideals of urban democracy.

In the contemporary urban environment spectacular spaces of prosperity and affluence are located alongside abandoned spaces of poverty, deprivation and decline. Divisions are evident both in the emergence of vastly different (and highly segregated) residential environments, as well as in the widespread development of privately owned leisure spaces, including the suburban shopping centres which are replacing the 'main street' as the principal shopping spaces of the middle and upper classes in many cities. Such urban development trends have also contributed to considerable physical decline and decay particularly in the traditional city centre, and provoked changes to the ways in which public space is used and perceived (Worpole 1991, 1992; see also Chapter 6). Of significance too in transforming urban form and its uses and in contributing to inequality and spatial polarization have been the privatization and regulation of leisure and recreational spaces, such as public parks and gardens (Worpole 1991, 1992; Zukin 1997). These are the places where once people of different social classes and racial backgrounds mingled freely but from which the poor and the marginal are now directly and indirectly being excluded. This exclusion is happening in response to middle-class unease about the increased presence of such people in these places.

The growing number of people now living in poverty has led to a considerable rise in urban homelessness. With this rise and the associated perception that there has been an upsurge in criminal and antisocial activities have come calls for civic authorities to address both the 'inappropriate' use of cityspace and the physical signs of urban decline. As a result, both overt and more subtle strategies have been implemented in an effort to control 'deviant' behaviour, including increased policing and surveillance measures, and making creative use of urban design (Davis 1990; Zukin 1997). For instance, the construction in parks and at bus stops of benches that cannot be slept on has become quite common in major cities around the world. Also on the urban rehabilitation and social control agenda is the formulation and implementation of redevelopment and reimaging strategies for entire urban precincts (like declining city centres, public parks and abandoned industrial sites). These redevelopments are intended to turn deteriorating urban spaces into areas for the middle class and their residential and recreational priorities and to rid the areas of the poor, the criminal and the homeless (see Chapter 6). In the cities of the 'haves' and 'have-nots', surveillance and policing are fusing with urban design and architecture to ensure that the poor are kept apart from the affluent – effectively insulating one class (or racial group) from another. According to Marcuse (2000: 272), 'we may almost describe many of our contemporary cities as entirely fragmented, composed only of a collection of separate areas of concentration of different people all desiring to stay apart from all others'.

Mike Davis (1990: 224) goes even further, claiming that 'we live in "fortress cities" brutally divided between "fortified cells" of affluent society and "places of terror" where police battle the criminalized poor'. With the increased demand for policing has come a corresponding rise in the activities of private security firms which are taking on roles that were once the sole province of publicly funded and accountable police forces. These security firms patrol public, private and quasi-public spaces but are not accountable to the public. Rather, they act in the interests of private corporations or individuals largely to protect private property. This trend is most pronounced in the United States but has become a feature of most cities in the west since the 1980s. And as part of a trend that has been labelled the 'aestheticisation of fear' (Zukin 1997: 26), there has been a rise also in domestic security involving the use of private firms and/or the installation of elaborate electronic security systems. There has also been an increase in the establishment of gated or walled residential estates not just for the rich but for the middle class as well, along with corresponding changes to domestic architectural styles involving the incorporation of many defensive elements into the design aesthetic (Blakely and Snyder 1997; Marcuse 2000). Those unable to live in fully secured residential enclaves or apartment blocks frequently rely on formal and informal neighbourhood surveillance programmes, such as Neighbourhood Watch (Morgan 1994). It is in this context that Steven Flusty (1997) describes the elaborate performance that entering his parents' suburban Los Angeles house has become in recent years:

> Over the past decade ... the simple act of entering the residence has grown dauntingly complex. Next to the door is a small metal plate with an illuminated red L.E.D., warning of the presence of an activated alarm. Upon disengaging the dead bolt and opening the front door, I have thirty seconds in which to deactivate the alarm by entering a sequence of digits into a small key pad in the entry hall. Should I forget the number ... a shrieking siren wakes the neighborhood. Next the deadbolt must be reengaged and a separate switch, located elsewhere in the house, must be tripped to deactivate the pressure pads strewn beneath the floor and contacts embedded in the interior doorways. At that point the house's interior becomes safe for passage and the alarm may safely be reactivated as a perimeter defense. At any time, the alarm may be intentionally activated by hitting the 'panic buttons' sprinkled throughout the house at strategic locations. The exterior of the house, once illuminated only by a porch light, now basks in the glare of multiple 150-watt security lights in the back and side yards, switched on from dusk to dawn by photoelectric sensors.
>
> (Flusty 1997: 46)

This house, says Flusty, is actually one of the 'less obtrusively secured' in the neighbourhood.

Cities, therefore, are becoming places where far from encountering difference, people actively contrive to avoid it. Different social classes, increasingly, are forced to follow different trajectories through space, they inhabit different zones for work and leisure, and rarely, if ever, do they unexpectedly encounter the 'other'. Their ideal urban environments are places of control rather than disorder. This city of difference is not a place where diversity is celebrated on the ground. It is a place of watchfulness and suspicion – of enclaves of homogeneity, perhaps even of community – a place where mingling with strangers is to be avoided. Like Marcuse, Mike Davis (1990) argues that urban division is the result of structural power and the major divisions are those of class and race. In Marcuse's (2000) view, there needs to be recognition of the bases of such inequality. This knowledge, in turn, he suggests, should inform strategies designed to allocate urban resources more evenly and foster interactions between different groups. In other words, what is required is that the social, economic and spatial effects of economic and industrial change (in particular, globalization) are addressed. As Harvey (1992) has claimed in his assessment of the 'battle' over Tompkins Square Park in New York City:

> We cannot understand events within and around the park or strategize as to its future uses without contextualizing it against a background of the political-economic transformations now occurring in urban life . . . to be seen in terms of social processes which create homelessness, promote criminal activities . . . generate hierarchies of power between gentrifiers and the homeless, and facilitate the emergence of deep tensions along the major social fault-lines of class, gender, ethnicity, race and religion, lifestyle and place-bound preferences.
> (Harvey 1992: 591)

In this context, Marcuse points out that exploring the link between urban division and globalization has become a central concern of many debates within urban studies. In addition, globalization is an important issue in the study urban cultures. Thus it has been recognized that processes of globalization are important elements framing the contemporary relationship between capitalist economic power, the city and local cultural identity and in accentuating the spatial consequences of social and economic inequality (see Chapter 6). Of concern, particularly for Marxists, have been the uneven economic, social and cultural effects of globalization within and between cities around the world, and within and between western and non-western nations. These debates hinge also on notions of heterogeneity and homogeneity.

Global trends and local diversity

In little more than a decade the rhetoric of globalization and its implications has come to dominate academic, political and popular discourse as many cultural and economic trends and exchanges seem unconstrained by the geographic and administrative boundaries of nation states (see also Chapter 6). These trends effectively operate with few opportunities for the mediations of national governments and scant regard for the local consequences of decisions that have been made not just elsewhere in the world, but often in no one specific place. There is a logic to the discourses of globalization that marginalizes and disempowers communities and regions. As individuals and collectivities, people seem unable to intervene effectively either to prevent change or direct is trajectory. Moreover, those who dare to challenge the assumptions underpinning globalization face accusations of conservative parochialism. Globalization is now, simultaneously, the almost incontestable explanation and rationale for unemployment, deindustrialization and the emergence of 'rustbelt' cities and regions (Stevenson 1998). The imperatives of globalization are reconfiguring social, cultural and regional inequality to such an extent that it is very hard to dispute Wenner's (1996: 235) observation that globalization (in all its guises) is 'hard to like'.

Both as idea and process, globalization is complex. Similarly, the effects of globalization are uneven and unpredictable. For instance, tensions between 'the west and the rest' are played out perhaps most sharply in the local effects of western media and economic processes that are becoming increasingly global. The question which emerges relates, in particular, to whether or not this globalization necessarily results in westernization and the annihilation of local or indigenous cultural identity. At one extreme is the fear that the global penetration of dominant 'systems of meaning, action and symbolic forms' (King 1990: 398) usually conceptualized as being those of the United States is annihilating local cultural diversity around the world. This argument is difficult to sustain, however.

Even though the global expansion of American culture and its incursion into other geographical and cultural landscapes are empirical realities, the outcome of globalization is not necessarily the destruction of local cultural diversity and vitality (Featherstone 1990). Rather, the more likely scenario is that the artefacts and practices of the globalizing culture will in some way be transformed or subverted in the very act of coming into contact with a particular local culture. And although this local culture may well be changed as a result of this contact it will not be destroyed. Indeed, it has been pointed out that the local 'response to globalisation' (King 1990: 398) is often an increase in the production of difference rather than in the universal production of sameness. This takes the form of a celebration of local idiosyncrasies and practices sometimes, it must be acknowledged, to the level of parody. Some theorists have argued that one response to the pressures of globalization has been a 'resurgence of indigenous cultures, sometimes led by religious fundamentalism' (McGuigan 1999: 96). So while the increasing globalization of culture is undeniable, it is untenable to speak of the existence of an all-encompassing, emerging global culture (Featherstone 1990: 11).

McGuigan (1999) in his discussion of globalization also draws attention to the ways in which academic theorizing has, inadvertently, become implicated in supporting forms of global domination. For instance, he points out that universal positions have been criticized because they endorse the imposition on non-western cultures of western values and political ideals, including equality, individualism and democracy (McGuigan 1999: 88). Similarly, the champions of 'otherness' and difference are accused of focusing on a 'we' and a set of values that are essentially western. The core of this critique is neatly summarized in the following passage: 'Crises of identity and epistemology, the chronic choices of those freed of tradition and modern restraint, do not much concern the famine stricken and dying in Africa. They are specifically western problems that do not touch upon the material and cultural realities of the Rest' (McGuigan 1999: 89).

A concern with the local consequences of globalization has not just focused on 'the west and the rest', however. Since the 1980s, a realization that the effects of global economic change are geographically uneven led to a specific interest in the uniqueness and specificity of different cities and localities within western nations, and their responses to the often-devastating effects of globalization (Massey 1984; Urry 1985; Cooke 1989; *Environment and Planning A* 1989, 1991). Partly influenced by cultural theories of difference and in response to the general challenge being mounted against structuralist epistemologies, the task has been to find fruitful ways of conceptualizing the relationship between society and space that takes account of both the micro and the macro. What is required is a way of exploring the effects of globalization on local cultures and economies that does not slip into relativism. This has been the intellectual terrain where, according to Zukin (1988: 433), the debates and theoretical insights associated with postmodernism and cultural studies have had the greatest effect on mainstream urban thought.

It was in this context that social science research was conducted during the 1980s in a number of localities in the United Kingdom into the consequences of national and international economic restructuring (Savage et al. 1987; Cooke 1989; Bagguley et al. 1990; Harloe et al. 1990). These 'locality studies' were the subject of several conferences and initiated spirited debates largely within British urban sociology and human geography focusing on their perceived methodological and epistemological strengths and limitations. As a central figure in locality research, Doreen Massey (1991) has claimed that national and international changes in the economy and in the nature of industrialism unevenly affect regions and locations. It is, she argues, important that an understanding of the extent and the nature of these differential effects inform policies and platforms for political action. 'Localities', Massey (1991: 275) suggests, 'are not just about physical buildings, nor even about capital momentarily imprisoned; they are about the intersection of social activities and social relations and crucially, activities and relations which are necessarily, by definition, dynamic, changing.' In other words, these studies are about 'place' and local cultural identity.

Such a focus has been criticized by adherents to more orthodox urban theoretical perspectives, however. It is argued that research focused on the local (including the politics of culture and difference) is a conservative practice that trivializes the significance and extent of class-based inequalities, thus undermining the potential for fundamental social change. Harvey is one who has been a vocal critic of aspects of locality research saying for instance: 'Every sentence in [Massey's influential book] *Spatial Divisions of Labour* is so laden down with a rhetoric of contingency, place, and the specificity of history, that the whole guiding thread of Marxian argument is reduced to a set of echoes and reverberations of inert Marxian categories' (Harvey 1987: 373). In Harvey's view, this concern with 'the local' has shifted the focus of Marxist urban research from being a materialist endeavour concerned with structural inequality and the capitalist mode of production, to one which concentrates overly on the importance of consumption. In response, Massey (1992: 12) has argued that it is important to distinguish between 'place-based politics' and politics which is 'place-bound'. This task requires Marxists to move beyond notions of the revolution of the proletariat to conceptualize and engage with, what John Urry (1989) terms, the 'small-p' politics of civil society. Increasingly, these politics are about culture and consumption.

It is argued, in this context, that society is becoming increasingly 'fragmented' and individual goals, for example those associated with issues of personal identity, consumption and lifestyle are replacing commitments to once-fundamental collective objectives and priorities, in particular those of the relations of productions. Scott Lash (1993: 252) claims there has been a 'displacement of politics from production to consumption, from the material to the cultural'. All the while, however, cities and urban cultures continue to be constructed, deconstructed and reconstructed by powerful commercial interests (predominantly those of white, middle-class men) which, increasingly, are global in scope. Thus the major forms of social inequality, such as class and gender, continue to be reproduced and inscribed locally in the landscape. The challenge for urban research since the 1980s has been to address these contradictions. Something the locality research with its focus on the relationship between the global and the local has tried to do.

Locality studies seek to do three things. First, they attempt to engage with the important challenges and insights of cultural studies and its focus on difference and the micro. Second, they retain a fundamental concern with macro processes, such as globalization and capitalism that continue unevenly to build and destroy localities. Third, locality theorists seek to deal with the centrality of culture and consumption to the contemporary urban experience. Cultural theorist Meagan Morris (1992, 1993) argues that a concern with the 'place-based . . . may well provide in future more concrete ways of articulating and practising a politics of "space" than those traditions of theorizing that think themselves universal have so far been able to achieve'. Despite his reservations, even Harvey (1987: 376) has acknowledged that some consideration of the local level can be important in the 'search for global solutions' to urban crises. As is explored further in the chapters to follow, an examination of **urban texts** (both written and built) can also provide incisive revelations about these processes. The methodological and theoretical tools of cultural enquiry can deepen our understanding of the dynamics of social structures, social action and lived urban cultures.

Conclusion: the micro and the macro

The issue of diversity is fundamental to the demography and the experience of the city. It has, thus, been an important theme in the urban studies literature. Researchers variously have grappled with the distribution, consequences and causes of difference. This chapter has surveyed some of the major urban studies approaches to addressing these concerns, highlighting that the endeavour has been both uneven and contradictory. On the one hand, structural theoretical frameworks, such as Marxist political economy and early Feminist urban studies have argued that the key issue is not difference but inequality, and the task of urban research is to unmask its causes and the processes which reproduce it. On the other hand, those that celebrate difference argue against totalizing explanations of inequality grounded in overarching notions of social and economic structures. For Marxists, urban form and inequality are both outcomes of the capitalist mode of production and the distribution of urban resources, including access to facilities and the quality of residential environments, is the result of fundamental shifts in the nature of capitalism. The foundational work of Castells prompted analyses of the relationship between collective consumption and the reproduction of capitalist labour power. Even those Marxists unconvinced by Castells's fixation on the object of sociological analysis that was unique to the city, remained focused on exploring the urban effects of capitalism and the class-based nature of inequality. Many early Feminists also accepted the importance of capitalism in shaping the urban landscape but to this they added gender. Feminists demonstrated that the home-based work of women was also important to the reproduction of the workforce. They argued that the built environment reinforced gender differences and inequalities, while practices, such as urban planning were underpinned by patriarchal ideologies that positioned women in the home and the suburbs and men in the city. Fear has also been identified as a major axis influencing (structuring) women's relationship the built environment.

The shift from a concern with inequality to one with difference that came with the influence of cultural studies is an important one. Even though cultural theorists talk about gender, ethnicity, race and their expression in the built landscape, difference is not synonym for inequality. Where the theories of inequality are concerned with underlying cause and fundamental change, the celebration of difference rejects the existence of overarching power structures to argue that power is situational and negotiated in struggles over discourse. For instance, they claim that it is just not possible to speak with one voice for *all* women because all women do not have the same relationship to space. Each one has a range of (often contradictory) subject positions through which they engage with the urban. The recognition of urban difference prompted Young (1990, 1995) to argue that it could be the basis for a reconceptualization of politics – a way of moving beyond restrictive notions of community and individualism. Young's insights are important but trends in contemporary urbanism suggest that, rather than fostering the experience and celebration of difference, city building and the priorities of city dwellers are increasingly creating homogeneous, predictable environments where encounters with difference are, if not avoided completely, then controlled. Analyses of these urban trends indicate that somehow ways must be found to address both the structural and the lived dimensions of space. This is a problem that has framed recent attempts to explore the ways in which localities have been affected by, and responded to, the globalization of capitalism and culture. The tensions inherent in the study of difference and inequality pivot on negotiating yet another dichotomy – that of the micro and the macro.

The next chapter develops some of the themes introduced in this chapter and considers the contributions that key cultural theories can make to the study of the urban (including those underpinning conceptualizations of difference).

Further reading

Fincher, R. and Jacobs, J. (eds) (1998) *Cities of Difference*. New York: Guilford.
Marcuse, P. (2000) Cities in quarters, in G. Bridges and S. Watson (eds) *Companion to the City*. Oxford: Blackwell.
Saunders, P. (1981) *Social Theory and the Urban Question*. London: Hutchinson.

4 MEANING AND MEMORY: READING THE URBAN TEXT

> The city as we imagine it, the soft city of illusion, myth, aspiration, nightmare, is as real, maybe more real, than the hard city one can locate on maps, in statistics, in monographs of urban sociology and demography and architecture.
>
> (Raban 1974: 2)

Introduction: the culture of cities

It has now become commonplace to acknowledge that cities play a pivotal role in the construction and experience of the cultures of everyday life and, within their spaces, collective and individual meanings are made and unmade, and identities formed. As discussed in Chapter 3, cities are comprised of multiple histories and a myriad of coexisting and competing presents. Such observations seem so much a part of the language of contemporary urban studies that it is easy to forget how relatively recently the theoretical and methodological tools needed to make them (and to explore the complexities of urban culture) become available. It is easy to forget, too, that it was not the insights of academics writing within any established urban studies tradition that, initially, proved influential in this regard. Rather, it was the theories and methods of an emerging interdisciplinary field of cultural enquiry that, albeit unintentionally, effectively reshaped the parameters of urban scholarship. Influenced by poststructuralism and with little knowledge of (or interest in) established traditions in urban thought, many cultural theorists of the 1970s and 1980s became fascinated with the phenomenon of place, and by the form and culture of cities. From this fascination, city spaces came to be conceptualized as 'texts' that were inscribed with the multifaceted, sometimes overlapping, traces of time, experience and use. It was argued that these texts could be read (or deconstructed) to reveal both a complex tapestry of meanings and underpinning relations of power.

If utopian visions for a better society achieved through the transformation of the city had guided urban studies throughout most of the twentieth century, these new cultural approaches were decidedly counter-utopian. In particular, they pivoted on celebrating urban chaos and difference, and advocated exploring the city as it is, not as it might be.

This chapter further investigates cultural studies approaches to the city commenced in Chapter 3. Considered, in particular, are conceptualizations of the relationship between the urban landscape, the construction of meaning, and the negotiation of identity. To this end, the chapter begins with a discussion of the foundations of cultural urban thought before moving on to examine semiotics, which provides a methodological frame for many analyses of the city as 'text'. The chapter then considers the seminal work of Walter Benjamin, whose writings on nineteenth-century Paris explored the 'knowing' of that city through the work of artists as well as through the experiences and meanderings of the urban *flâneur*. Benjamin's work, in particular, underpins many of the so-called postmodern approaches to studying the city and urban cultures. Also considered is the suggestion that spatial practices create a myriad of narrative maps which, although mythological, imaginary and partial, are central to the process of transforming cartographic space into places of meaning and memory. As a result, within a single urban landscape, a multiplicity of places will exist that have been defined through use, imagination and cultural practice. It also points to the likelihood that such a confusion of meaning and references can lead to a fixation on surfaces at the expense of depth and 'true' experience. The significance of place-naming to this process is also discussed.

The city experienced

It is not possible to talk about cultural studies as a unified domain of enquiry or as a discipline like sociology or philosophy. It is highly fragmented and has its roots in a number of quite divergent disciplines and often-competing 'ways of seeing' and interpreting the world. Seminal has been the work of a range of scholars, including Roland Barthes (1968, [1957] 1972), Michel Foucault (1972), Jacques Derrida (1976) and those associated with the Centre for Contemporary Cultural Studies at the University of Birmingham in the United Kingdom (e.g. Hall and Jefferson 1976; Willis 1977). Cultural studies approaches have also been influenced by poststructuralist theories of language, representation and subjectivity, and often endorse the view that the project of modernity has been rendered obsolete and the world has entered a period of postmodernity. This is a world supposedly dominated by simulations, images and the fragmentation of identity (McGuigan 1999). What is fascinating is the extent to which the city and the urban, as cultural texts, have become central to many cultural studies analyses. In addition, the notion of space has emerged as pivotal to explorations of subjectivity and, more generally, as metaphor, now permeates the language of (postmodern) cultural enquiry (Zukin 1992). Also of significance is the idea of postmodernism as an aesthetic form which is most notably associated with architecture and urban design (see Chapter 5). Notions of postmodernism have had a significant impact on cultural approaches to the urban, with the idea of the 'postmodern city' being particularly important.

The theories and methods of cultural studies resonated with urban scholars, many of whom were (as discussed in Chapter 3) becoming dissatisfied with established theoretical and analytical frameworks by the end of the 1970s (Hall 1992). The key features and orientations associated with the so-called cultural 'turn' in urban analysis are succinctly summarized in the following passage from Julie Graham (1988: 60) 'modernism, homogeneity, rationality, mass production, metanarrative, tract housing and space are dead. Long live post-modernism, pluralism, power and desire, small batch production, local narrative, indigenous architecture and place'. According to David Harvey (1989), the first indication that a shift in urban theory and analysis was underway emerged in the early 1970s with the publication of *Soft City*, Jonathan Raban's (1974) rather idiosyncratic celebration of life in 'his' city of London. When considered in retrospect, Harvey (1989: 3) suggests it is possible to see that this book flagged the emergence of new ways of thinking and talking about the city and the 'problems of urban life'. Specifically, in Harvey's view, *Soft City* marked the arrival of the idea of the postmodern city and its representation of urban life can be seen as emblematic of what has come to be associated with the 'postmodern condition' (Lyotard 1984).

Whether this theoretical shift is to be embraced as transcending or augmenting existing modes of explanation and analysis, or rejected as a retrograde denial of structures, remains a vexed question. For Harvey, however, the approach articulated in *Soft City* is, ultimately, unconvincing. Of particular concern is that Raban explicitly dismisses the relevance and utility of traditional overarching explanations of urbanism – those grounded in notions of rationality. In their place he proffers an analysis situated in the lived moments of individual everyday urban experiences and imaginings. The significance of the rejection of the metanarrative cannot be underestimated because, until this time, the formulation of (and, indeed, necessity for) totalizing theoretical explanations had been accepted as de rigueur in all the social sciences, including urban studies, and underpinned the practical interventions in cityspace of urban policy and planning. In rejecting such explanatory frames, Raban espouses a view that articulates with perhaps the most trenchant of the theoretical challenges to come from scholars loosely associated with a postmodern cultural critique: the rendering as contestable the epistemological assumptions underpinning all social research, including those associated with the urban. In particular, the foundations of Marxist political economy (discussed in Chapter 3) and the ecological theories of the Chicago School (see Chapter 2) are destabilized.

According to Raban, his actions and those of his fellow city-dwellers are fundamentally irrational. Indeed, everything about London – the place and its people – is, in his view, fragmented and deeply contradictory. The discordant rhythms of the city have their genesis in the accidental intersections of time and space. Raban's city is a city of signs, images, surfaces, movement and transient moments; it is an 'emporium of style' (1974: 57–84) where people assume different identities almost at will. Raban tells of his escape from the oppressive boundaries and surveillance of the communal rural village and of finding freedom in the confusion and anonymity of the metropolis. His metropolis is a place that Simmel ([1903] 1995) would recognize where the 'freedom of the city is enormous. Here one can choose and invent one's society, and live more deliberately than anywhere else. Nothing is fixed, the possibilities of personal change and renewal are endless and open' (Raban 1974: 225). But freedom has its consequences, and Raban remains at heart a country mouse – wary of the dangers of the city he 'run[s] from bolthole to bolthole, unequipped to embrace that spaciousness and privacy of city life which so often presents itself as mere emptiness and fog' (1974: 225). Hence the city of freedom is, simultaneously, a place of danger and, indeed, the book's opening anecdote is of an inexplicable act of urban violence (1974: 2–3). The following passage reveals the depths of his urban trepidation: 'Cities are scary and impersonal, and the best most of us can manage is a fragile hold on our route through the streets. We cling to friends and institutions, exaggerate the importance of belonging, fear being alone too much' (1974: 225).

No doubt influenced by the work of Simmel, this tension between urban freedom and urban fear is at the core of Raban's postmodern city. In addition, Raban directly takes issue with the urban sociology of the influential Chicago School theorists, Park, Wirth and others (discussed in Chapter 2). While urban sociology had sought traditionally to identify the patterns and rules governing urban life and their underpinning rationality, Raban (1974: 152) dismisses this quest as both misguided and impossible. The city for Raban is unknowable and its boundaries fluid – it is an ambivalent space. In many respects Raban's unknowable, incoherent city can be read as a metaphor for a postmodern society. It is also tempting to categorize *Soft City* as a kind of postmodern ethnography in the tradition of community studies and the Chicago School (discussed in Chapter 2). But this is patently not the case. The fundamental difference between *Soft City* and urban ethnography is that Raban is not interested in penetrating the backstage of everyday life in order to learn more about a particular group – perhaps the residents of a neighbourhood, or an urban gang – and to uncover their reality. For Raban there is no reality outside of personal experience, and the personal experiences he seeks to explore are his own.

The intellectual influences on Raban's analysis are many and eclectic; however, it is difficult, as Harvey (1989: 6) notes, not to be aware of the significance of Roland Barthes's (1968, [1957] 1972) theories of signification and symbolic meaning. The following passage is illustrative of Barthes's influence:

> Most of the goods we consume come in two kinds: as objects of nutrition and investment, or, in slightly modified form, as epigrammatic ideas, liberated from their strict function ... Their most important function is to tell us something about the people who buy them; they belong to the hazardous but necessary urban art of self-projection.
>
> (Raban 1974: 98)

Within this conceptualization, Raban suggests that food, motor cars, houses and suburban location have been 'transformed' into 'badge[s] of affiliation to a caste, a symbol not of status but of taste and identity' (1974: 103). In broad terms, Raban is reading as texts his city, its artefacts and its life. While Raban's use of Barthes is perhaps subtle, cultural urbanists since have engaged quite explicitly in urban semiotic analysis; it is thus important to explore the underpinnings of this approach and its analytical strengths.

Texts and contexts

Building on the structural linguistics of Ferdinand de Saussure (1960) and the anthropology of Claude Lévi-Strauss (1955), in particular, Barthes's ideas about signification, myth and ideology had a profound influence on the development of interdisciplinary cultural studies and the emergence of culturally informed approaches to the study of the city. Semiology, or the 'science of signs', provided Barthes with both taxonomy, and the theoretical and methodological starting point from which to analyse the complex relationship that exists between everyday texts (such as photographic images, magazines and items of clothing) and power (Barthes [1957] 1972).

It was his original contention that many fundamental social ideologies and values are embedded in cultural artefacts and practices but are rarely evident – these are the 'mythologies' of everyday life. Barthes argued that in every culture there are core values and beliefs that are accepted as 'givens'; for instance, there are socially ascribed ways of being a man or a woman, and associated acceptable forms of femininity and masculinity. These values and beliefs, in Barthes's view, support particular historically and culturally specific power relationships. To this end, he sought to use semiotics to analyse the production and reception of meaning through texts. From this analysis he aimed to expose those ideologies and values embedded in the texts but which appear as natural or 'common sense' to those who share a culture. He argued that in order to uncover the layers of meaning ingrained in texts and reveal political significances, it was necessary to understand the language-like system of communication that links the signifier (the carrier of meaning) and the signified (the abstract concept referred to by the sign).

Central to Barthes's semiotics then is the concept of the cultural text which, according to Duncan and Duncan (1992), he defines in a

> broad fashion as a space in which there is a weaving together of symbols to create an irreducible plurality of meaning. It is a signifying practice that abolishes the distinction between writing and reading, production and consumption. A text does not occupy space as does a work on the library shelf, but is a field within which there is an activity of production, of signification.
>
> (Duncan and Duncan 1992: 27)

A cultural text, as a combination of signs, can be static and seemingly fixed (like a photograph, a poster, an item of clothing, or a room and the furniture within it viewed at a particular moment in time), or dynamic, such as the same room observed at different times, a busy urban street, a building, or even an entire neighbourhood. An *urban* text, therefore, can be a physical structure, like an individual building, a monument or a building facade, or it can be a particular 'lived' space – a neighbourhood, a park or shopping plaza. An urban text can also be any of the various official and unofficial ways in which the city is represented, including architectural elevations, maps, planning documents and real estate publications (Gottdiener and Lagopoulos 1986a: 3), as well as those influential representations of city life and spaces featured in films, music, art, literature and other cultural forms (see Chapter 7). Urban texts can be read in isolation or in combination. What is of significance are the 'discourses, symbols, metaphors and fantasies' (Donald 1992: 422) through which culturally specific meanings are assigned to the urban environment and urban life. The coding and decoding of these meanings is an interactive process with the users of the city being actively engaged in a dialogue with its spaces.

Barthes explored landscape and urban texts in a number of works published at different times during his life; indeed, his famous anthology *Mythologies* ([1957] 1972) includes two essays that analyse place as a system of communication. These essays are 'The blue guide', which is a semiotic exploration of travel guides as the socially and culturally constructed lenses through which travellers 'see' landscapes, and 'The Eiffel Tower', which is a semiotic analysis of the famous Paris landmark. Less well known is his essay 'Semiology and the urban' (Barthes [1970–71] 1986) which appeared in print more than a decade after *Mythologies* at a time when (partly influenced by the psychoanalytic theory of Jacques Lacan) he was in the process of re-evaluating his rigid structuralist approach to semiotics in favour of one that emphasized the centrality of the body and individual sensory pleasure in the reception and interpretation of texts – including those of the urban (Gottdiener and Lagapoulos 1986b; Duncan and Duncan 1992). This move away from the cultural and the historical to the personal and the bodily, makes the insights put forward in 'Semiology and the urban' very different from those contained in his earlier works, such as 'The blue guide'. Indeed, according to Gottdiener and Lagapoulos (1986b: 88), 'Semiology and the urban' is, in contrast to previous works, more psychoanalytic than social.

In what is, thus, like Raban's, a highly personal interpretation of cityspace, Barthes argues that the urban text is one where unstable and transient signifieds are continuously being transformed into signifiers – forming an 'infinite chain of metaphors whose signified is always retreating or becomes itself a signifier' (Barthes [1970–71] 1986: 95). What this means is that, as all users of the city write their own relationships with space, there can be no scientific, knowable basis to the interpretation of the landscape – no straightforward relationship between the signifier and the signified. Rather, the urban text is experienced and thus read in a myriad of highly idiosyncratic ways. According to Barthes, and at odds with his earlier theorizing, the relationship between the signifier and the signified (the key elements in the transmission of meaning) is intrinsically unstable. Indeed, in this formulation, the signifier is conceptualized as being largely independent of the signified. In other words, the circulation of meaning and the connection between the signifier and the signified is never straightforward, and neither meaning nor interpretation is 'fixed' even at the level of myth. Rather, '[a]ll signifying systems are productions of historical and cultural conventions' (Duncan and Duncan 1992: 19). Although still a form of communication, the grounds on which to make interpretations and generalizations are no longer firm. This highly individual process of reading or knowing a city is thus described by Barthes ([1970–71] 1986: 92) as follows: 'The city is a discourse and this discourse is truly a language: the city speaks to its inhabitants, we speak our city, the city where we are, simply by living in it, by wandering through it, by looking at it.' And, with reference to Victor Hugo's 'intuition', Barthes ([1970–71] 1986: 95) further suggests that 'the city is writing. He who moves about the city, e.g., the user of the city ... is a kind of reader who, following his obligations and his movements, appropriates fragments of the utterance in order to actualize them in secret.'

It is in the acts of 'wandering' and 'looking' that one reads and interprets the urban landscape. Hence, to follow this logic a little further, it is in relation to shifting personal histories that urban texts are interpreted and reinterpreted. In accumulating urban stories from the multiple users of the city, from the 'native to the stranger' and piecing together their fragmentary readings, it may be possible to gain insights into the city and its 'language' (Barthes ([1970–71] 1986: 97). In contrast to his earlier formulation of semiotics with its emphasis on ideology and structural power, this approach totally neglects the social and political contexts within which the urban text is produced emphasizing, instead (as Raban does), the primacy of personal readings and sensory experiences.

The final decades of the twentieth century saw a proliferation of 'readings' of the urban landscape, with shopping centres/malls (often represented as the quintessential spaces of postmodernism) being a particular favourite (Gottdiener 1986; Fiske et al. 1988; Morris 1988; Winchester 1992). Such semiotic analyses of the urban landscape were influenced both by Barthes's structuralism and his poststructuralism, as well as by the work of other semioticians, such as Umberto Eco (1976). In spite of these differing influences, however, the major semiotic approaches within urban studies have tended to divide along the fault-lines evident in Barthes's work. With one approach being primarily concerned with signification in its own terms and for its own sake and having little regard for social contexts, and the other seeking to explore social, political and ideological imperatives through the study of signification and urban symbolism (Gottdiener and Lagopoulos 1986a). One outcome has been that many semiotic readings of the built environment (those undertaken within the first analytical tradition) are little more than amusing contributions to what often appears to be a faddish academic game.

In focusing solely on the text and individual psychological responses to the text, and in ignoring the social contexts within which the text is produced, many such works are context-bound, relativist and highly individualistic – like the work of Raban. If undertaken as part of a broader sociology of the city, however, it has been demonstrated that urban semiology can provide insights into the extent to which the urban landscape is implicated in the construction, representation and reproduction of cultural meanings and power relations (Stevenson 1998). When explored in the context of changing social relations including those associated with gender, class, ethnicity and so on, a semiotic reading can reveal the dynamic (and insidious) dimensions of social power not otherwise evident. For instance, Feminist readings of the urban landscape have exposed its embedded masculine codes and revealed both the obvious symbolism of urban skylines dominated by high-rise buildings, as well as the unequal gender relations more subtly inscribed in urban monuments and the design of streetscapes (Morris 1988; Monk 1992). They have also provided alternative urban geographies that draw on the experiences of women rather than of men (Wilson 2001). Similarly, my own work into city reimaging and urban redevelopment highlights the ways in which urban symbolism can be manipulated to consolidate and reproduce existing power relations, reinforcing the economic and political interests of those who have long controlled the urban development agenda (Stevenson 1998, 1999b).

One of the most compelling figures in cultural urban studies that has come to be closely connected with processes of reading and interpreting the urban landscape and the experience urban life is the urban *flâneur*. The *flâneur* was popularized by the Marxist cultural critic, Walter Benjamin, who was interested in the interrelationship between the city, as a multilayered meaningful space, and the act of uncovering these layers of meaning. At the same time, Benjamin was disturbed by the inequality starkly evident in the modern capitalist city. As Savage and Warde (1993: 123) explain, Benjamin's work 'addressed urban meaning as the interface between personal memories and experiences, and the historical construction of dominant meanings and values'. Benjamin's work also provides a way of seeing 'the manner in which an urban sensibility structures our narratives of the real' (Keith 2000: 411). It is thus important to explore his ideas in a little more detail.

Into the 'labyrinth'

Determining just who the *flâneur* is (or was) and exactly what *flânerie* involves (and what this understanding might mean for a sociology of the city) is a highly complicated process (see, for instance, contributions to Tester 1994). Essentially, though, the *flâneur* is a literary construction of the nineteenth century. He is a poet, an artist and, most importantly, a 'stroller'.

An amateur 'street detective' (Morawski 1994; Shields 1994) who passed his time moving effortlessly and, seemingly, invisibly through the spaces of the emerging modern city of the nineteenth century, in particular through the newly constructed arcades of Paris. But in the act of strolling the *flâneur* did not just observe urban life, he was, according to Benjamin, engaged in an 'archaeological' process of unearthing the myths and 'collective dreams' of modernity (Frisby 1986: 224). *Flânerie*, then, becomes a way of reading urban texts, a methodology for uncovering the traces of social meaning that are embedded in the layered fabric of the city (Featherstone 1998: 910).

It was largely through the work of Benjamin that the *flâneur* developed as an intriguing (albeit mercurial) figure in urban discourse. Benjamin's work, however, is incomplete and often contradictory (see Buck-Morss 1995). In addition, he had considerable difficulty getting much of it published in his lifetime and significant parts either did not appear until well after his death or were never published (see the letters between Adorno and Benjamin reproduced in Taylor (1980) for a discussion of some of the intellectual objections he encountered from fellow Marxists). It was even longer before many of his key works were translated into English and began to influence wider academic debates about cities and urban cultures. It was to be in his Arcades Project (*Das Passagen-Werk*), commenced in 1927, that Benjamin intended fully to explore his ideas about the city. Although this work is unfinished what were to be its central themes are set out in a number of related articles and a collection of framing notes written over a period of 17 years (see Buck-Morss 1995). Significant relevant works include 'One way street' (Benjamin [1928] 1979), 'Paris: capital of the nineteenth century' (Benjamin [1935] 1995) and various essays about the nineteenth-century poet Charles Baudelaire and his celebrations of the *flâneur* (Benjamin 1973).

For Benjamin the nineteenth century was a period of tension between antiquity (a time of dreaming) and modernity (the awakening), and his exploration of the city, architecture and the use of public space was but one aspect of his quest to investigate the origins of modernity within that century (Frisby 1986: 221). To this end, Benjamin's aim was to examine the impact of industrialization on contemporary cultural practices, including art and the urban, and to examine the 'mythic forces' present in the emerging forms of creative expression (such as Surrealism) associated with industrial capitalism (Sontag 1979: 10; Buck-Morss 1995: 256). Like Georg Simmel (see Chapter 2), Benjamin saw the city and urban architecture as central to modernity; however, where Simmel was interested in examining individualistic ways of coping with urban life, Benjamin wanted to investigate city environments as repositories of collective memories and experiences. His was a search for the signs, metaphors and illusions of modernity (Frisby 1986).

Benjamin's intention, however, was not to form these 'traces' into a definitive linear historical narrative; rather, they were to remain as fragmentary glimpses of previous worlds able to be connected and reconnected in a range of ways to illuminate forgotten/alternative histories. Benjamin's overarching aim, therefore, was hardly modest in that he sought to 'interpret for his own generation [the collective] dream fetishes in which, in fossilized [material] form, history's traces survived' (Buck-Morss 1995: 39). He believed that key sites in which to uncover these traces were the decayed and/or abandoned spaces of the city, in particular, the arcades of Paris.

In Paris during the 15 years following 1822 something like 30 luxury pedestrian shopping arcades were created by the erection of glass roofs across inner city streets or 'passages' (Benjamin [1935] 1995: 46–7). These arcades were in many respects the forerunners to the modern department store, which developed also in the nineteenth century. The arcades intrigued Benjamin because here for the first time, he argued, were truly modern urban spaces designed specifically for the conspicuous consumption of the commodities of capitalist production. They were also places of architectural innovation in that extensive use was made of glass and a new 'artificial' building material – iron. The architectural and commercial style of the arcades was subsequently adopted by cities around the world – perhaps the first example of the serial reproduction of a modern built form. Buck-Morss (1995) explains the significance of the Parisian arcades to Benjamin's work, as follows:

> The covered shopping arcades of the nineteenth century were Benjamin's central image because they were the precise material replicas of the internal consciousness, or rather, the *un*conscious of the collective dreaming. All the errors of bourgeois conscious could be found there (commodity fetishism, reification, the world as 'inwardness'), as well as (fashion, prostitution, gambling) all of its utopian dreams. Moreover, the arcades were the first international style of modern architecture, hence part of the lived experience of a worldwide, metropolitan generation.
>
> (Buck-Morss 1995: 39)

Benjamin saw the arcades as entry points to the 'labyrinth' that is/was Paris. They were the 'crucial architectural trace of lost fantasies' (Frisby 1986: 210). In his notes for *Passagen-Werk*, Benjamin attempts to identify the users/inhabitants of the arcades and to speculate about their relationship to these spaces and to each other. Accordingly, as prostitutes and *flâneurs* where among those most highly visible in the arcades they became for Benjamin archetypes of the 'modern metropolis' (Shields 1996: 230). As Shields

(1996) explains it, Benjamin took on the task of uncovering the mythical underpinnings of the everyday activities, interactions and non-interactions of these 'types' to reveal the distinct ways in which they experienced the urban landscape and created alternative (unofficial) cultural traditions and urban histories. These were histories and traditions that had long since been 'forgotten'.

Benjamin's associated ideas about the uniqueness of individual buildings, neighbourhoods and cities and the essence or 'aura' of originality also afford a rich vein of insight to analyses of cities and urban cultures. The specificity of place, according to Benjamin, is the result of the relationship that exists between a particular building or city, and the histories, cultures and social practices embedded in that place. For instance, even though the architectural style of the Parisian arcades was copied/adopted by other cities, in Benjamin's view they were never actually replicated. Rather, they remained deeply embedded in their place and time, melded to the collective histories and memories of the uniqueness of Paris and the people who inhabited both the city and the arcades. Here Benjamin's work links closely with the discussion of urban symbolism (see pp. 58–62). Covered arcades may have been symbols of such signifieds as progress, bourgeois consumption and power, but they remained inextricably connected to the specificity of place. In other words, the replication of built form does not result in any replication of the traditions, practices or aura of the original city or space (Savage and Warde 1993: 137). Nor are the replicas like anywhere else – they too are embedded in a particular place and time.

Later in the nineteenth century, the department store usurped the arcades as places of conspicuous consumption, and the construction of Georges Haussmann's boulevards reshaped inner Paris (see Chapter 5). The emergence of the department store and the 'end' of the arcades signalled also the demise of the *flâneur* – in Benjamin's ([1935] 1995: 52) enigmatic words the department store was the space of the *flâneur*'s 'last practical joke'. Significantly, the development of the department store facilitated the emergence of a more highly 'feminized' public space and was, in part, responsible for forging new connections between (bourgeois) women and consumption. The department store provided women with options for experiencing and being in (quasi)public space that had previously not been available to them. Along with the emergence in the nineteenth century of white-collar occupations for women, such as clerks, hairdressers and shop assistants (Jordan 1999), the development of highly feminized spaces like department stores not only increased women's presence in public space, but also 'transformed the middle- and lower-middle-class woman's experience of public life' (Wilson 1995: 68). As has been pointed out repeatedly in the literature, the *flâneur* was unquestionably male, and *flânerie* was a way of experiencing and occupying urban space that was available only to men.

This does not mean, of course, that women were not present in public space or that they were excluded completely. Prostitutes, for instance, were highly visible (archetypal) occupants of the Parisian arcades, and other working-class women were also frequent users of public space (Wilson 1991, 1995, 2001). Wilson (1995) has suggested also that often women were present in public space in disguise. But, as Janet Wolff (1985) explains, there was no role as *flâneuse* available to women. They could be prostitutes, widows, lesbians or murder victims but the 'respectable' woman 'could not stroll alone in the city' (Wolff 1985: 41). In addition, Wolff (1985) argues that women's presence in nineteenth-century urban space has largely been rendered 'invisible' by literature and official discourse (including history). Clearly, these issues connect with broader debates within urban studies about gender (including women's relationship to public space) and the relevance of difference to the study and lived experience of cities and urban cultures that were discussed in Chapter 3. They are also relevant to pronouncements within cultural planning about developing an urban public culture (see Chapter 6).

In a tradition no doubt inspired by the work of Walter Benjamin, it has become increasingly common for artists, photographers and filmmakers today to work explicitly with the 'traces' of the built environment in the production of their art. They are the *flâneurs* (and *flâneuses*) of the contemporary city. To this end, artists often explicitly attempt through the visual and metaphorical 'excavation' of place to represent collective histories, nostalgia, memories and belonging. For instance, prominent Australian-based sculptor Anne Graham (1999) describes her planning for the artwork *Passage* (commissioned for Martin Place in central Sydney as part of the City of Sydney Sculpture Walk) as a process of working with the 'footprints' of the buildings that previously inhabited the site. She details a meticulous historical research process which informed, and was expressed through, the artwork produced – in particular, through the use of mist (Stevenson and Paton 2001). The issue of the city and its representation – the city *in* text rather than *as* text – is explored in Chapter 7.

Benjamin has made it possible for urbanists to recognize the lived complexity of the city in that he provides a framework for investigating the ways in which cultural identities and histories are inscribed in space. In particular, he has made it possible to conceptualize the city not as a single monolithic space, but as many places which have been constructed through use and experience. But he still retains an overarching concern with the social and with inequality – something which is frequently forgotten in the cultural studies analyses his work has informed. Recently, a focus on the experiential dimension of cities and their alternative uses has found resonance with those analyses of cities concerned with their significance as sites of resistance – themes which have been most eloquently developed in the work of French cultural theorist Michel de Certeau (1988).

Walking and the tactics of everyday life

De Certeau is concerned with the 'tactical' ways in which everyday activities or 'practices', such as reading, cooking and shopping, are used by the less powerful to subvert dominant social ideologies and power relations. In highlighting the creativity of everyday life he argues that the resources of a more powerful 'other' are routinely appropriated by and used to serve the interests of the subordinate. Such tactics, he suggests, are often overlooked or dismissed as part of the 'obscure background of social activity' by those academics concerned with more technocratic, systematic conceptions of power (de Certeau 1988: xi). Building, in part, on the work of Foucault, de Certeau identifies practices which 'elude discipline' while remaining within the 'field in which it is exercised' (1988: 96). In other words, these actions take place within existing (imposed) regulatory frameworks but manage to avoid the nets of surveillance, policing and discipline. For example, a renter might remake a flat as their 'own' through the socializing they do there, their choice of furnishings, the placement of personal effects, and the uses they make of different rooms (a room designated 'lounge room' may be used as a bedroom). In a range of ways, but always within the parameters set by the formal agreement they have with the landlord, the renter tactically claims as their own a space they do not possess in any economic sense. These tactics can (albeit in a small way) serve to disrupt or undermine capitalist social relations and the power derived from the private ownership of property. Through the ways in which it is occupied and used, the flat also plays an important role in framing and expressing the identity of the tenant.

Similarly, following de Certeau, John Fiske (1989a, 1989b) argues that young people routinely take the objects or commodities of capitalism, like clothing, magazines and other popular cultural forms, and use them creatively to express identities and values which, frequently, are in opposition to those of the dominant. Safety pins, for instance, were never intended by their manufacturers to be worn through noses, as they were by many punk rockers in the late 1970s. This tactic was for the punks an act of resistance and a marker of collective identity. Of course, the opportunism of capitalism is such that styles created by subcultural groups as markers of resistance frequently are (re)appropriated by mainstream culture – punk is just one subcultural style to emerge first in the repertoires of fashion designers and then later in mass-produced chain store form (Rowe 1995). The creativity of popular culture and everyday life means that new styles are continually being adopted as tactics of resistance. The city (or more accurately, the street) through the uses that urban dwellers make of its spaces, is, according to de Certeau, another important site of bottom-up tactical resistance.

Just as Benjamin recognized the contribution of urban walking to the construction and investigation of a culture, walking, as both activity and metaphor, is central also to the work of de Certeau. Of interest are popular practices – the cultures of the street. In addition, de Certeau is fascinated by the city as a 'lived text' and in this respect he has been deeply influenced by Barthes's work on signification, myth and the reception of meaning (discussed on pp. 58–62). De Certeau's point of departure is an analysis of the 'spatial practices' or 'tactics' which subvert the overarching meanings that have been inscribed or imposed on the landscape by official processes or 'strategies' such as architecture, planning and design. In opposition to the rational official 'concept-city', which de Certeau accepts exists as a knowable, totalizing space, he posits an unknowable dynamic city. This is a city which works within and against the mapped theoretical city. An understanding of this city (as a collection of spaces) begins with a consideration of its smallest elements – footsteps in the street.

Through walking, de Certeau argues, urban users both experience and create a city they cannot 'see' in the sense that it is possible to be only in the space one is occupying at a given time. The route one is following (where one has been and is going) and the shape of one's journey through urban space can be held only in memory or imagination, both of which would have been informed either by previous experience of this particular space or by its representation in map or pictorial form (see Chapter 7). De Certeau argues that it is in the act of walking that a 'myriad' of users write and rewrite the city as 'their' space – creating fragmentary stories that link and intersect with other fragmentary stories. It is also through these trajectories and connections that the city is given form (1988: 97). He explains this process and its significance as follows: 'The networks of these moving, intersecting writings compose a manifold story that has neither author nor spectator, shaped out of fragments of trajectories and alterations of spaces: in relationship to representations, it remains daily and indefinitely other' (de Certeau 1988: 93).

De Certeau goes on to claim that while it is possible to trace or mark a walker's journey on a map such representations fail to capture the quality or nature of the experience or act of walking. They are stripped of content and 'a way of being in the world [is] forgotten' (1988: 97). In addition, representations fail to reveal the tactical quality of 'the walk' and the ways in which space is claimed and interpreted through the act of walking. For the city-dweller, the 'invention' of place through practice also involves the remembering of stories associated with the place which, in turn, contribute to their connection to the place. These are the 'poetic spaces' of imagination, which Bachelard (1969) describes as framing a place-bound nostalgia. De Certeau also highlights the importance of physical and symbolic boundaries (such as place names) to the processes of experiencing and remembering the city, and in constructing the lived culture of the urban street. He suggests that the boundaries which delineate a space have both a spatial and a narrative form.

Raban (1974) describes the limits to 'his' London within the parameters of the 'official' city as follows:

> The Greater London Council is responsible for a sprawl shaped like a rugby ball about twenty five miles long and twenty miles wide; my city is a concise kidney-shaped patch within that space, in which no point is more than about seven miles from any other. On the south, it is bounded by the river, on the north by the fat tongue of Hampstead Heath and Highgate Village, on the west by Brompton cemetery and on the east by Liverpool Street station. I hardly ever trespass beyond those limits, and when I do I feel I'm in foreign territory, a landscape of hazard and rumour . . . I mark my boundaries with graveyards, terminal transportation points and wildernesses. Beyond them, nothing is trusted and anything might happen.
>
> (Raban 1974: 161)

Boundaries serve an important role in delineating one's place in the world – defining who one is as an occupant of cityspace. Geographer Doreen Massey (1992: 13) has argued that boundaries are pivotal to defining 'identity through negative counterposition with the Other beyond the boundary'. In other words, spatial cues, defined in terms of inclusion and exclusion, are employed in the negotiation of identity. Frequently, in the absence of personal experience, the identity of a delineated place is defined according to popular perceptions of the place and the dominant impressions that are ascribed to it deliberately or otherwise. This process is a significant factor contributing to the development of positive and negative images of place, including the stereotype of the stigmatized neighbourhood, suburb, city or region and in framing imagined urbanism (Stevenson 1998). In addition, the importance of naming to this process of mental mapping/ stereotyping cannot be underestimated.

De Certeau suggests that the official city exists, in part, as an outcome of having been named – the name unifies and sets apart. This is equally the case with streets and suburbs. However, names (or at least 'proper' names) also give places 'a meaning . . . that was previously unforeseen' (1988: 104), and thus a symbolic dimension which 'eludes' the official or imposed. For instance, according to de Certeau (1988: 104) 'names make themselves available to the diverse meanings given them by passers-by; they detach themselves from the places they were supposed to define and serve as imaginary meeting-points on itineraries'. There are also those names which linger in popular usage long after 'the place' has gone and which confuse the casual visitor or newcomer. In fact, they are key elements of place-based insider–outsider narratives. 'Bank Corner', 'Pommy Town' and 'Frog Hollow' are three examples from my own knowing and experience of place.

In many respects the symbolic unification of previously unrelated spatial fragments begins with the official and unofficial naming of the space. Paul Carter (1987: xxiv) asserts that place-naming is the act that transforms symbolically anonymous spaces into particular places for which a mythical past can exist and an imagined future is possible. This act of naming is central to the process of bringing a place into existence. The popularity of songs about named places (particularly in the United States) is another dimension of this process. Through being invoked in song often (relatively) anonymous places (such as Arizona, Memphis and Albuquerque) are constructed by, and become elements of, the mythologies of popular culture. In this context more songs have probably been written about New York than about any other city in the world.

There is an intricate connection between the naming of places and encoded cultural meanings. However, these spatial meanings are not essential, nor are they fixed or stable. Rather, meaning is problematic, requiring continued definition, redefinition, constitution and reconstitution through discourse including through popular culture and the activities of walking and occupying space. Equally, spatial meaning, including naming, is vulnerable to manipulation by particular interest groups for a range of ends, be they political, social or commercial objectives – issues which articulate with those discussed in Chapter 6.

Conclusion: surfaces and depths

Since the mid-1970s there has been a burgeoning interest in investigating the ways in which people use and experience the city, and in uncovering the meanings they derive from this engagement. As has been suggested in this chapter and in Chapter 3, this interest was initially prompted by two factors. Initially important was the development a theoretical vocabulary with which to discuss urban experiences and the complexity of everyday urban life. Second, there was by the 1970s increasing dissatisfaction with the established theoretical frameworks of urban sociology. Where traditional urban analyses sought to identify the regularities and rules governing urban development, urbanism and urban inequality, the point of departure for work concerned with notions of experience was that the city had no identifiable and consistent rhythms. Thus, there was little point in searching for and invoking overarching factors, such as capitalism and patriarchy, as explanations of urban phenomenon. Instead, culturally informed research focused on the actions and interactions of urban dwellers – life as it is lived on the streets and in the neighbourhoods – and framed their analyses principally in terms of these micro-situations.

This emerging body of work also sought to explore the symbolic and the interpretative dimensions of urban life and, thus, supposedly to move beyond the structural, the predictable, and the political to delve into the irrational and serendipitous. An endeavour compellingly undertaken in Raban's book *Soft City* which is discussed in the chapter as being both pivotal to, and emblematic of, this cultural (postmodern) approach to the city. The aims of Raban's book are deceptive in their simplicity. He seeks to investigate 'his' city of London and his own deeply ambivalent relationship with its spaces. He is not interested in drawing on totalizing explanatory frames for this discussion, nor does he attempt to generalize from his experiences to those of other urban dwellers. The relationship he describes has been formed in the context of his own personal biography and not as a result of larger historical forces. *Soft City* is a highly idiosyncratic account of one person's experience of urban life. But the book is not atheoretical. As is discussed in this chapter, the language and insights of *Soft City* have been informed by a range of disparate theoretical perspectives, some from within mainstream urban studies and others from the interdisciplinary field of cultural studies. In addition, Raban connects (sometimes obliquely) with a number of the central concerns of social and cultural analysis, in particular, those associated with the challenge to structuralism. But his, ultimately, is a city of surfaces.

The themes of the symbolic and the interpretative recur in the cultural studies literature on the city. In this respect, much of it links with, and makes use of, the insights of several key cultural theorists many of whose ideas continue to be overlooked within mainstream urban studies. However, this neglect ignores the potential of this body of work to provide fruitful ways of dealing with the conceptual breach between the social and personal. A way of overcoming the chasm between analyses of the micro and those macro approaches focused on social structures. A way of coming to terms with both the surfaces and the depths of the urban. To this end, the chapter explored the contributions that three significant cultural theorists – Barthes, Benjamin and de Certeau – have and can make to the study of the city. The chapter demonstrates that a cultural analysis is fruitful for investigating, not just personal meaning systems, but also broader political and ideological factors and contexts, their subtleties and the relationship between them. For instance, Barthes's early work demonstrated the significance of texts in the reproduction of dominant social and political values and power relationships. Similarly, Benjamin's development of Baudelaire's idea of the urban *flâneur* was much more than a personal rendering of urban space. Rather, it was a way of delving into the traces of social meaning embedded in the built environment. As Benjamin conceptualized it, *flânerie* was a highly complex and intricate endeavour capable of uncovering the collective memories, experiences, signs and metaphors of modernity and De Certeau's probing of the creative tensions that exist between the 'concept city' and the lived city of experience also provide keen insights into the symbolic and mythological dimensions of urban space.

In different, often contradictory ways, the theoretical themes investigated in this chapter and other insights from cultural studies discussed elsewhere, can do more than just explore the relationship between the built environment and the negotiation of personal meaning. Rather, when undertaken in the context of a broader analysis of urban processes, cultural theories and methods can provide incisive ways of understanding the connectedness of the lived and the structural elements of urban life. Nowhere is this relationship more evident than in the practices of architecture and urban design and the discourses that legitimize them. After all it is within built space that cultures are negotiated and feelings of belonging expressed. These issues are developed in the next chapter, which considers the key trends in city building beginning with the reconstruction of Paris in the nineteenth century.

Further reading

Gottdiener, M. and Lagopoulos, A. (eds) (1986c) *The City and the Sign: An Introduction to Urban Semiotics*. New York: Columbia University Press.
Harvey, D. (1989) *The Condition of Postmodernity: An Enquiry into the Origins of Cultural Change*. Oxford: Basil Blackwell.

DESIGNING THE URBAN: FROM THE CITY BEAUTIFUL TO THE 'END' OF MODERNISM

> Then will come the dream city gleaming white impalpably through swathing mists of steam that jet across the vast shining façades that will pile up, mass upon mass, tower upon tower into the heavens and the myriad of uncountable windows will catch and reflect the rays of the setting sun, causing the whole enormous piled up mass to flash and glitter in the sunset yellowy like a fairy city built of clouds, orange and yellow and delicate white, that goes sailing into the sunset.
>
> (Devereux 1925: 52)

Introduction: boulevards, skyscrapers and pastiche

The uniqueness of any city lies in the specific arrangement, form and function of its spaces and the intersection between these spaces and individual and collective experience. In other words, it is in the idiosyncratic coincidences of time, space and culture that individual urban identities are forged and the rhythms of city life created. Pivotal here are the aesthetic and strategic practices of architecture and urban design which, through a complex of formal and informal processes contribute to the creation of urban cultures as well as giving shape to distinctive city image. This nexus of built form, imagination and social interaction operates at both the micro- and the macro-levels, applying as surely to creating and defining the character and 'feel' of a particular neighbourhood as it does to delimiting the city as an imagined unity. Cities divide into geographically discrete precincts which rarely conform to imposed administrative or political boundaries. Rather, they form around the activities of commerce, sociability, domesticity, and/or collective identity. The resulting precincts have a vitality and a 'look' that marks each as unique. In addition, the built environment can define a city in ways that are frequently iconic providing the world's 'great' cities with readily recognizable markers of their distinctiveness and status in the international urban hierarchy as well as framing specific place-based experiences. For instance, it is undeniable that the towers, canyons and brash modernism of New York City both are instantly familiar and structure an urban culture that is palpably different from that experienced within the low-rise, post-imperial grandeur that is London.

It is the relationship between the constructed landscape and the processes of forming and reforming urban cultures that underpins the concerns of this chapter. In particular, the chapter explores some of the ways in which urban design and architecture frame city life as theory, aesthetic and lived experience. To this end, the legacy of Haussmann's reconstruction of Paris is introduced in relation to the building of urban landscapes which are direct expressions of political power. Conversely, however, these same places can also facilitate public engagement and foster community. Also discussed in the chapter is the immense influence on city life of the modernist aesthetic philosophy that form should follow function. In the 1960s, for example, this essentially anti-urban philosophy was used to justify massive slum clearances, the destruction of neighbourhood communities, and the building of alienating public spaces, such as high-rise housing developments for low-income earners and vast networks of freeways. If this is the urban legacy of the modernist concern with the general, the minimal and the formal, though, the theory and practice of postmodernism are shaping a very different urban aesthetic. With an emphasis on 'the local', playful echoes of the present and the past are combined to create urban environments that frequently seem little more than a pastiche of ornamentation and form. Although legitimized in terms of the idiosyncrasies of place, they often appear mass produced and artificial.

Landscapes of power

The City Beautiful is the name given to an approach to urban design that emerged during the nineteenth century with the radical rebuilding of the central districts of a number of European cities, most famously Paris and Vienna. It was in the twentieth century, however, that the movement found its most widespread expression. In particular, in the plans and built form of the major cities of many emerging, often postcolonial, nations, such as India, Australia and the United States, and those of the 'new' totalitarian empires of that century, including the Soviet Union and Nazi Germany (Hall 1992). With the City Beautiful movement the connection between the urban landscape and power that invariably underpins all urban development and public architecture was made explicit. With differing emphases, it has been power in all its manifestations, including political, military, gender, religious and economic that singularly or in various combinations has been significant. In cities around the world, the power relations informing the City Beautiful have legitimized the design and construction of potent symbols of supremacy in the form of monuments, streetscapes, buildings and in the location and design of parks and gardens. The spaces of the City Beautiful are those of the civic or public realm – the sites of ceremonies, parades and imposing public architecture (Alonso 1963), of movement and congregation. They are places where large numbers of strangers can mingle in ways not possible in the cramped streets and lane-ways of Renaissance or medieval city centres.

The most famous nineteenth-century practitioner associated with the City Beautiful was Georges Haussmann, whose reconstruction of Paris under the auspices of Emperor Louis Napoleon III transformed the look and feel of that city from a place of dark and narrow streets – and the arcades romanticized by the poet Baudelaire (discussed in Chapter 4) – to one of boulevards, civic buildings and a lively street culture. It was Haussmann who, as Prefect of Paris, oversaw the wholesale clearance of slum areas in the centre of the ancient city and in their place ordered the construction of the elaborate system of boulevards, markets, parks, cultural buildings and bridges that is contemporary Paris. Places which are now important markers of the city – internationally recognizable symbols of its supposed way of life and identity as a city of sophistication, romance, creativity and the avant-garde. Thus the urban culture (both real and mythologized) that developed with Haussmann's rebuilding of Paris continues to resonate in the contemporary popular imagination as elemental to the experience of this city.

The massive rebuilding project that Haussmann set in train was revolutionary, even visionary, in its time. Indeed, Marshall Berman (1988: 150) describes the network of boulevards which have come to be seen as emblematic of the reconstructed Paris as being 'the most spectacular urban innovation of the nineteenth century and the decisive breakthrough in the modernization of the traditional city'. Something like a quarter of the city's workforce was directly employed in Haussmann's rebuilding projects. Once completed, the new spaces facilitated trade and fostered local economic development, at the same time they provided sweeping vistas across urban space and made possible both the congregation and easy movement of people (including the police and military personnel) within and between city precincts (Berman 1988). The boulevards, in particular, became places of both commence and community. It was in the shops, restaurants and pavement cafés that lined the boulevards that large numbers of people could come together for a range of novel (modern) urban experiences.

Unlike the objectives of the Garden City and other late-nineteenth-century urban reform movements (discussed in Chapter 2), however, the transformation of Paris initiated by Napoleon and overseen by Haussmann was not an attempt on the part of the powerful to promote health and sanitation or improve the living conditions of the urban poor. Rather, underpinning Haussmann's interventions in the Parisian landscape was the linking of power and social control to architecture and urban design. In effect, the massive slum clearances that were undertaken were done, in part, for reasons of law and order – being an explicit strategy for crowd and riot control – as well as to facilitate trade and commerce. As many urban commentators have noted, the boulevards of the 'new' Paris were intended to make it more difficult for potential revolutionaries to erect barricades and partition the city as their predecessors effectively had done. In addition, the boulevards became places for military parades and symbolic displays of the supremacy of Emperor Napoleon. As Miles (1997: 23) neatly explains, '[w]hilst medieval streets were gaps between buildings in the Baroque city they became avenues of procession'.

The use of the Parisian boulevards for this, and other forms of political urban spectacle continued throughout the twentieth century. For instance, during the Second World War the invading Germans used a parade down the Champs Elysées as a way of symbolically claiming the city for the Third Reich, while the newsreel footage of Charles de Gaulle leading the parade down the same boulevard that marked the liberation of Paris is an enduring post-war image. Urban historian Lewis Mumford ([1938] 1958: 96) succinctly describes the connection between the symbolic, the military and the City Beautiful as follows:

> military traffic was the determining factor in the new city plan . . . The esthetic effect of the regular ranks and the straight line of soldiers is increased by the regularity of the avenue: the unswerving line of march greatly contributes to the display of power, and a regiment moving thus gives the impression that it would break through a solid wall without losing a beat.
>
> (Mumford [1938] 1958: 96)

The reshaped Paris provided a redevelopment model for 'emerging and expanding cities in every corner of the world, from Santiago to Saigon' (Berman 1988: 152). For instance, in the United States, the City Beautiful influenced the monumentalism of Washington, DC, the nation's capital city and inspired renowned architect and urban planner Daniel Burnham.

Burnham's famous 1909 plan for the redevelopment of the city of Chicago explicitly sought to reproduce the form and character of Paris. Like Haussmann, Burnham oversaw the demolition of slums, and the building of parks and roadways. Interestingly, Burnham's plan was innovative for its time in that it sought to connect the city to its waterfront, with the major roads leading to 'a green park next to the inland sea' (Sennett 1990: 95). Burnham was backed in his endeavours to rebuild Chicago by local business interests who saw the redevelopment as crucial to the economic revitalization of the city. This is a connection which has framed and made possible countless urban redevelopment projects (City Beautiful or otherwise) throughout the twentieth century. Indeed, the City Beautiful has been described as 'an expression of the political power of the business community with little concern for social equity' (Short 1991: 121). However, as already argued, it would be misleading to suggest that it has been the power of the 'business community' alone that, initially or subsequently, has been influential in framing the urban agenda. Nevertheless, the role of business can never be underestimated.

Elsewhere in the world, the urban strategies of the Fascist regimes of the 1930s were intended to create urban spaces that were symbolic expressions of the absolute power of these totalitarian regimes. Indeed, Hitler reportedly had a detailed knowledge of the City Beautiful designs for Paris and Vienna, including information about the exact dimensions of the Champs Elysées (Hall 1992: 198). The designs and landscapes associated with Facism perhaps have come to represent the City Beautiful ideal at its most sinister. Interestingly, though, in the opinion of renowned urban planning historian Peter Hall (1992: 192), Canberra, the capital city of Australia, should be regarded as the 'city beautiful exceptional'. Hall argues that the crucial factor contributing to the earning of this mantle was the lengthy period of time that elapsed between when the vision of American architects Walter Burley-Griffin and Marion Mahoney for the new city was accepted by the Australian government and when it finally took shape (more or less) as they planned.

Overtly and subtly, the influence of the City Beautiful philosophy on the form of cities throughout the world has been considerable. The planned cities of the City Beautiful all share common features although each redevelopment may have been driven by different sets of interests, including intriguing alliances between visionary architects and the powerful (be they emperor, business interests, government or dictator). More generally, though, the City Beautiful has informed in a variety of ways the ideas, practices and accepted symbolism of nineteenth-, twentieth- and twenty-first-century city-centre design and architecture. Specific expectations and images frame collective views about how a city centre should look, what activities should take place there, and what role these spaces should play in announcing a town or city as a 'place' and in defining its ceremonial role. In addition, the formalism of the City Beautiful articulated with other modernist approaches to the building of cities emerging at the same time and, in combination, provided the twentieth century with its most enduring built icon, the skyscraper (Stern et al. 1987). It also legitimized the massive urban renewal projects undertaken during the 1960s in cities, such as New York (Berman 1988). Of significance as well, of course, was Le Corbusier's ideal of the 'Radiant City' (discussed on pp. 82–7). Underpinning the emergence of modernist architecture and design was the teleological view that form should follow function. Indeed, as Hall (1992: 183) suggests, the 'City Beautiful rapidly gave way to the City Functional'. With this shift came the fusing of everyday life with the machine-like products of modern architecture, land-use zoning, instrumental rationality, and the tyranny of 'the road'.

A 'sidewalk ballet'

Any consideration of modernism as a specific architectural style invariably raises bigger questions about the complex and contradictory features of modernism as an identifiable cultural movement (see McGuigan 1999). It also drifts into the allied conceptual concerns of modernity and modernization. At the very least it points to them as silences. However, any in-depth exploration of these vexed issues is beyond the scope of a book such as this, as is any attempt to tease out their interconnections. That said, it is important to acknowledge that both as concepts and lived phenomena, cultural modernism, modernity and modernization are intricately linked with the linguistic and intellectual distinctiveness of each often being difficult to sustain. The following passage from Charles Jencks provides a neat summary of how each might be conceptualized in relation to the others. According to Jencks (1996: 8), 'Modernism . . . is a troubled cultural movement relating directly to modernity – the social condition of living in an urban, fast-changing, progressivist world governed by instrumental reason. This in turn stems from modernisation (continual economic growth dependent on industrialisation and progressive technology).'

While it is not possible here to delve into definitional explanations or unravel the range of interrelationships, the theories and practices of architecture and urban design are deeply embedded in broader intellectual, aesthetic, technological and social contexts. Indeed, the core concerns of modernity, including the fundamental values of the Enlightenment, in particular those associated with a belief in rationality, the certainties of truth, the triumph of reason, and 'man's' ability to dominate nature were fundamental, indeed seminal to the emergence of the distinctive modern urban landscape. In many respects, it was in architecture and the urban that, during the twentieth century in particular, the aesthetic, the rational, the technological and the modern fused in a most spectacular and visible way in the form of the skyscraper. However, such underpinning connections must be treated here as 'givens' and discussed only to illuminate specific contexts. The concerns of this book are to investigate the connections between cities and urban cultures, and to discuss how they have been conceptualized within urban studies. This focus requires the negotiation of a precariously narrow intellectual pathway that highlights some of the key issues in the conceptualization of modernism as an urban aesthetic and the role that this aesthetic has played in framing the look and experience of western cities since the nineteenth century.

It is always difficult to identify with any precision just when so-called 'movements' in aesthetics, including architecture, begin; however, the emergence of modernism is generally traced to the mid-nineteenth century and to the streets and salons of the pre-Haussmann Paris (Harvey 1989). According to Foucault (1986) the work of the poet Baudelaire (in particular, his essay 'The painter of modern life' – see Chapter 3) was pivotal in marking an aesthetic break with the past and heralding the arrival of the modern. In a similar vein, Marshall Berman (1988: 132) says that Baudelaire 'did more than anyone in the nineteenth century to make the men and women of his century aware of themselves as modern. Modernity, modern life, modern art – these terms occur incessantly in Baudelaire's work . . . [which] set agendas for a whole century of art and thought'. Jim McGuigan (1999: 42) argues that Baudelaire had an 'essentially aesthetic' conception of modern life in that it was concerned with 'art and personal sensibility' rather than with the 'conditions of knowledge'. In particular, Baudelaire's aesthetic vision of the modern was framed around the debonair figure of the *flâneur* whose role as observer of, and commentator on, life in the streets and arcades of Paris was presented as the counterpoint of modern man (Foucault 1986: 40; see also Chapter 3).

The *flâneur*, of course, was not only the denizen of the emerging modern metropolis but also its creation. He simultaneously embodied a way of occupying and relating to public space that was possible only in the new urban environment while also being defined in terms of this relationship to space. So in addition to providing an aesthetic rendering of the modern world, Baudelaire's vision was, at its core, an urban one that celebrated the spectacle, the energy, the creativity and the cultures of the 'street' (Berman 1988). So from the outset the modern was deeply ingrained in the spaces of the metropolis and both the *flâneur* and the urban landscape itself were its stars. De Certeau (1988: 95) is another who highlights the indivisibility of the modern and the city in claiming that 'the city is simultaneously the machinery and the hero of modernity'.

Hence, it was in the cities of the nineteenth century that the consequences of modernization were most visible. Cities were places of rapid population growth, and social change and unrest, as well as being where new forms of cultural expression developed. The streets of the great cities of the world, including Paris, London, Berlin and New York, were where the most significant social, economic, political and creative upheavals of the century were played out (Berman 1988: 174). However, the emerging modern city belonged as much to Haussmann as it did to Baudelaire, and although the foundations of modernism were fermented in the chaos of the urban, soon the urge to control this chaos become compelling. Indeed, the quest to impose order on urban disorder became the leitmotif of modernist urban planning and development from the late nineteenth century on. The city came to be conceptualized as a machine-like unit where every part (zone) was expected to have a specific function – roads were for traffic not people, the suburbs were for people not industry. What is more, it was believed that the problems (disorder) of the city could be solved by imposing the technical solutions supplied by experts (Hall 1992). Increasingly, the place of the street as Baudelaire had described it became precarious in the idealized planned modern city. Indeed, the 'street' was being replaced by the 'road', a change Berman (1988) describes as follows:

> for most of our century, urban spaces have been systematically designed and organized to ensure that collisions and confrontations will not take place here. The distinctive sign of nineteenth-century urbanism was the boulevard, a medium for bringing explosive material and human forces together; the hallmark of twentieth-century urbanism has been the highway, a means for putting them asunder.
>
> (Berman 1988: 165)

Berman (1988: 309) goes on to argue that this period saw the 'splitting off' of modernism from modernization in the sense that artists no longer engaged in a 'creative dialogue' with the urban landscape in the way they had since the time of Baudelaire. Rational urban planning and development reached a climax after the Second World War with massive suburbanization on the fringes of cities accompanied by major urban renewal schemes in their centres that involved 'slum' clearances and the construction of major roads and other infrastructure. This was the time of 'high' modernism in architecture and urban planning of which the city of New York (dominated as it is by the vertical and the horizontal) is perhaps emblematic.

In post-war New York, planner Robert Moses oversaw an unprecedented public works programme that included carving a network of expressways through established neighbourhoods, such as the Bronx. The justification for this redevelopment was to facilitate motor vehicle (commuter) traffic and to 'fight' urban 'blight' (Hall 1992: 292). But this renewal came at an enormous social cost, in particular the annihilation of tight-knit neighbourhood-based working-class communities. One of the most trenchant and passionate critics of Moses's redevelopment projects was the New York resident Jane Jacobs, whose book *The Death and Life of Great American Cities* (1961) is a sustained attack on what she considers the failure of modernist urban planning. This book became a rallying point for those opposed to wholesale urban renewal and who wished to protect their neighbourhoods and lifestyles. The strength of Jacobs's work is the bottom-up view she provides of life in the streets of a neighbourhood marked for destruction. She describes as an 'intricate sidewalk ballet' (1961: 50) the myriad of activities and interactions that take place in her street over a 24-hour period. This is a celebration of heterogeneity. In the course of a day a variety of people, such as commuters, residents, shoppers, trades people, office workers and visitors, used the street in a range of different ways. Jacobs asserts that the urban street comes alive as a result of the various uses people make of it and the resulting serendipitous encounters enrich lives and urban experiences. Indeed, urban density and diversity, she argues, actually foster the development of community life as well as facilitate privacy and anonymity – themes which, subsequently, were echoed in many cultural theories of urban difference discussed in Chapter 3.

At a time when top-down planning, systems theory and a faith in the infallibility of the expert were the dominant discourses in planning, Jacobs's work was a quiet but powerful oppositional voice that signalled the start of a shift (at least rhetorically) to a more consultative urban development agenda (Sandercock and Forsyth 1992). Academic works published around the same time (many of which were ethnographies in the tradition of the Chicago School), including Young and Willmott's ([1957] 1962) atheoretical but influential study of neighbourhood relationships in a poor working-class area of East London added weight to Jacobs's position. Like Jacobs, they found that the quality of the relationships of people living in so-called slum areas had not been eroded or degraded by urbanism but were in fact very similar to the *gemeinschaft* relationships that Wirth and others believed existed only in the country (see Chapter 2). Ironically, though, at the same time as providing a powerful case against high modernist planning and urban renewal, it is possible with hindsight to read Jacobs's book as a manifesto for the gentrification of traditional working-class areas by the middle class. Gentrification is an urban development trend that internationally since the 1960s has displaced the poor from their urban neighbourhoods just as surely as did the renewal schemes of developers like Moses (Zukin 1989).

While Robert Moses may have been the ideological and aesthetic heir to Haussmann and the City Beautiful movement, it was the philosophy and urban design ideals of the modernist movement in architecture and, in particular, of the Paris-based architect Le Corbusier that, perhaps, influenced him even more directly. Le Corbusier, more than any other architect, has come to be most closely associated with urban renewal and late modernist architecture.

The vertical city

Modernism emerged as an identifiable architectural movement and set of building design principles during the final decades of the nineteenth century and the first of the twentieth. Although the foundations of the movement lay in Europe (which was also the base of several of its most high-profile advocates), it was architects associated with the mid-western United States city of Chicago (including Daniel Burnham and Louis Sullivan) who are credited with popularizing the new style, and generally are regarded as having 'laid the foundations of modern commercial architecture' (Furneaux Jordan 1988: 307). These architects put into practice technological and aesthetic innovations that broke sharply with those of the past. Not only was Chicago the city where the first skyscraper was constructed, but also it was the place that boasted

> the first scientifically planned foundations for high buildings, the first systematization of a type of high office block, and the development of aesthetic programmes to suit the new techniques.
> (Furneaux Jordan 1988: 307)

The result was an approach to construction that made extensive use of glass, iron and reinforced concrete, and was underpinned by a modernist concern with efficiency, rationality and simplicity. The highly visible result, as Furneaux Jordan (1988) points out, was a radically new design aesthetic. Materials, technology and ideology thus combined in the form of buildings which had facades and interiors that were relatively free from 'unnecessary' ornamentation and references to the past (Sennett 1990: 171). In many respects, modern buildings were as much bold affirmations of progress and scientific knowledge as they were celebrations of new construction techniques and materials – they were potent symbols of the machine age, evidence of an historical rupture. Of course (as was discussed in Chapter 1), it was in New York that the skyscraper found its most eager enthusiasts. Robert Hughes (1997: 405) points out that 'between 1927 and 1933 New York went skyscraper-crazy and produced some of the most daring, exuberant, and flat out original buildings in the history of architecture'. The skyscrapers constructed during this period include perhaps the most iconic of all skyscrapers – the Empire State building, the Chrysler building and the Rockefeller Center (see also Chapter 1). In combining height and utility with French art deco style these buildings are not simply functional, they are beautiful.

By the beginning of the 1930s the skyscraper had become the unchallenged symbol of modern American architecture (and, indeed, of modern United States). However, one important factor that characterized the modern era and distinguished it from earlier periods was the pace and extent to which its principles and innovations were adopted elsewhere. Architects and planners around the world embraced the design and building approaches of the Chicago architects at a speed that effectively signalled the arrival of the first truly international style of architecture and design. Architecture had become enmeshed in an emerging international network of ideas and practice to an extent not previously experienced, as Furneaux Jordan (1988: 307) explains: 'The Renaissance, after its birth in Florence, took nearly two centuries to establish itself in England. Today any new idea, any technical advance is planetary knowledge within a week.'

During the twentieth century, two discrete schools of modern architecture emerged, which although grounded in the same ideological and design values pivoted largely on the use of different building materials. One primarily made use of glass and steel and is often associated with Mies van der Rohe, whose minimalist approach to architecture and design is neatly summarized in his famous dictum 'less is more'. The preferred material for the other school of modern architecture was reinforced concrete, which was used extensively for domestic, public and commercial construction. The architectural style of this school came to be termed the 'New Brutalism' and was closely linked with the work of Le Corbusier and the Congrès International de l'Architecture Moderne (CIAM) in Paris, of which he was a leading figure. Exemplified by his assertion that houses were 'machines for living', the core principles of the industrial (modernist) era – efficiency, rationality and mass production – underpinned Le Corbusier's architectural manifesto. His was, in essence, a utopian vision fermented in the economic, scientific and social optimism of the 1920s. Nevertheless, his influence on urban design and architecture throughout the twentieth century was such that it effectively transformed urban landscapes around the globe.

Peter Hall begins the chapter on Le Corbusier in his book *Cities of Tomorrow* (1992) – the title of which directly references the title of one of Le Corbusier's ([1929] 1947) own publications – perhaps unfairly with a most damning and uncompromising assessment of his work and legacy. Hall (1992: 204) asserts that the 'evil that Le Corbusier did lives after him; the good is perhaps interred with his books, which are seldom read for the simple reason that most are unreadable'. More than any other architect or planner Le Corbusier has come to personify all that is now considered 'bad' about modernist planning and design. A harsh assessment perhaps but as Hall points out, the social consequences of Le Corbusier's ideas being put into practice in the working-class housing estates that were built around the world during the 1950s and 1960s were devastating. And, in fact, Hall goes on to explain, it was not the buildings or the estates that Le Corbusier himself actually designed or saw built that are so criticized but those built by others according to the doctrine he set out in his writings, including *The Radiant City* (1933) and *The City of To-morrow and its Planning* ([1929] 1947).

Le Corbusier espoused the principles of linear design, advocated the use of concrete in construction, and detailed what he believed to be the liberating potential of 'rational' city planning and design. In particular, he felt that the skyscraper was the most efficient building form of all as it allowed land values to be maximized at the same time as freeing up space for parks and gardens. In this he rejects the cluttered unplanned high-rise chaos of the Manhattan skyline as a 'tragic hedgehog' (Hughes 1997: 407). The key was to build towers that would take up only between 5 and 15 per cent of the available ground, allowing the rest to be turned over to grass, trees and recreational spaces. Hence the Corbusian ideal city was a vertical one and, like the blueprints for all utopian cities from Thomas More's to Ebenezer Howard's (discussed in Chapter 2), it too prescribes the number of residents to an urban zone. Le Corbusier's 'radiant city' was designed to accommodate 3 million people at a density of 1200 inhabitants to the acre. Le Corbusier believed that skyscraper design would simultaneously ease congestion in large cities as well as increase population densities – a prescription that has come to be known as the Corbusian paradox (Hall 1992). For Le Corbusier, therefore, the design of buildings was intricately linked to his manifesto for urban life and the ideal contemporary city. Le Corbusier's prescriptive vision clearly owes much to Ebenezer Howard's Garden City (see Chapter 2), but with a sinister high-density, high-rise twist. In the following passage, Le Corbusier ([1929] 2000) describes his vision splendid with the conviction of the evangelist and the awe of the believer:

> The square silhouettes of the terraced roofs stand clear against the sky, bordered with the verdure of the hanging gardens. The uniformity of the units that compose the picture throw into relief the firm lines on which the far-flung masses are constructed. Their outlines softened by distance, the skyscrapers raise immense geometrical facades all of glass, and in them is reflected the blue glory of the sky. The overwhelming sensation. Immense but radiant prisms.
>
> (Le Corbusier ([1929] 2000: 343)

Le Corbusier envisioned a city that was built according to strict geometrical principles – comprising repetitive grid-lines of X-shaped towers. This city, however, was also one sharply divided according to class, with the workers (who supposedly never went into the city) living in tower blocks located in self-contained 'garden' suburbs on the periphery, while middle-class 'citizens' who worked in the city were housed in high density accommodation in the centre. These were the affluent cosmopolitan urban dwellers who could afford all that city life had to offer; urbanism for them was about consumption and lifestyle. There was no place on the streets of Le Corbusier's contemporary city for the performance of Jacobs' sidewalk ballet. Rather, street-based community life was to be annihilated and the street given over to either or both the 'delicate organs' of 'gas, water and electricity' (Le Corbusier [1929] 2000: 339), or cars and other motor vehicles. Le Corbusier (like Robert Moses, who followed him) was an 'enemy' of 'the street' (Sennett 1990: 170) so celebrated by Jacobs.

Le Corbusier believed that his dream of the modern city should replace the crumbling disorder of existing urban environments and obliterate any link to their urban pasts. According to his manifesto, the old had to be destroyed to make way for the new – and in this Le Corbusier made no exceptions; had he had his way hundreds of acres on the Right Bank of Paris (including its medieval quarter) would have been early casualties. Sennett (1990) explains this impulse to destroy and rebuild – of 'negation and creation' – as follows:

> this compulsion to empty in order to build reflects a belief the modern artist holds about his or her social status as an inventor. The inventive person stands in a hostile relation to the existing society . . . The desire to create is burdened by the belief one must in the process negate; indeed, the act of creation produces an image of this denial, a picture of the very possibility of creating a blank canvas, a clean emptiness – these spaces of negation which seem the promise of freedom.
>
> (Sennett 1990: 172–3)

The highpoint for modernist architectural *theory* was the period between the two world wars. However, for modernist architectural *practice* the highpoint came later as a direct result of the Second World War reconstruction in Europe, and after that the long boom in commercial property development in places like the United States and Australia (Crook et al. 1992). After the Second World War Le Corbusier's ideas shaped urban redevelopment and reconstruction initiatives around the world. For instance, they underpinned the design of high-rise housing estates built for low-income earners in many countries, including in the United Kingdom. They also influenced the urban renewal strategies of Robert Moses and others in the United States and elsewhere. In every case they legitimized massive slum clearances and the creation of 'green field' sites. As critics have pointed out, such renewal was the triumph of ideology over local values and ways of life (Jacobs 1961). Elsewhere, Le Corbusier's architectural principles articulated with the agenda of the City Beautiful and many civic buildings in planned cities, including Canberra in Australia and Chandigarh in India, were directly inspired by his work. The result in these places was, in effect, a blending of the Radiant City (that had already blended with the Garden City) with the City Beautiful, as Jacobs (1961) explains:

> The architecture of the City Beautiful centers went out of style. But the idea behind the centers was not questioned . . . the idea of sorting out certain cultural or public functions and decontaminating their relationship with the workaday city dovetailed nicely with the Garden City teachings. The conceptions have harmoniously merged, much as the Garden City and the Radiant City merged in a sort of Radiant Garden City Beautiful.
>
> (Jacobs 1961: 15)

By the 1970s the Le Corbusian dream had unravelled. Housing estates designed and constructed according to his principles were being acknowledged as social failures and some had even been demolished. Ideas of community, participation and the local, which were anathema to the utopian dream of the rational, radiant city, were gaining currency as countercultural movements challenged the values and dominance of modernism in all its aesthetic and political forms, including architecture and design (Harvey 1989: 38). The core principles of the Enlightenment that underpinned modernism were also questioned, as was the legitimacy of overarching theories of society. Many now suggest that the origins of postmodernism and an associated shift in the nature of society and knowledge lay in the anti-modernism movement of the late 1960s and early 1970s.

Postmodern landscapes

Harvey (1989) regards the publication of Jonathan Raban's book *Soft City* (1974) as an important marker of the emergence of the idea of the postmodern city and of a postmodern understanding of urbanism (see Chapter 4). With a slightly different emphasis, the architectural theorist Charles Jencks (1984) has chosen a far more spectacular event to mark the end of urban modernism and, arguably, the birth of the postmodern. According to Jencks (1984):

> Modern architecture died in St Louis, Missouri on July 15, 1972 at 3.32 p.m. (or thereabouts) when the famous Pruitt-Igoe scheme, or rather several of its slab blocks, were given the final *coup de grâce* by dynamite. Previously it had been vandalised, mutilated and defaced by its black inhabitants, and although millions of dollars were pumped back, trying to keep it alive (fixing broken elevators, repairing smashed windows, repainting), it was finally put out of its misery. Boom, boom, boom.
>
> (Jencks 1984: 9)

This 'death' has been interpreted as proof that technology is not capable of solving social problems, evidence that the hegemony of modernism had been broken (Jencks 1996). Jencks, like Harvey (1989), Ellin (1999) and others, goes on to argue that one result of the 'end' of modernism was the emergence of an architectural style that (at least rhetorically) was grounded in the histories and identities of local people and places – one that was resonant with context rather than pretext. In contrast to the alienating spaces of modernism, such as high-rise housing for low-income earners, postmodern architecture supposedly offered 'a more humane scale, a less bleakly functional line, a greater diversity of spaces' (Crook et al. 1992: 63). But, of course, in architecture and urban design as in other areas of aesthetics, the so-called 'break' between modernism and postmodernism was not simple nor was it complete. The destruction of Corbusian-inspired housing schemes like Pruitt-Igoe may have marked symbolically both the death of the modern and the birth of its architectural post. However, actually unpacking the complexities of this break and identifying what is meant by postmodernism are deceptively difficult tasks.

As with interpretations of cultural modernism, explanations of postmodernism must similarly be undertaken in the context of a discussion of broader developments in society and technology as well as within culture. Interestingly, in undertaking such an analysis, Crook et al. (1992) argue that postmodernism is actually a more difficult concept to define than is modernism. They suggest that while in architecture it is possible to see modernism in terms of identifiable 'schools' it is just not possible to do this with postmodernism which, they claim, is 'part-field and part-style' (1992: 64). The key feature of postmodernism in both conceptual and design terms seems to be fluidity. Other scholars have questioned whether postmodernism should be seen as a radical break with modernism at all or interpreted more subtly as a shift in emphasis within modernism – a 'revolt' or reaction from inside against the 'high modernism' of the post-Second World War period (Harvey 1989: 42).

Since the revolutions which prompted their spectacular growth in the nineteenth century, cities have been messy, disorderly and contradictory. And even the most authoritarian modernist attempts to impose order and rational solutions on this chaos were at best only partially successful and at worst social and environmental disasters. In addition, all were resisted in some way. Postmodernism is, in many respects, about recognizing the failure of high modernism in its own terms. The graffiti, the broken lifts, the wasted parklands and the smashed windows described by Jencks (1984: 9) can readily be interpreted, following de Certeau, as the powerless using the resources they have at their disposal to resist the power and the values of the dominant, and to protest being forced to live in inappropriate housing. While the logic of modernism sought to control but failed, postmodernism sought to recognize and celebrate disorder – to work with local values in building and design rather than impose formulaic, theoretically pure 'solutions'. In addition, while high modernism was certainly the dominant theory and style of architecture in the decades following the Second World War it was not the only one.

The hegemony of modernism was forged primarily in the realm of the design and construction of prestigious, highly visible commercial and public buildings in central business districts, and in the practices of city-wide urban planning and development. But oppositional styles and approaches did exist. These styles were largely found in the domestic sphere where the design and ornamentation of many (perhaps even a majority of) private dwellings continued to be grounded in the local vernacular even if informed in the abstract by the ideas of modernism (Crook et al. 1992). High modernism did not annihilate the old or the different everywhere 'on the ground', although it certainly did so discursively. Arguably, therefore, postmodernism, as a reaction to the hegemony of modernism, in part involved the assertion of already-existing ideas and aesthetic practices. It is also possible to argue, as Harvey (1989) has, that the shift to postmodernism was a cultural response to broader changes that were taking place in capitalist production and accumulation. Similarly, Frederic Jameson (1991: xiv) also suggests that the cultural phenomenon of postmodernism is an outcome of changes occurring in the economy, in particular, to emerging 'forms of economic production and organization thrown up by the modification of capitalism – the new global division of labour'.

In Jencks's (1996: 29) view, effective architectural postmodernism can be understood as containing a 'double-coding'. By this he means 'the combination of modern techniques with something else (usually traditional building) in order for architecture to communicate with the public and a concerned minority, usually other architects'. First, postmodern forms of architecture supposedly make valuable links between architecture, history and the city (context). Second, it should communicate successfully with the ultimate users of buildings as well as with experts. In other words, postmodern buildings simultaneously should 'speak' the fundamentally contradictory languages of tradition and of change. Postmodern buildings often do this by making playful use of symbolism, ornamentation and historical references intended to invoke the past at the same time as asserting the fashionable and the technologically sophisticated (Ellin 1999). In Jencks's view modernism had failed to communicate effectively to anyone other than an architectural elite. The movement was unable to deal with both tradition and change. Moreover, the modernist desire was to annihilate all historical quotation, whereas architects of the postmodern explicitly attempt to work with, and with reference to, local traditions. Where modernism sought to impose its international style across city spaces irrespective of the 'place', postmodernism set out to consider and incorporate the specificity of the local – thus moving the emphasis quite sharply from 'space' to 'place' (Stevenson 1998).

Jameson (1991) claims that one result of postmodernism has been a fundamental change in the relationship between subjectivity and space (Wexler 1991). The result, he claims, is depthlessness and confusion. He illustrates this point by undertaking (what is now seen as) a classic analysis of the Bonaventure Hotel in Los Angeles, which he regards as a 'full blown postmodern building'. He argues that the subject becomes lost within the confusing, disorientating spaces of this hotel. The spaces of postmodernism are illegible, the referents or codes that people previously could rely on to orient themselves, are variously absent, confused or contradictory. There is no essential logic or meaning to be uncovered or decoded within the postmodern, 'this latest mutation in space – postmodern hyperspace – has finally succeeded in transcending the capacities of the human body to locate itself, to organise its immediate surroundings perceptually, and cognitively to map its position in a mappable external world' (Jameson 1991: 45). Patton (1995) points out, though, that many of the elements of this postmodern building which Jameson found so confusing in the late 1980s/early 1990s, are now fairly common (and easily navigated) aspects of the urban landscape.

In response to the postmodern challenge, the trend in urban planning over the final decades of the twentieth century was away from city-wide, single-use zoning to a smaller-scale, mixed-use approach that also supposedly embodies a double coding. In line with the ideological shift that was occurring in architecture, this trend was underpinned by the recognition of the diverse and fragmented nature of the urban environment and experience. Single-use zoning increasingly came to be viewed as both wasteful and incapable of taking account of the priorities and lived experiences of a multiplicity of urban communities. A leading critic of modernist planning and advocate of the so-called **Europeanization** of the city, including a celebration of 'the street' and a return to a concern with the human scale, was Leon Krier. Among other things, it was Krier who introduced the idea of the urban *quartier* which is now often used in urban planning and redevelopment discourse, in particular, cultural planning approaches (see Chapter 6).

The rationale for the all-encompassing 'masterplan' of modernist urban planning was thus challenged by calls for a celebration of the urban expression of local history, diversity and the 'aesthetics' of urban places (Boyer 1990, 1992) – a shift from seeing the city as a machine to seeing it as dynamic system (Ellin 1999). But, as was the case with architecture, the irony has been that, rather than being rendered obsolete, masterplans continue to be developed for 'postmodern' redevelopments. In particular, they are being formulated for the wholesale redevelopment of large tracts of redundant former industrial, often waterfront sites (see Chapter 6). In an effort not to appear top-down, however, these blueprints explicitly incorporate references to the local, albeit often in ways that are clichéd and tokenistic, such as continually highlighting the maritime past of a particular site by adopting a nautical theme in decoration and in the use of props such as fishing nets. Frequently, too, this incorporation of the local is co-optation in disguise (Stevenson 1998, 1999b). Likewise, just as domestic architecture could be seen as a point of resistance to modernism, much contemporary domestic architecture continues outside the 'rules' set by the architectural hegemony of postmodernism. In effect the 'postmodern style' has been simplified to the point of caricature and mass-produced by project homebuilders across a rapidly expanding suburbia on the edges of contemporary cities throughout the world. House after house features mass-produced decorative and architectural features that supposedly reference the past. There is little room within such developments for successful connections with the local to be made or for the design to communicate effectively with residents. Instead, the local, the personal and the idiosyncratic emerge in domestic gardens and garden ornamentation, as people seek to turn an anonymous space into 'their' place. Just as the postmodern inhabited the modern, so, too, does the modern inhabit the postmodern.

Conclusion: from space to place

Architecture and urban design are fundamental to the emergence and experience of urban cultures. In exploring this relationship the chapter began by discussing the City Beautiful urban design movement that was fostered by the rebuilding of a number of European cities in the nineteenth century. This discussion also highlighted the close connection that exists between urban design and power in all its manifestations, including economic, political, gender and military. For instance, in carving a network of boulevards through the centre of Paris, Georges Haussmann was not seeking to address problems of overcrowding and disease in poor inner-city areas. Rather, under instruction from Emperor Louis Napoleon III, he was seeking to control urban unrest and revolution, facilitate the movement of commercial goods in and out of the city, and create spaces for the display of imperial power. Similar objectives have underpinned the adoption of the City Beautiful approach in cities elsewhere in the world. Such redevelopments conversely also have a profound effect on the ways in which people use the urban environment. In Paris the boulevards became areas of movement and exchange fostering new expressions of urbanism and the development of distinctly modern forms of creativity.

During the twentieth century the principles of City Beautiful merged with those of the influential modernist movement in design and architecture to inform massive slum clearances, the construction of high-rise housing and commercial spaces, and the building of roads and freeways. The person who has come to be most closely associated with this manifestation of modernism is the architect Le Corbusier and his dream of the 'radiant city in the park'. But urban modernism had other 'villains' with Robert Moses and his destruction and reconstruction of the neighbourhoods of New York being another high-profile exponent. The chapter went on to discuss how Moses's urban renewal schemes (and the top-down rational approach to planning that legitimized them) prompted harsh criticism most notably from journalist Jane Jacobs. Jacobs and others focused attention on the lived dimension of the street, the intricacies and complexities of street culture, and the 'community' networks that develop from the density and diversity of city life – themes which connect with those discussed in Chapter 3.

Criticisms, such as those of Jacobs, coupled with a more widespread challenging of the hegemony of high modernism, ultimately found expression in postmodernism. Where modernism sought to impose rational solutions on the chaos of urban space, postmodernism favoured the celebration of the local and idiosyncratic. One of the most significant trends of the so-called postmodern turn in architecture and urban design has been the conceptualization of the landscape of the city as a spectacle. This trend has involved both the building of spectacular precincts for the purposes of consumption and the staging of festivals and special events within urban space. Such strategies are intended to revive declining cities and urban economies. It is a consideration of these issues that is undertaken in the next chapter.

Further reading

Berman, M. (1988) *All that is Solid Melts into Air: The Experience of Modernity*. New York: Penguin.
Jacobs, J. (1961) *The Death and Life of Great American Cities*. London: Jonathan Cape.
Jencks, C. (1996) *What was Post-Modernism?* London: Academy Editions.

THE CITY AS SPECTACLE: CULTURE AND THE REIMAGING OF CITIES

> The spectator's consciousness, imprisoned in a flattened universe, bound by the *screen* of the spectacle behind which his life has been deported, knows only the *fictional speakers* who unilaterally surround him with their commodities and the politics of their commodities. The spectacle, in its entirety, is his 'mirror image'. Here the stage is set with the false exit of generalized autism.
>
> (Debord 1977: 218)

Introduction: making cities fun

Cities are stages for the great triumphs and tragedies of humanity – sites for the events and interactions which define the ages. People are drawn to the city for work, politics, pleasure, crime and conquest. They are the places of contemporary spectacle. Indeed, not only does the majority of the world's population live in cities, but also they are among the most visited places on earth. More and more, it is the built fabric of the city as much as the activities that take place there that is both the object of the 'tourist gaze' and a marker of urban identity. Interest in the duality of the urban spectacle and the spectacle that is the urban landscape developed as capitalism became increasingly global, production moved from Fordism to post-Fordism, and postmodernism usurped the modern as the dominant form of cultural expression. In the city, the result has been a change in the relationship between its material and symbolic aspects with attention becoming focused on consumption and the nature and potential of urban cultures, diversity and creativity and their spaces, rather than on production and its spaces. To the fore have come urban identity and the urban experience, with lifestyle and tourism emerging as the major pivots of the 'new' service economy. How a city looks and feels, and the attractions it offers both visitors and residents mark it as being different from all others – as a unique and desirable place to visit, work, live and invest. Since the 1980s, concerted attempts have been made to harness and/or manufacture these unique elements of the urban. These then form the basis of strategies intended to position a particular city favourably within the world hierarchy of cities. It is such issues that frame the concerns of this chapter.

The chapter begins with a consideration of the background to, and significance of, the global competition of image and liveability within which major and provincial cities alike are enmeshed. It then goes on to suggest that it is possible to see the dominant approaches to city reimaging and place marketing as comprising something of a spectrum. At one end are those developments that emphasize pleasure and entertainment through the integrative use of thematic architecture and 'event' shopping experiences. In this context, the chapter investigates the serial building of spectacular themed urban precincts frequently located in the inner city or on the waterfront. Constructed on the abandoned sites of industry (production), these formulaic inner-city redevelopments are intended to be centres of recreation and tourism (consumption). They are designed principally to facilitate city reimaging and to be the impetus for local economic rejuvenation. Alongside a discussion of underpinning assumptions about the nature of urbanism that are framing such redevelopments and repositioning cities as landscapes of consumption, the chapter considers the related trend for cities to stage festivals and events of local, national or international significance.

At the other end of the reimaging spectrum is a range of more low-key approaches. These emphasize local cultural identity, the promise of 'authenticity', and the idea of creativity. Through a discussion of cultural planning and the 'creative city', the chapter considers the pivotal role being played by the creative arts and cultural industries within these strategies. Cultural planning seeks to express local identity and history, and rejuvenate the public sphere. As community gathering places and sites of commercial exchange, public space has long played a significant role in framing and facilitating urban culture and politics. Indeed, it is frequently argued within cultural planning discourse that such spaces are fundamental to democratic citizenship. However, as the chapter suggests, many cultural planning commentators seem to harbour nostalgic longings for public spaces reminiscent of the imagined *polis* of antiquity and seek to use the arts and cultural industries as a way of recreating such spaces.

Urban decline and the global

An important consequence of an increasingly global economy and the changes associated with this development, such as progressively mobile capital, a shift to post-Fordist production, and the emergence of an international division of labour, has been a declining place for an interceding national economic body – a role traditionally played by the nation state (Held 1989; Crook et al. 1992) – and a corresponding increase in the autonomy and significance of regions and cities as competitive economic entities. These trends are often associated with claims that the 1980s heralded the advent of the self-reliant 'world' or 'global' city (Sassen 1993, 1994). Places, such as London, New York and Tokyo, have emerged as the dominant spatial pivots or 'command centres' (Sassen 1993) of the complex international urban network of finance, communication and information flows. These cities, frequently, are regarded as having more in common with each other than with their surrounding districts and nearby cities (Bridge and Watson 2000). Increasingly, in political and economic terms it is such cities rather than nation states that have international hegemony being 'more like city-states, separate in many respects from their hinterlands and with enormous significance for their national economies. In global cities we see the clearest signs of cities becoming independent economic actors' (Bridge and Watson 2000: 108).

While the global city status of London and New York (and one or two others) is relatively unproblematic, there are many who see the positioning or classification of other cities as 'global' cities as being rather tenuous and somewhat arbitrary. Almost every city, it seems, aspires to be recognized as a global city so assuming or ascribing this status depends first on determining the 'selection' criteria. For instance, is Los Angeles a global city in the same way as New York? Clearly, different cities play different roles in the global economy. In an effort to deal with such complexities there are some commentators who suggest that cities are best ranked on a continuum according to their varying roles as commercial, financial and informational hubs of international activities like commodity exchange, insurance, communications and taxation (Berry and Huxley 1992). In King's (1993: 84) view being a world city is as much about the role that a city plays in the globalization of culture as it is about the global economy (see Chapter 3). In this respect, both the possibility and composition of a global network of cities, as well as the globalization of perceptions of the urban as a cultural form have salience. Lash and Urry (1994) point out that the global economy is 'disordered' and 'de-centred' comprised of a series of 'flows' of tourists, migrants, ideas, money, information and so on. Following from this insight it is reasonable to expect that cities will be positioned differently in relation to these global flows and to other cities.

Hence, it is perhaps best to speak of the existence of intersecting continua (flows) that are comprised of the cities of the world, rather than of a single hierarchy of world cities. Such a formulation recognizes the existence of a complexity of global networks and flows that simultaneously link and separate cities, as well as the existence of ranks within flows. Within these networks, cities occupy differing positions vis-à-vis other cities, nation states and other networks of cities on a range of issues and in a variety of instances. The positions occupied may be oppositional or reinforcing, material or symbolic. These comments and the preceding observations, however, are not intended to deny the significant, often determining, effects of the premier global circuits of political and economic activity and their national, regional and local effects. Debates about global cities, therefore, necessarily articulate in a number of crucial respects with a range of other theoretical debates, such as those about the existence of a world economic system (Wallerstein 1987; Sassen 1994), exchanges on the globalization of culture, and of the impacts of the 'technological revolution' (Castells 1991). In each of these debates, however, there is agreement that the nature of, and relationship between, space, place and temporality have fundamentally changed (Giddens 1985; Harvey 1989).

Whether conceptualized as encompassing a worldwide network, or as being semi-autonomous sites linked at particular conjunctures of time for a range of idiosyncratic reasons, built environments around the world are being shaped and reshaped by the fluctuating global movement of investment capital in and out of the urban economy and the spatial structure. Predominantly, financial investment has been moving away from the sites and spaces of mass production and into the urban spaces of consumption. As a result, some places within every nation have prospered at the expense of other areas in the same country (see Chapter 3). As the processes of globalization stimulate and facilitate the dominance of international networks of cities and the decline of the nation state so, too, is it shattering the economic and physical structures of many regional, often industrial, cities, such as Liverpool and Manchester in the United Kingdom, Baltimore and Pittsburgh in the United States, Newcastle and Wollongong in Australia. For countless regional industrial cities, often also facing a decline in state intervention and support and very few avenues of effective access into the global urban networks, the spatial impact of industrial and economic change may well be irreversible and, ultimately, fatal. The reality of the uneven effects of globalization provides part of the rationale for undertaking locality research (see Chapter 3).

Economic growth and globalization have impacted unevenly on cities, regions, nations and urban neighbourhoods. For instance, within individual cities (whether world, regional or 'developing'), there are people and places that have been affected differently by the withdrawal of capital and changes in industrial production. As Sassen (1994, 1996) points out, even the richest of 'global cities' are both rich and poor. Some even argue that only certain areas of great cities can claim the status of 'global city' (Jopson 2002). These 'cities within cities' have more in common with other 'cities' in the global networks of cities than with their surrounding suburbs. Many so-called world cities have become, simultaneously, 'mega-cities' of poverty and decay having spawned under-serviced and neglected urban spaces. These include shanty areas that are home to an ever-growing number of poor, displaced, often rural people, and the abandoned sites of industrial production. Sassen (1996) describes the class-based spatial divisions that are visible in Manhattan as follows:

> The overall sense, particularly in Manhattan, is that residential space has increasingly been occupied by a growing urban gentry and the infrastructure of shops it requires; by a growing number of immigrant communities containing various sub-economies; and by a growing number of poor displaced people who occupy devastated areas of the city, some of which eventually become incorporated into the expanding gentrification process or, alternatively, into the expanding immigrant communities.
>
> (Sassen 1996: 29)

Castells (1991) utilizes the established sociological concept of the divided city (see Chapter 3) in his exploration of the effects on the ground of the international growth of the 'informational mode of development' and the resulting interplay between technology and labour. Such factors and associated restructuring processes have disadvantaged large segments of the population, in particular the traditional working class. The result is starkly inscribed on the urban landscape where many low-cost areas and working-class spaces have been devastated, while the residential, work and consumption spaces of the 'professional-managerial' class have flourished. Sassen (1996: 40) explains that all the major cities of the developed world are experiencing the 'emergence of the dualities in economic power and cultural representation' which have spatial consequences. In addition, the brutal reality of urban decline frequently has been a factor defining the terms of what has developed as a global competition between cities. This competition, increasingly, is being played out on the terrain of consumption and lifestyle, and often involves the building of spectacular themed urban precincts and the development of the arts or cultural economy (Zukin 1997, 1998). Urban space, amenity and urban cultures have become valuable commodities for sale in the global marketplace.

Selling the city

As a result of globalization, deindustrialization and economic restructuring a growing number of cities and regions are being forced to look to consumption, entertainment and finance activities in order to compete with other cities for the capital investment needed to facilitate their economic and spatial survival. For many declining industrial cities (and spaces within cities) competing on the basis of image and amenity is now the 'only game in town' (Hall 1989: 281). Often prompted by coalitions of local business and government interests, and in an effort to reverse urban decline and consolidate a place within, or provide an entrée into, the global network of cities, more and more cities are initiating comprehensive urban redevelopment schemes and city enhancement programmes. Central to the majority of these initiatives is a reassessment of the image that the city projects. Not just in terms of how people respond to and interpret the place, but also a consideration of the configurations of meanings, feelings and expectations which are involved in the perception of the city (Ashworth and Voogd 1990; Madsen 1992; Kearns and Philo 1993). Therefore, when selling the city the commodity being promoted through place-marketing and city-reimaging campaigns is not just the city and the physical spaces of the city *per se* but the city's symbolic spaces as well. Selling and defining place is a complex transaction which requires the sale of what the city means, how it feels, and what it looks like – both the tangible and the intangible attributes of particular urban spaces. These qualities must be identified and packaged, not just to potential investors and visitors, but also to local residents and communities of interest (Holcomb 1993; Stevenson 1999b).

The dynamic interplay between political procedures and symbolic meanings – or urban symbolism – underpins many urban redevelopment schemes and city reimaging programmes (see Chapter 4 for a discussion of urban semiotics). Pivotal here is the *idea* of the city which operates on a number of discrete but reinforcing levels – the political, the economic and the symbolic. These levels are constituted as much in terms of the existence of the idealized city as 'myth' (Goodwin 1993) and of how such an imagined city might look, as in terms of what globally significant activities are actually undertaken there. Through often quite intricate media marketing campaigns attempts are made to intervene in the production and transmission of urban images and to reinterpret these images as the basis of a strategy for 'selling' the city. The overarching aim is to distinguish a particular city from all others as a unique and attractive place to live, visit and work, and as dynamic and prosperous centres for commerce and industry to (re)locate – a process neatly summarized by Mulgan (1989: 270) in the following passage: 'The advertisements for the new towns (Telford, Milton Keynes) and old ones like Swindon offer semi-rural paradises: small cities promote themselves by pretending not to be cities at all – Throughout the world cities now compete in terms of league tables of "liveability".' Or as Harvey (1989: 92–3) says, 'Cities and places now, it seems, take much more care to create a positive and high quality image of place . . . [that is] blessed with certain qualities, the organisation of spectacle and theatricality.'

A frequently devised strategy used to repackage the city as a tourist destination is the spectacle of the urban festival – a celebratory event or carnival which is designed to focus regional, national or international attention on a city (Roche 2000; Stevenson 2000). Through saturation media coverage, a high-profile event like the Olympic Games, for example, can focus regional, national and international media attention on a particular city for a concentrated, if limited, period of time. Such visibility can help to market renewing cities while offering the enticing promise of positive long-term local economic benefits. The staging of a mega-event frequently also involves a programme of major building and urban redevelopment. For instance, preparations for the 2000 Olympic Games in Sydney saw the construction of an entire new suburb, several major stadia and other sporting facilities as well as the wholesale transformation of sites across the city centre – including renovating existing sporting facilities, building bus shelters, painting hoardings, and even substantially remodelling major leisure and recreation sites. There were also several government initiatives to move the poor and the homeless out of the centre of the city at least for the duration of the Games.

The production of smaller-scale events, such as local cultural festivals is also seen as an effective way of raising the profile of urban centres in the tourism and city image marketplace. These initiatives, too, can involve some manipulation and upgrading of the urban environment. No matter what the scale, the development and improvement of urban cultural resources and the production of events and festivals almost always occurs in conjunction with a concern about whether or not the city is perceived favourably by outsiders as a desirable place to live or to visit.

The term 'urban tourism' has been coined to name the contrived repackaging of declining industrial cities into centres for tourist consumption (Rowe and Stevenson 1994). Although Law (1992, 1994) points out that the actual tourist pursuits on offer in these places, in fact, differ very little from those offered by traditional tourist centres, with cultural spaces, such as museums, exhibition centres, retailing and the like, being dominant. What distinguishes urban tourism from traditional tourism is the way in which what is on offer has been packaged and marketed. According to Law (1992: 599) as localities respond to the forced shift away from being centres of production and take on the task of reinventing themselves as centres of consumption, '[t]he older industrial city has to raise its profile in the marketplace of visitors and substantially improve its attractiveness'. Thus a range of regeneration strategies might be formulated, either for whole cities or for precincts within cities, including the staging of events. Here leisure, enjoyment, spectacle and pleasure are produced, packaged, marketed and consumed.

Through redevelopment, image-making and place-marketing exercises focused on the production of commercialized leisure spaces, governments and various business interests aim to attract new commercial investment to the city and the city centre, in particular, to stimulate the interest of tourists, and to trigger local economic recovery. It is often hoped, too, that these redevelopments will provide the impetus for more widespread processes of urban renewal that will further stimulate employment opportunities in the region (Hoyle 1988). In the quest to reimage or redevelop cities and parts thereof, two approaches have emerged internationally as significant. These Bianchini and Schwengel (1991) term **Americanization** and Europeanization. Where one blueprint – Americanization – pivots on the construction of spectacular spaces, frequently located on the waterfront, the other – Europeanization – focuses on local cultural industry development and is frequently undertaken under the banner of cultural planning. These two approaches are explored in the next two sections of this chapter, beginning with an analysis of Americanization that includes a consideration of the reasons why this initiative is increasingly being described as a redevelopment cliché.

'An urbanism of universal equivalence'

The construction of saleable consumption spaces and a renewed urban image may involve only very minor manipulations of the built environment, for example, the fashioning of performance or exhibition spaces from abandoned industrial buildings. But it is very common for these small redevelopments to occur within the context of a much more ambitious building and rebuilding programme. In its most extreme form this process could consist of the wholesale transformation of entire urban districts or precincts and the remodelling and demolition of all the existing buildings within that space (Law 1994). This type of redevelopment became an architectural and planning fashion during the 1980s in particular. It involves the redevelopment of redundant, often decaying urban sites frequently located near the waterfront into ambitious, derivative urban 'experiences' commonly known as 'festival marketplaces'.

Festival marketplace developments were pioneered by the American property developer James Rouse, who devised the formula originally in the 1950s for the redevelopment of the derelict Boston waterfront (Hannigan 1998; Harvey 2000). Here the reconstruction of the waterfront set in train an ongoing process of inner-city revitalization, commencing with Scollay Square and the Quincy Markets (Tunbridge 1988). The redevelopment consisted of a combination of theme-park entertainment, leisure shopping, street theatre and other services and soon become a focus for tourist activity (Hall 1989: 281). The perceived success of Boston provided a development model for other depressed cities to emulate, first in the United States and later around the world. Along with the Quincy Markets, other high-profile exemplars include Baltimore's Harbor Place, New York's South Street Seaport, London's Docklands, Sydney's Darling Harbour and San Francisco's Pier 39. The Rouse Corporation became so synonymous with festival marketplace developments that in the United States they are often referred to as 'Rousifications' and their proliferation across that country described as the 'Rousification of America' (Tunbridge 1988: 70; Hall 1992: 348).

Festival marketplaces are urban spectacles both in their architectural form and in the nature of the activities that take place. Indeed, Harvey (1989: 90) describes how the building of Harbor Place in Baltimore developed from the Baltimore City Fair as the 'institutionalized commercialization of a more or less permanent spectacle'. Festival marketplace developments, initially, were also reactions against the modernist urban renewal of the 1960s (see Chapter 5). So a totally different (postmodern) architectural aesthetic was adopted. This is one which Harvey (1989: 91) describes as an 'architecture of spectacle, with its sense of surface glitter and transitory participatory pleasure, of display and emphemerality, of *jouissance* . . . an eclectic mix of styles, historical quotation, ornamentation, and the diversification of surfaces'. Thus the construction of urban precincts that are both the means and the ends of the provision and experience of pleasure is a distinguishing feature of the Americanization approach to city reimaging. The manufactured environment is simultaneously an object of intrinsic sensory pleasure, and, as the setting for a range of leisure activities, acts as the facilitator of the experience of pleasure.

The essence of the festival marketplace is its contrived packaging of time and place. Often, however, the result is the construction of simulated urban landscapes that are devoid of both content and context. Like the synthetic urbanity which Michael Sorkin (1992) attributes to Disneyland, the built spaces of the festival marketplace resonate with an 'urbanism of universal equivalence' (Sorkin 1992: 217). The essential paradox of this city reimaging panacea, therefore, is that in the quest to create difference, a sense of place and a destination attractive to tourists and potential investors, the result is frequently the manufacture of sameness, substitution and simulation. Or as M. Christine Boyer (1990: 96) puts it, the 'recursive' and 'serial' 'mass production' of identical city places across space. It is very difficult to tell one festival marketplace from the other. They all look alike, feel the same, have the same architectural codes, play with the same contrived notions of place and localness, and offer the same suite of attractions and facilities (including aquariums, festival shopping spaces, convention centres, themed restaurants and most recently, sporting arenas).

The festival marketplace is touted as a strategy that will achieve a range of social objectives, for example a reduction in unemployment, through the trickle-down of the benefits of local economic recovery. These claims have been widely challenged, however. For instance, Andrew Church (1988: 194) on conducting a review of the London Docklands and the operations of the London Docklands Development Corporation suggested that the development had brought 'few benefits to the unemployed residents of Docklands'. Other commentators, for example Tweedale (1988: 196), have claimed that the festival marketplace formula 'only addresses the physical half of the problem and ignores totally the social processes'. Similarly, Harvey (2000), while acknowledging the spectacular economic success of the Baltimore development (visited by more people per year than Disneyland), notes that most of the social problems of the inner city remain – just around the corner and conveniently out of sight.

The formula of the harbourside festival marketplace development has gained currency worldwide. This trend is closely linked to the globalization of culture, the imagining of the global city, and of ideas about the architectural and urban design icons that mark this status (Stevenson 1999b). Thus it has not just been the world's 'major' cities which sought to assert their status through the symbolism of the built environment, including by building a festival marketplace. Countless regional cities have also sought such status. For instance, it was against this background that politicians and elite business interests in the deindustrializing regional Australian city of Newcastle formulated a strategy intended to change the negative image that the city was seen to have acquired because of its past as a centre for heavy industry (Metcalf 1993; Metcalf and Bern 1994; Rowe 1996). Pivotal to the strategy was a proposal to redevelop a large tract of the urban waterfront, known as Honeysuckle, into a festival marketplace. This redevelopment strategy was sold as a risk-free way of marking the regional port city both materially and symbolically as 'great'. In this quest, popular – indeed mythological – ideas about what such a city should look like were central to the urban development proposal put forward and to the public relations and media campaigns adopted to gain local support for the proposal.

The blueprint for the Honeysuckle site was first revealed in October 1991 in a promotional video that featured three-dimensional computer images of the barren waterfront site transformed into a festival marketplace development of enterprise, entertainment and high-cost living (New South Wales Property Services Group 1991). The artistic impressions of the reimaged Honeysuckle site that appeared in the video, the accompanying brochure and the official masterplan all depict manufactured water features, quaint replica sailing ships, high-quality marina spaces and the integrative use of symbolic architecture. Moreover, it was explicitly claimed in the promotional literature that the Honeysuckle Development would see Newcastle take its place alongside the 'great port cities of the world' including London, Boston and Vancouver, at the same time as providing the key to Newcastle securing its economic, social and cultural futures (New South Wales Property Services Group 1991). In other words, the festival marketplace redevelopment was promoted as the trigger that would transform the image and appearance of industrial Newcastle from that of a stigmatized, second-rate, 'coal town' into a vibrant, attractive and enviable 'great' port city.

The point is that the potency of this redevelopment proposal for local residents came primarily from the symbolic status believed to accrue to cities that adopt certain urban redevelopment strategies, such as the waterfront festival marketplace, in response to the material and symbolic challenges of de/reindustrialization. The construction of particular landscapes is deemed necessary if a city is going to gain a position somewhere within the global networks of cities – in this instance a position as a 'great port city'. As already argued, these networks mesh the economic with the political and the symbolic in a competitive game of attaining and retaining urban status. For a regional deindustrializing city, such status is intimately associated with the symbolism derived from the connectedness of the imagined and material forms of metropolitan centres and the global status which certain architectural structures (including festival marketplaces) are seen to announce. Thus it was the festival marketplace strategy that was chosen for the Honeysuckle site over more low-key alternative proposals that focused on local cultural development (Stevenson 1998, 1999b).

Festival marketplace developments or the Americanization of the inner city, can be considered the most extreme example of the city reimaging/urban tourism spectrum. Cultural planning or, to use Bianchini and Schwengel's (1991) term, Europeanization, although drawing on many of the same discourses and also often involving some manipulation of the built environment, pivots on the nurturing of local cultures and seeks to incorporate the expressive arts and broadly defined cultural activities into the reimaging process. There have been numerous examples of depressed cities and regions that have explored the potential of spatially based arts activities and the development and promotion of local cultural forms as triggers for community and economic rejuvenation of depressed cities and regions.

Cultural planning and the 'creative city'

Since the 1980s, local cultural development came to assume a central place on the policy agendas of cities and regions in developed countries around the world. In the United Kingdom, Australia, the United States and Canada, in particular, city-based cultural planning has emerged to be the most significant local cultural policy innovation of recent years. At the same time the rhetoric of the 'creative city' has become almost a civic boosterist cliché (Landry and Bianchini 1995; Greenhalgh 1998). The emerging cultural development priorities of the Council of Europe (Bennett 2001) and of the fledgling parliaments of Scotland and Wales also highlight the importance that is being placed on fostering the creativity of cities and regions as the basis for strategies to revive local economies and to mark places, symbolically, as 'different' (Stevenson 2003). Cultural planning pivots on the claim that, through the coordination of urban and cultural policy formulation and implementation, local government, perhaps more than any other tier of the state, is well placed to address the challenges of urban decline. While it would be misleading to present cultural planning as a cohesive body of thought or of policy interventions (indeed, the term 'cultural planning' is not even used universally), it is, nevertheless, correct that, worldwide, similar blueprints are being developed and intersecting claims being made for locally focused and coordinated cultural planning/creative city approaches to city reimaging.

This emerging discourse of city reimaging and cultural policy formulation is one which is said to draw (albeit in theory) on perceptions of the 'form and feeling' of European cities, and takes the idea of a marketable 'local culture' as its point of departure (Stevenson 2000). Central to such strategies is the rhetoric of local difference and diversity. Initiatives associated with cultural planning may endorse the construction of cultural precincts, the identification and promotion of local distinctiveness, and the nurturing, through creative practice, of a positive (and marketable) sense of place and belonging (Bianchini et al. 1988; Landry et al. 1996). Locally based cultural planning is simultaneously positioned as being the solution to the crises that have befallen the once glorious cities and landscapes of modernism and (as is explored below) touted as a framework for fostering local participatory democracy and citizenship.

Cultural planning is presented as a mechanism for placing local cultural activity on the urban agenda in order to improve city life and the fabric of the built environment. As an aspect of this quest, urban cultural activities, such as the expressive arts are reconceptualized in conjunction with broader economic, urban and social policies (McNulty et al. 1986; McNulty 1988, 1991). Conceptually, therefore, cultural planning is concerned with considerably more than simply delineating a role for artistic endeavour in the city. It is claimed that when articulated with such diverse urban policy matters as public transport, the standard of roads, street lighting, urban safety and other issues and activities (Landry et al. 1996), a comprehensive local government cultural policy for leisure, recreation, artistic and entertainment pursuits is capable of achieving wide-ranging social objectives and considerably improving the 'quality' of urban life (Evans 2001). As Mercer (1991a) explains it:

> a broad and enabling [cultural] policy framework ... can simultaneously address the (soft) 'intangibles' of affirmation, identity, quality of life, celebration and social justice and the (hard) 'tangibles' of economic development, leverage, industry strategies, infrastructure development, training programs, domestic and inbound tourism revenue, urban design, town planning and transport.
>
> (Mercer 1991a: 3)

As a consequence, in part, of its underlying anthropological definition of culture, the scope of cultural planning is vast with its exponents asserting the legitimacy of all forms of cultural activity, including the popular and commercial. Cultural activities and cultural resources are thus conceptualized as being dynamic and pervasive processes and not as a static range of artistic objects and practices – the definition that has traditionally dominated cultural policy discussions. Culture 'is what counts as culture for those who participate in it' (Mercer 1991b: 5). And by arguing from this definition that cultural planning should articulate with such urban issues as the design of the built environment, housing policies, retailing, policing and a range of economic activities and initiatives (Bianchini et al. 1988; Bianchini 1991: 27; Mercer 1991a), cultural planning is specifically being presented as a new way of approaching urban planning (Evans 2001). In fact, cultural planning is concerned with both the design and the governance of the city (Mercer 1991c). As Bianchini (1991: 26) suggests, 'policy-makers should positively and consciously make cultural policies an integral part of urban development strategies. In this context, the overarching and integrating concept of "cultural planning" ... could become a precious instrument for policy-makers.' Just as Boston and Baltimore are perhaps the most famous exemplars of the Americanization festival marketplace formula, Glasgow in Scotland has become one of the most celebrated examples of the Europeanization or cultural planning approach to city reimaging and urban regeneration. It, too, has become something of a model which other cities have tried to copy.

Beginning with the 'Glasgow's Miles Better' marketing slogan, Glasgow in the 1980s actively fostered the expressive arts and cultural activities as part of its strategy for reimaging. This programme included upgrading the urban environment, opening new museums and instigating a programme of cultural festivals which culminated in 1990 with the city's designation as the 'European City of Culture' (Bianchini 1991). These cultural policy initiatives articulated with a range of government-sponsored community housing projects (Hague 1990), the restoration of historic buildings and the construction of new office space. This was a combination of projects which led to claims that the development of local cultural resources and activity can be the impetus for 'successful' city redevelopment and reimaging and prompted many observers to describe Glasgow as an urban renewal success story. Assessing the nature and extent of this 'success', however, is difficult to do (see Spring 1990). There is emerging evidence to suggest that the revival may well have been something of a mirage or a mask that obscured a considerable widening of the gulf between rich and poor. There is also some evidence pointing to the limitations inherent in cultural planning strategies that are based too heavily on events and which fail to develop the cultural infrastructure of the entire city (Stevenson 2003).

Nevertheless, the example of Glasgow continues to be a positive referent for the cultural planning approach to inner-city redevelopment and reimaging. It has proved influential in shaping redevelopment strategies around the world. Indeed, there has emerged an intriguing global circuit of cultural planning consultants selling a 'just add local culture and stir' version of cultural planning, modelled in part on the Glasgow example. Needless to say, this is a trend which works totally against the local cultural industry development objectives that underpin the rhetoric of cultural planning (Stevenson 2003).

A powerful discourse of civic pride and citizenship also pervades the cultural planning literature and positions the (re)development of city cultures and the public realm at the centre of this process. Some commentators claim that as a result of the physical 'destruction' associated with urban decline, the symbolic role and ambience of the city centre is also under threat (Bianchini et al. 1988; Montgomery 1990; Bianchini and Bloomfield 1996). It is argued that the revival of the city centre through cultural planning strategies is crucial to the reconstruction of the local identity believed to be fundamental to an empowering experience of urbanism (Worpole 1992). It is at this point that cultural planning strategies become implicated in discussions of cultural democracy and citizenship, with the renewal of local cultures being regarded as pivotal to the renewal of the public realm. It is necessary to discuss some of the ways in which the concept 'civic' and notions of citizenship have been used in the cultural planning literature and to highlight the importance of public space to this formulation and to the reimaged city centre.

Planning cultural citizenship

The urban culture that is being imagined within cultural planning discourses is one which is grounded squarely in the belief that an empowering 'civic culture' (Montgomery 1990) is fundamental to democratic politics and local citizenship (Bianchini and Bloomfield 1996; Ghilardi 2001). Central here is the rhetoric of civic redevelopment and the creation of 'active citizenship' – 'Civic identity, community identity, ethnic identity, gender identity. [Cultural planning is] effectively a way of addressing . . . citizenship' (Mercer 1991a: 8). The crux of this position appears to be the view that the 'cultural' revitalization of the inner city and the reconstruction of the public realm are pivotal to reviving local democracy and building 'community identity'. The public realm is conceptualized as being 'a realm of social life in which the different ages, ethnic groups, sexualities, genders, (dis)abilities and political tendencies that together make up the contemporary city can (re)discover each other in human terms, and at the same time rediscover their own city and its history' (Griffiths 1993: 109). The building of the public realm is predicated on the existence of traditional forms of public space (parks, town squares and the like) and the animation of this space through cultural activity.

The issue of citizenship is of particular concern for the British exponents of cultural planning seemingly as an outcome of the tradition's social democratic origins. For example, at a local level the British Labour Party has actively been involved in the formulation of a cultural planning approach to urban issues (Mulgan and Worpole 1986; Bianchini et al. 1988; Worpole 1992; Greenhalgh 1998) and, nationally, cultural planning is on the agenda of the Blair Labour government. In British cultural planning discourse notions of citizenship are imbued with a range of meanings which are grounded specifically in the history of the labour movement, the welfare state and local political configurations like the relationship between the tiers of British government. The following passage from Mulgan and Worpole (1986) both defines this view of citizenship and encapsulates the ideology that underpins its current usage in British cultural policy discussions:

> The key word in post-war Labour Party vocabulary was 'civic'. It expressed the strong sense of active citizenship which came out of the war; it expressed a sense of there being such a thing as a 'civic culture' – the reciprocal responsibility between state and citizen, and amongst citizens towards each other. 'Civic responsibility' and 'civic pride' were transformed into 'civic halls', 'civic baths', 'civic gardens', 'civic theatres' and so on . . . This is where the heart of such cultural policy as there was at a local government level was expressed through very patrician forms of municipal provision.
>
> (Mulgan and Worpole 1986: 27)

This particular understanding of citizenship and the allied concept 'civic' establishes a rationale that justifies the scope and objectives of cultural planning as it is currently being promoted in Britain and elsewhere. The cultural strategies which are being presented as the keys to reviving local citizenship are those which have been devised to protect what is seen as the integrity of public buildings and public space, in particular, those buildings and spaces in the inner city or civic centre – spatiality is at the heart of the citizenship and cultural planning rhetoric (Ghilardi 2001). Initiatives such as the promotion of cultural activity, the development of cultural precincts and other leisure and recreational spaces are intended, in part, to revive urban life and animate the city at the same time as reviving core social democratic traditions of local participatory democracy and 'collective morality' (Mulgan 1989: 263).

Despite the social democratic origins of cultural planning in Britain, the neo-conservative perspectives of urban writers, such as the American Richard Sennett, and idealized notions of the Roman *piazza* and the Greek *polis* are deeply implicated also in the cultural planning claims of the need to foster citizenship and public life through local cultural policy and city reimaging strategies. Mulgan (1989: 275), for example, has argued that there is a link between politics and city life that can be traced back to the Greek *polis*. This is a link, he suggests (1989: 276), which is 'withering as public spaces are privatised' and which, in turn, is threatening the 'cultural roots of democratic, public life'. He further argues that:

> Any plans for the creation of convivial, communicating cities inevitably find themselves struggling with a long erosion of the traditional political structure of the city within which people think, argue and organise.
>
> (Mulgan 1989: 275)

Mulgan's position is representative of a view that goes beyond the discourses of cultural planning and holds that the cities of earlier centuries were places of public debate and the free exchange of ideas. Jürgen Habermas (1991) is one commentator who has documented in detail the issue of open political debate, the public sphere and changes to both over time. Similar themes are also intriguingly being mobilized in the emerging discourses associated with cyberspace (see Chapter 7).

In his writings on urban culture, Sennett has argued that the history of modern urbanism has been a process of 'wall building'. According to Sennett (1990: xii), modern city spaces trivialize urban life and actually separate people from the experience of the outside world. At the root of this change, he argues, is fear. An outcome of this fear is the desire to construct urban spaces that will protect city dwellers from the threat posed – or perceived to be posed – by other users of the city (by difference and diversity – see Chapter 3). Sennett considers the Greek *polis* and its particular organization of space to be a use of urban space and an acceptance of the 'reality' of urbanism that is superior to the current experiences. The *polis* thus provides a model and a way of thinking about public space that Sennett believes is capable of overcoming the isolation and separation caused by contemporary city design. Sennett's argument appears to be not that the modern urban experience of difference and confusion is new, but that modern attempts to deny these experiences and to insulate or isolate people from them are. There are clearly synergies between these ideas and those of Young (1990), discussed in Chapter 3. Zukin (1997) also makes a related point:

> the culture of cities retain a residual memory of tolerance and freedom. The very diversity of the population and their need for cultural and economic exchanges create unpredictable spaces of freedom: the markets, restaurant kitchens, designated landmarks, and the parades that become both sites and sights of new collective identities. This is the city that people cherish. It is this transcendent narrative of opportunity and self-respect that lends hope to common public culture. But if entire cities, led by their downtowns, continue to be ghettoised by public rhetoric and private investment, the dream of a common public culture will fall victim to an empty vision.
>
> (Zukin 1997: 294)

As a result of the trend towards division and separation, Sennett (1977: 338) argues that there has been an eroding of the 'balance between public and private life, a balance between an impersonal realm in which men [sic] could invest one kind of passion and a personal realm in which they could invest another'. Sennett later summarized his concern in a radio interview, saying that it is important that simpler urban spaces are again designed and built because these, he envisages, will 'produce . . . more social complexity, more social interaction' (Ravlich 1988: 473). It is noteworthy, though, that many have argued that Sennett's project, a 'concern for the recovery of a "public philosophy" and a "less intimate" society is grounded essentially in conservative pluralist assumptions of consensus' (Rodgers 1985: 207).

It is, in part, by using Sennett's work as a point of departure that others, such as Mercer (1991b), see cultural planning is a reimagining tool that is capable of reviving the 'outside' as a 'dimension of human experience'. Cultural planning, therefore, is seen as addressing what Sennett identified as a fundamental urban problem – the disequilibrium between '*urbs* and *civitas*, stones and rituals, shelter and emotions, commerce and citizenship, outside and inside' (Mercer 1991b: 1). Cultural planning based on the European model of city life is conceptualized as the means by which 'the walls' which separate urban dwellers can be removed. Mercer (1991b: 2) suggests that this quest to attain a 'modern urban culture' has several pivots including treating the city as a 'stage', utilizing the gamut of cultural capital, and linking economic, social and cultural objectives. Mercer (1991b: 9) also suggests that a redefinition of the 'nature and meaning of the . . . civic realm' should be addressed by cultural planning. Such a task is complex and must take the vast critical literature on citizenship as its point of departure. To date, however, this task has not been undertaken seriously by anyone writing within cultural planning, although Bianchini and Bloomfield (1996) make a start. Given the centrality of conceptions of citizenship and of the democratic public realm to cultural planning recommendations, this failure is alarming. For instance, Watson (1992) suggests that cultural planning can offer women the chance to represent the diversity of their urban experiences. However, as I have argued elsewhere (Stevenson 1992, 2003), for this to happen there must be fundamental changes to the theories and the practices of cultural planning, including an evaluation of their underpinning conceptions of citizenship and of the relationship between women, citizenship and public space. A starting point might be the ways in which (and reasons why) fear structures women's use of public space (see Chapter 3). In addition, cultural planning pronouncements on reviving city and civic life pivot on romantic notions of a golden age of urbanism – an age before modernism – that are underpinned by an imagined (lost) *gemeinschaft* (Stevenson 1992).

Conclusion: fantasy cities

Beginning with a consideration of the idea of the global city and of the relationship of this urban form to the increasing flow of people, ideas, culture and finance around the world, this chapter has argued that cities within each nation are positioned differently in relation to each other. While some cities are centres for certain sets of flows and not others, an increasing number (particularly regional deindustrializing cities) are either locked out, or on the margins, of the international networks. In order to compete with other cities for the financial and capital investment needed to survive, it has become necessary for cities to find ways of raising their profile in the international marketplace. This means trying to appear as attractive and vibrant places for business and industry to relocate and for tourists to visit. In addition, while some cities in every nation have prospered at the expense of others, there are often large areas within cities (even major cities like London and New York) of disadvantage and decline. For instance, changes in the nature of industrial production and the global movement of capital investment have left tracts of redundant land usually near the inner city and/or on the waterfront. Through a host of reimaging strategies often involving considerable modification of the built environment and the redevelopment of redundant sites, more and more cities are attempting to raise their profile in what has become a global competition of image, liveability and culture. To this end, careful manipulation of city image is usually combined with clever marketing campaigns, the injections of public funds and urban redevelopments schemes. The chapter explored two key urban redevelopment and city reimaging approaches that have been adopted by cities around the world in an effort to offset the negative spatial, cultural and economic effects of deindustrialization and global economic change. These approaches were the Americanization or festival marketplace approach and cultural planning which seeks to reproduce the form and feel of European cities by fostering local cultural industry development.

The festival marketplace blueprint for urban redevelopment was pioneered originally in the United States in the 1950s. This approach involves the wholesale transformation of redundant former port/industrial land. Festival marketplaces have a number of key features, such as the use of integrative postmodern architecture. They also support a range of fairly predictable activities, including leisure, special events and shopping. Most also have an aquarium, a convention centre, four- and five-star hotel accommodation, theatres, restaurants and often even a sports stadium. The chapter argued that festival marketplaces have been widely criticized on a number of grounds. In particular, for their sameness (anywhere could be everywhere), the fostering of middle-class consumption and leisure activities, and for being presented as solutions to a range of social and economic problems they have not been able to ameliorate. Festival marketplaces are also criticized for ignoring local cultures and for failing to support the development of local cultural infrastructures. These concerns are at the centre of the other influential approach to city reimaging discussed in the chapter – cultural planning or Europeanization.

The origins of cultural planning lie in an uneasy blending of social democratic principles of access and equity underpinned by an anthropological definition of culture, and a neo-liberalism that endorses, in particular, treating the arts and cultural activities as industries. The result is a hybrid model that fosters using culture (in conjunction with a range of social and economic policies) as a tool for animating the urban landscape, reviving local economies, nurturing community cultural identity, and fostering social equity. Not surprisingly given the scope of these promises and the tensions implicit in its theoretical foundations, cultural planning has rarely achieved such wide-ranging objectives – often being little more than an elaborate arts policy. The chapter also considered the importance of notions of cultural citizenship and participatory democracy to cultural planning discourse, arguing that they merge ideas of public space (often grounded in imagined notions of the *polis* of Ancient Greece) and citizenship in ways that require detailed investigation.

Many of the dominant ideas about city form that are recognized globally and regarded as ideal or as symbols of urban supremacy have developed resonance not through people's actual experiences of these places but through the imagery encountered in marketing campaigns, film and other forms of popular culture. It is this relationship between the real and the imaginary city – the city and its representation in cultural texts – that is investigated in the next chapter.

Further reading

Boyer, M. (1992) Cities for sale: merchandising history at South Street Seaport, in M. Sorkin (ed.) *Variations on a Theme Park: The New American City and the End of Public Space*. New York: Hill and Wong.

Mulgan, G. and Worpole, K. (1986) *Saturday Night or Sunday Morning? From Arts to Industry: New Forms of Cultural Policy*. London: Comedia.

Sassen, S. (1993) *The Global City*. Princeton, NJ: Princeton University Press.

7
IMAGINING THE CITY: MOVIES, MAPS AND CYBERSPACE

> And I can't believe it's changed. Driving in from the airport yesterday in the taxi, past the flat neat factories and warehouses that were once flat neat farms, mile after mile of caution and utilitarianism, and then through the centre of the city with the glitz and the European-style awnings and the paving stones, I could see it's still the same. Underneath the flourish and the ostentations is the old city, street after street of thick brick red houses, with their front porch pillars like the off-white stems of toadstools and their watchful, calculating windows. Malicious, grudging, vindictive, implacable. In my dreams of this city I am always lost.
>
> (Margaret Atwood, *Cat's Eyes*, 1999: 14)

Introduction: inner cities

Cities are understood and experienced in a range of contradictory yet reinforcing ways. Fundamental is the interplay between the 'real' city of lived personal experience and the 'imaginary' city of representation and fantasy. One is a tangible city of surfaces – of footpaths, buildings and roadways. The other is the place of literature, popular culture, anecdote and memory. While the real city appears to be soundly located and constructed within personal biography and the physical world, the imaginary city somehow seems to defy time, space and identity – the London of Virginia Woolf can exist alongside that of Dickens but 'belong' to neither. Of course, the city of experience is also the city of dreams and nightmares (as the passage from Margaret Atwood so eloquently describes). It is a city of emotions, of friendship, loneliness, fear, avoidance, memory, love and home. The imagined city thus intersects with the real to construct intimate personal relationships with place. In addition, the city encountered and experienced in imagination informs vigorous searches in 'real' space for the tangible built markers that will confirm the imaginary as real, while the physical destruction of the city of memory can be devastating.

Representations of the city can serve as anchors that confirm we are (or have been) here/there/somewhere/anywhere. It is possible to locate oneself in space using the coordinates on a map, we recognize and relate to the buildings and places we have gone to and those we have only ever seen in movies or read about. For artists, poets, novelists and filmmakers the city has been an endless source of fascination and inspiration. For some, exploring the city through art is an aspect of a much bigger political project, while for others it is an expression of their passion for a particular city – an attempt to claim it as theirs, to co-opt it to the service of their story. However, the creative and political intentions underpinning the production of art do not determine its reception, which always occurs within social and personal contexts and in relation to alternative representations of the same and other cities. Such concerns underpin the matters explored in this chapter, which considers themes and issues associated with the representation of the city in cultural texts. The chapter provides an introduction to the significance of such texts in defining the symbolic parameters of what is meant by the term 'urban' and in framing imagined urbanism.

The expressive arts have long been powerful commentators on the city and the quality of therein. As discussed in Chapter 2, this has frequently meant denoting a powerful anti-urbanism often in opposition to a celebration of the rural idyll and the imagined differences between the rural and the urban – *gemeinschaft* and *gesellschaft*. However, this rendering has been more complex than the established rural = good/urban = bad categories. As a considerable number of creative artists, writers and filmmakers in the twentieth century actively celebrated urban life in opposition to a menacing rural. The chapter argues that these themes and contradictions re-emerge also in representations of the suburbs. Throughout the twentieth century, the representation of urban form became increasingly global and immediate. With the development of international circuits of information and communication, most significantly the production and consumption of film and media imagery, it is now possible for selected representations of urban landscapes and urban life to be conveyed routinely to audiences around the globe. For instance, popular culture provides people who have never been to the 'great' cities of the world with strong impressions of their physical and symbolic form – Central Park, skyscrapers and the wastelands created by elevated railways are prominent features of the imagined New York. At the same time the traffic jams and the, seemingly, featureless sprawl of suburban Los Angeles also have salience. Futuristic anti-urban film imagery, such as the Los Angeles of *Blade Runner*, is frequently threatening, decaying and dehumanizing, while Fritz Lang's classic 1920s film *Metropolis* remains a powerful metaphor for a class-divided society. Finally, the chapter investigates the significance of cyberspace and the development of so-called 'cyber communities' and 'virtual cities' as new discourses of urbanism and, indeed, of anti-urbanism. But first to a consideration of the significance of maps and mapping as influential ways of representing the imagined and the real.

Mapping the landscape

Children often play a word game that involves locating themselves and their 'place' within a series of ever-expanding spaces starting with their house, street, suburb and then moving to the relevant city, region, state, nation and so on until they reach the end-point of this hierarchy of imagined space – the universe. More recently, some tourism marketers have sought to represent a similar sense of specific location in infinite space by producing postcards and other souvenirs that depict a particular city or region as an infinitesimal, but disproportionately significant, point in the galaxy. Such exercises rely on a shared understanding of the spaces being imagined and their relationship to each other. Invariably, this commonly held knowledge has been built through exposure to a range of spatial referents including representations such as maps, which traditionally have been regarded as objective renderings of reality. Indeed, the relationship between space and its representation in map-form is widely assumed to be unproblematic. According to Neil Smith and Cindi Katz (1993: 69–70), 'the function of mapping is to produce a scale representation of . . . space, a one-to-one correspondence between representation and represented, such that the outcome – the representation – is considered "accurate" for some specified purpose'. Recently, however, some incisive arguments have emerged from within social science and cultural studies which challenge the orthodoxy of scientific impartiality that underpins the practice of cartography and the popular perception of its products, as well as exposing the political and ideological nature of maps and mapping (see for example Harley 1992; Pickles 1992; King 1996). In spite of seeming innocuous, the drawing of maps is neither an objective nor purely technical process while interpreting or reading them is never benign or solely cognitive. Rather, maps are constructed and read 'in the context of other symbolic, ideological and material concerns' (Pickles 1992: 211). Or as Harley (1992: 232) explains, 'cartography . . . belongs to the terrain of the social world in which it is produced'.

The mapping of physical space has a long history that simultaneously transcends, unites and divides cultures and constructs 'places'. In the west, maps have been used not simply to delineate space but, deliberately or inadvertently, they have played a crucial role in the politics of conquest, domination and imperialism, asserting the authority of powerful interests, including supporting the hegemony of sovereigns, states, economic systems, and religions (Harley 1992). As Smith and Katz (1993: 70) point out, 'mapping involves exploration, selection, definition, generalization and translation of data, it assumes a range of social cum representational powers . . . the power to map can be closely entwined with the power of conquest and social control'. For instance, for most of the twentieth century, Britain and the nations of its Empire/Commonwealth were coloured pink on maps of the world. Clearly, this uniform shading was an expression of the dominance of imperial Britain. And, indeed, it gradually came to be viewed that way by many people growing up in (former) British colonies, such as Australia. Here seeing the nation shaded pink was regarded initially as a sign of collective identity and belonging but, increasingly, came to be seen as representing the nation's subordinate status for which a festering resentment was emerging.

In addition to the mapping of physical space which is undertaken within the largely positivist practice of cartography, there are well-established traditions of mapping within theoretical and applied social science, including urban sociology and human geography. As well as providing valuable insights into the spatial distribution of difference, these practices are also outcomes of academic and social priorities, and thus can have significant political and ideological consequences. As discussed in Chapter 2, the principal concern of the founders of the Chicago School of urban sociology was to map the distribution of particular social phenomena across space. This task included identifying and marking concentrations of ethnic groups and deviant activities in particular urban neighbourhoods or zones. More recently, cultural planners have sought to map the diversity of creative activity across the city as the first step in developing strategies for local cultural development and tourism (Grogan and Mercer 1995; see also Chapter 6).

Not only do maps show/mark the situation of one place in relation to others and serve as a readily decodable means of locating oneself or a set of activities in 'real' space, but also they actually flatten difference and variety – this is particularly so with regard to the city. The difficulty, as de Certeau (1988) points out, is that cities are lived spaces and maps depict 'concept cities' where the lived messiness of urban life is necessarily evacuated (see Chapter 3). In addition, there will inevitably be more than one map/representation of a single city or space. Iain Chambers (1993) describes the complexity of, and contradictions involved in, mapping the urban landscape as follows:

> Yet the very idea of a map, with its implicit dependence upon the survey of a stable terrain, fixed referents and measurement, seems to contradict the palpable flux and fluidity of metropolitan life and cosmopolitan movement. Maps are full of references and indications, but they are not peopled. You often need a map to get around a city, its subway system, its streets. But that preliminary orientation hardly exhausts the reality in which you find yourself. The city plan is both a rationalization of space and time; its streets, buildings, bridges and roads are temporal indices. It permits us to grasp an outline, a shape, some sort of location, but not the contexts, cultures, histories, languages, experiences, desires and hopes that course through the urban body. The latter pierce the logic of topography and spill over the edges of the map.
> (Chambers 1993: 189)

In a similar vein, Rob Shields (1996: 228) suggests that maps and planning documents are actually 'still life portraits' of the city – 'treacherous metaphors' that serve to 'remind' us of cityspace by '*summarizing*' its 'complexity . . . in an elegant model' (emphasis original). In Shields's view, maps have come to be treated as 'natural objects' that exist outside ideology and everyday experience. However, he argues, that in spite of appearing benign once a space has been represented in map-form the representation becomes a potent reification – a construct, which is both treated as reality at the same time as it shapes it. For instance, as I have argued elsewhere (Stevenson 1998, 1999b), architectural elevations and, increasingly, computer-generated and video representations, of 'concept masterplans' for major urban redevelopment schemes are usually presented as benign illustrations of land-use ideas intended to help people visualize a possible future for a specific (often redundant) site. However, these representations insidiously frame the terms of the redevelopment debate and guide a host of building and zoning decisions that may not have occurred in the absence of the imagery. There may be insufficient funds available to build what is being represented and rarely have the requisite planning approvals been sought before the images are produced. Indeed, such approvals are frequently deemed irrelevant as the final shape of the redevelopment is to be determined by 'market forces' and/or 'community consultation'. The point is, however, that once imagined, the representation assumes a reality that is unassailable. It is impossible to disentangle analytically or discursively the site as it is from the way in which it is being represented and its future imagined. And these 'realities' are inseparable from how the site is remembered. In other words, the representation is simultaneously the real and the real is the imaginary, and the negotiation of both is political.

According to Shields, such outcomes confirm the unsustainability and inadequacy of the established analytical distinction between the real and the represented (imagined). Shields calls for the theoretical debate to be broadened and for scholars to explore approaches capable of dealing with this 'coexistence' while also 'guard[ing] a place for the paradox of the street, the irony of contrasting representations and the complexity of everyday life' (Shields 1996: 246). To this end, he considers the usefulness of the work of several theorists who have been influential in cultural studies but who he feels have been 'neglected' within mainstream urban studies, including de Certeau and Benjamin (see Chapter 3). Like Harley (1992) and others, he goes on to suggest that Derrida's theory of deconstruction is particularly useful in providing a method for uncovering what is invisible (including embedded power relations) in language systems and texts, such as maps.

Deconstruction is a method for exposing the assumptions underpinning accepted dualities like the 'real' and the 'imagined', the 'urban' and the 'rural', the 'good' and the 'bad'. For instance, as Shields (1996: 232) points out, the second term of any dualism is invariably devalued/subordinated by the first whether spoken or not. Each term is dependent on the other 'for its distinctness and definition' – the 'real' is implicitly what the 'imagined' is not. Following Derrida, Shields (1996: 233) argues that rather than understanding one word in a conventional dualism in terms of the other, what needs to be asked is 'what operations must be brought to bear to distinguish' one from the other, including 'what technologies, sciences and other professions are brought into existence to accomplish this feat of definition?' This means also locating the contradictions and the tensions embedded in the dualism. I would add that it also means recognizing that like representations, dichotomies, such as the rural and the urban, connect with powerful social values and thus support some interests over others. Harley (1992: 240) argues that when deconstructing or dismantling a map the starting point should be the footnotes and 'inconsequential marginalia', which will provide pointers to the priorities and values that guided the representation and the social, cultural and historical context within which it was drawn. Similarly, when analytical attention is turned to other forms of urban representation, in particular, art and literature, Derrida's theory of deconstruction, along with the semiology of Barthes (see Chapter 3), have proved useful tools for understanding what influential texts say about the society in which they were developed and the place of the city within that society.

The art of the city

Few encounters with the city and the complexity of living in them can be more evocative or confronting than those experienced through literature, film, art and television. In the media and the creative arts we come across many cities – from the city of fear, drudgery and loneliness, to the cities of Utopia (see Chapter 2). We can encounter entire cities (or parts thereof) that we may never have visited, as well as those we believe we know well. We may read passages or see images that evoke flashes of familiarity and affirm our own experiences of place or be introduced to aspects of 'our' city that we were barely aware of, gaining insights into lives and spaces that we had only ever glimpsed before like the backlight figures viewed fleetingly through half-drawn curtains that the poet Kenneth Slessor (1988) observed as he rode the 'last tram' (see p. x). The city of film and of the novel can be incidental to the narrative, or it can inhabit the screen or page like an omnipresence creating an 'atmosphere' that pervades the action. Equally, it can be afforded an even more central role as a pseudo-protagonist – an important pivot for the unfolding plot. Jane Augustine (1991: 73) suggests that until the twentieth century, English language novels largely treated the city as a 'backdrop to realistic dramas'. Since the 1900s, however, she argues that a literary tradition has developed which draws the city as 'quasi-human', a character capable of intervening in, or at least influencing the narrative and the actions of the 'human characters'. She claims that this development was probably an outcome of the massive changes that were occurring in society generally and, specifically, in the nature of urbanism. With reference to the work of twentieth-century novelists, including Theodore Dreiser, Saul Bellow and Alison Lurie, Augustine (1991) argues that there are a number of preconditions for the city to appear as 'quasi-character' in the modern novel, including when the central human character(s) is travelling, confused or encountering the erotic. In addition, the city can be personified in such a way that it seems to guide the actions or in-actions of the 'human characters'.

With regard to film, Helmut Weihsmann (1997: 8) argues: 'Ever since the first film camera reproduced the cityscape, a hundred years ago, there has been a continuing relationship between the cinema and the city.' Initially, this relationship involved film being used to document the form and structure of cities, a process whereby filmmakers walked through the busy urban streets recording images of its spaces and its people. Larry Ford (1994: 120) claims that in the early years of American cinema, cities were largely 'used as random, often unidentified, stages for action' playing no significant part in shaping the plot or effecting the psychological aspects of the drama, and they certainly did not assume a 'character'. Ford remarks that for Charlie Chaplin, Laurel and Hardy and other stars of the silent era, the city was 'just there'. Although as Stern et al. (1987: 79) point out Americans had an 'avid interest in urban life and particularly life as it was lived in New York'. The result was that before long 'the movie industry produced countless films utilizing cities as backdrops for action and often as major narrative elements' (Stern et al. 1987: 79).

In Europe, where film was regarded more as 'art' than as 'entertainment', a somewhat different creative relationship with the city emerged. As Ford (1994: 120) explains, German Expressionists during the 1920s were 'creating urban worlds . . . that where carefully contrived to contribute to a sense of mood and to enhance the emotional valence of films'. He gives the example of Fritz Lang's *Metropolis* where 'the city itself becomes a monster villain contributing directly to the misery of the human characters' (Ford 1994: 120). But there were many other films in this genre besides *Metropolis* (Weihsmann 1997). In the United States (with some notable exceptions, such as the 1930s film *King Kong* and *The Crowd* released in 1927), Ford argues that it was not until the 1940s and the emergence of *film noir* that the cityscape began to play a central role in influencing the narrative or atmosphere of the film. The importance of the city to films of this genre is perhaps not surprising, given that *noir* was greatly influenced by 'German Expressionism, French "poetic realism," and the hard-boiled tradition in American literature' (Selby 1984: 1–2). In the 'best' films in the *noir* tradition the city does not dominate the action nor is it depicted as unpleasant or frightening, but it is a potent presence – a 'setting that gradually contributes to the development of such feelings [as fear]' (Ford 1994: 123). Through the 1950s and 1960s, *noir* gave way to realism, actual streetscapes replaced stage sets, and colour supplanted black and white – as a result, filmic images of the urban became more complex and multifaceted. The city of film could be a place of community and pleasure, as well as of isolation and menace. And danger could haunt the city by day as much as by night. Although Miles (1997: 25) argues that urban images in film and other popular media became increasingly negative throughout the twentieth century, it would be more accurate to see this trend as part of a more complex engagement that developed between the city and its representation in film.

In all genres and national locations, film, literature and the popular media remain influential sources of images and ideas of urbanism and the urban landscape – they are intriguing markers of imagined urban cultures. As argued in previous chapters, representations of the urban have contributed to an understanding (and the experience) of what it means to be modern (and more recently postmodern) since the industrial revolution. Moreover, urban representations disclose much about nations, highlighting some of the dominant cultural myths that frame national identity (Short 1991). For instance, when Kenneth Slessor was writing his poetry (including 'Last Trams' referred to at the beginning of this book) in the first half of the twentieth century, the literature of Australia and the mythological construction of the nation were dominated not by the city but by a romantic ideal of the outback as a rugged landscape peopled by laconic, resourceful stockmen (Willis 1993). In part, Slessor hoped that his poetic explorations of city life would help to undermine the exalted place that 'the bush' had come to occupy in the imagination of this nation of urban dwellers (Semmler 1988). Similarly, Robert Hughes (1997) talks about the centrality of art and photography to the imagining of New York City especially in the early decades of the twentieth century – when this city was 'the prime subject of . . . [any] artist wishing to connect his work to modernity' (1997: 370). He suggests that in doing this some artists sought to poeticize or romanticize their subject matter, to soften its edges in part 'as a defense against the subject', while others confronted it 'head on' and tried to engage with its vastness, contradictions and brutality (Hughes 1997: 373).

According to Short (1991), myths of the city evident in the mainstream art and literature of the United States, Australia and England can be divided (at least in the first instance) into the 'pro-urban', the 'anti-urban' and the 'inner city versus the suburbs'. Short does not deal with the poetry of Slessor in his analysis of Australian myths of urbanism, but if he had I think he would locate his work in the pro-urban tradition, not because he necessarily depicts urbanism as 'good' but because in looking to the city for inspiration Slessor joined a prominent local avant-garde that included the artist Norman Lindsay, in their efforts to 'pilot [Australian] literature and art into the more exciting waters of cosmopolitanism' (Semmler 1988: vii). This was as much a political as it was an aesthetic endeavour. Short suggests that there is an established tradition that connects 'optimistic [political] radicals' with the urban. And the arts frequently have provided potent avenues through which these 'radicals' could express their belief in the liberating potential of the city (Berman 1988). For instance, the streets of nineteenth-century Paris provided considerable inspiration (and freedom) for writers, such as the poet Baudelaire. In the twentieth century, London and New York, as well as Paris have been sources of inspiration for many prominent writers, including Virginia Woolf and James M. Joyce (Kazin 1991; Squier 1991). Berman (1988) argues that writers of the nineteenth century demonstrated a much more nuanced and ambiguous relationship with modernity (including with the city) than did their twentieth-century counterparts. Nineteenth-century writers, he says, were 'simultaneously enthusiasts and enemies of modern life, wrestling inexhaustibly with its ambiguities and contradictions; their self-ironies and inner tensions were a primary source of their creative powers' (Berman 1988: 24).

Berman goes on to argue that twentieth-century writing does not demonstrate the same skill in identifying and grappling with the complexities and uncertainties of either the urban or the rural. Instead, he argues, the city and the country (urbanism and ruralism) are sharply polarized in twentieth-century works – with the city, perhaps, being associated with progress, liberty and the future, and the country with slavery, domesticity and the past. Or the city may be represented negatively as a place of 'swarming masses . . . who have no sensitivity, spirituality or dignity' (Berman 1988: 28), in contrast to life in simpler times and places. At the core of this polarization is a relationship to rationality and technology – a faith in which (indeed, love of) underpins much modern art, architecture and urban design (see Chapter 5), while hatred and suspicion of the same framed the critical work of T.S. Eliot, Marcuse and others (Berman 1988: 28–9). Short (1991: 47–8) suggests that the city in 'anti-urban' literature is frequently depicted as a wilderness – untamed, dangerous and inhabited by wild animals, 'a place of base instincts, ugly motives, subterranean fears and unspoken desires, a place which reveals the savage basis of the urban condition'. He goes on to argue that the portrayal of the city in futuristic films, such as *Escape from New York* (1981), can also be understood as being in this 'city as wilderness' tradition.

The anti-urban approach to the city which Short identifies has often been associated with conservative political and social agendas (Short 1991; Daniels 1992). For instance, Stephen Daniels (1992: 48) suggests that the practitioners of the 'picturesque' tradition of landscape art which dominated the late eighteenth and early nineteenth centuries in Britain 'could scarcely cope with industrialization' or, I would add, rapid urbanization. As a result, their work largely ignored emerging industrial landscapes in favour of those occupied by fine country houses and sweeping gardens – a walk through the galleries of the Tate Britain museum in London confirms this bias. But it is also the case that anti-urban art, literature and photography informed and fostered agendas for urban and social reform in the nineteenth century (see Chapter 2). Daniels asserts that the link between the anti-urban and a conservative politics was, in part, because many felt that the development of industrial capitalism was undermining the economic and political power of merchants. It is in this context that Daniels finds the work of the artist Turner particularly revealing. In contrast to the picturesque, Daniels (1992: 49) argues that Turner's early-nineteenth-century painting of the industrial city of Leeds is a depiction (and to some extent a celebration) of the 'complex implications of local industry – economic, locational, social, moral and political implications' in its own terms rather than in comparison with its rural 'opposite'. He further suggests that in not giving the painting a rural counterpoint, '[w]hat Turner depicts is not a contrast between the "country" and "city" but an integrated, wholly industrialized landscape . . . It is a scene of concerted energy – meteorological, technological and human energy – harnessed to industrial expansion' (Daniels 1992: 42).

The pro-urban and the anti-urban dualism is a useful starting point for categorizing the myths of the urban evident in film, literature and the arts, even though the dichotomy is unable to deal with ambiguities and contradictions, such as those Berman (1988) argues are evident or implicit in nineteenth-century literature. The other category which Short (1991) uses to explain the mythological content of representations of cityspace – the 'city versus suburbia' – is similarly cut through with contradictions. The ambiguity at the core of this dualism lies not so much between the city and the suburbs, but in the nature of suburbia itself. Suburbia is not quite urban but nor is it rural. It is a physical and discursive space located somewhere 'in between' the places of the city and those of the country, set in a seemingly featureless imaginative space beyond the 'real' city but not yet in the country. These issues will be explored with particular reference to discourses and representations of the suburban emanating from the most suburban nation in the world – Australia.

The imaginary suburb

According to Short (1991: 50) a 'major cleavage' that is a feature of most cities and informs the ways in which they are represented and imagined is the contrast between the (inner) city and the suburb. As with the pro-urban/anti-urban dichotomy, this division is also played out in terms of pervasive stereotypes and mythologies of place which, in turn, inform, and are commented on, in a variety of representations. Indeed, the suburbs and the quality of life therein have long occupied positions of ambiguity in both the intellectual and popular imaginations. Situated both mythologically and spatially between the places of the city and those of the country, suburbia is a 'liminal' or transitional zone constituted and reproduced through the contradictory discourses of ruralism and urbanism, and the opposition of the country and the city. In addition, the suburbs comprise a shadowland between work (which is the traditional world of men) and home – that space historically defined and peopled predominantly by women and children (see Chapter 3). In broad terms, dominant creative discourses on suburbia divide between those that support the idea of the suburbs and the quality of life they offer, and those which endorse the view that suburbs are 'non-places' where nothing exciting ever happens and no one interesting, different or creative lives. Suburbia is, simultaneously, 'hell' and 'green heaven' (Healy 1994: xvi). This division roughly follows the anti-urban/pro-urban divide and, intriguingly, draws on many of the same discourses.

As 'non-urban' spaces, the suburbs have tended to be regarded by anti-urbanists as nurturing many of the positive qualities that, traditionally, they have associated with the country. In contrast to what they see as the dangers, immorality and anonymity of the (inner) city, the suburbs have been viewed favourably as spaces for families, secure friendships, community and tranquillity (Stevenson 1999a). The suburb, in effect, is treated discursively as a rural substitute. Drawing, in part, on the utopian imaginings of the garden suburb (see Chapter 2), this view also supports single purpose land-use zoning that is intended to keep residential areas separate from the (less wholesome) activities of the city. However, it has not just been in terms of quality of life that the idea of the suburb has been merged approvingly with that of the country, but also through the mythologizing of the suburban environment. The suburbs have often been positioned as places of space and greenery, pseudo-rural environments where children have room to play and trees to climb. Although widely held, the anti-urban/pro-suburban discourse did not find resonance in the creative arts until relatively recently. As will be explored, artists and writers tended to belong to an urban elite who, if they considered the suburbs at all, almost invariably viewed them negatively (Glass 1994; McAuliffe 1994; Sowden 1994). It has been in popular culture, including films, television programmes and specialist women's magazines like *Home Beautiful*, that perhaps the most positive (and influential) renderings of the suburbs and suburban life are to be found. For instance, Bob Connell (1977) discusses how in the post-war period in Australia women's magazines sold the ideal of the suburban dream specifically to women. He describes the insidiousness of this process with reference to a serial that appeared in *Australian Home Beautiful* in 1946 called 'Joanna plans a home'. The Joanna of the story is a young serviceman's bride and in successive episodes of the serial Joanna (and the reader) is

> weaned away from her traditional tastes to a belief in modern design and new ideas in living . . . the sense that the reader might know her own mind about her environment [is] undercut and models of the formation of taste under the guidance of experts – architects, a wealthy friend with a 'very modern house', and, of course, the magazine itself – [are] substituted.
>
> (Connell 1977: 216)

Endorsed, in particular, is the ideal that a suburban existence in a home of one's own is the most desirable way of life for Australian families. Hollywood motion pictures and television serials of the 1940s and 1950s were also influential in framing a positive image of suburbia. Although mostly focused on life in idealized 'small town USA', the positive ways in which family life, residential homogeneity and place-based communities were portrayed, as well as the images of leafy streetscapes and low-density housing development, meant that these films and television programmes could conceivably have been set in either the suburbs of a major city or in a provincial town. Indeed, there is often a good deal of ambiguity evident in the portrayal of place in such programmes, with the one place variously appearing to be both suburb and small town depending on the requirements of the plot. In tandem with other forms of popular culture, such as magazines, American films and television programmes thus contributed also to establishing the legitimacy of widespread post-war suburban development and the hegemony of the 'suburban dream' in English-speaking countries around the world.

Another medium where positive ideas about the suburb have consistently been expressed has been in newspaper advertisements intended to sell both land (and life) in suburban housing estates on the fringes of the city, and the project homes 'designed' to be built there. Representations featured in such advertisements seek to appeal to potential residents' desire for the lifestyle being offered (Richards 1994). A central aspect of doing this has been repeatedly to evoke ideas of the country and rural life (thus referencing negatively the absent 'other' of the dualism). Such referencing is evident in the use of both words and pictures which promise a quasi-rural lifestyle within easy commuting distance of the metropolitan 'other'. This promising initially is revealed in the names developers give the various subdivisions. For instance, a cursory survey of the names of housing estates being advertised in a single issue of the daily Australian newspaper the *Newcastle Herald* illustrates this point. Names of the estates being advertised include Shamrock Hill, Avalon Forest, The Gardens and Kindlebark Estate. Significantly, all these names conjure notions of a rural that is not Australian. Instead, they draw on established pastoral myths that have their roots in pre-industrial Britain and which traditionally have underpinned the rural–urban dichotomy. When these estate names are considered alongside the images featured in the advertisements, the rural connotations are indisputable. Unlike the place names, however, these images draw primarily on myths of Australian rather than British nature. In particular, they evoke a sense of limitless space that is not an element of the English pastoral myth. Images include established trees, butterflies, homes with sweeping front lawns and driveways, birds, and children walking to school along leafy (and seemingly car-less) roadways. There is no indication that the houses featured are surrounded by other houses, no sense that these estates are part of a city (although mention is made of facilities such as schools, shopping centres, recreational spaces and travelling time 'to the city') and no indication is given that these places are intended to be home to anyone other than nuclear families. These images and place names are reinforced by the use of certain key words which recur; in particular, 'community', 'lifestyle', 'tranquillity', 'peace' and 'family' are common. I also recall an advertisement for a housing estate which ran regularly in this same newspaper several years ago that actually featured a horse and carriage! The words and images of such advertisements articulate with dominant expectations (dreams) of suburban life fostered in other forms of popular culture and, frequently, with dominant political rhetoric (Stevenson 1998).

In contrast to the pro-suburban/anti-urban theme there are the cosmopolitan 'pro-urban' thinkers who relish the creativity and diversity of the city and deride the suburbs (and its residents) as being bland and unimaginative. They find the suburbs lacking in terms of the quality of life found there, the absence of entertainment facilities, and the homogeneousness of the residents. In addition, they object to the environmental destruction caused by unchecked suburban development, the quality and characteristics of the housing stock that has been designed not by architects but by builders, and the physical layout of the estates. In arguing that the suburbs (at least those of the 1950s and 1960s) were aesthetic and intellectual wastelands, architectural critic Robin Boyd (1963, 1968) expressed sentiments that were fairly typical of the views of those architects, planners and artists who were committed to the aesthetic and design principles of modernism (see Chapter 5). Suburban life was also regarded as 'individualistic and selfish' (Wilson 2001: 105). Just as with the division between the pro-urban and the anti-urban, and positive assessments of the suburbs, this negative appraisal of suburbia has also been played out in the creative arts, literature and the popular media in a host of shifting, often contradictory ways (Rowse 1978; Glass 1994; Craven 1995). For instance, the comedian Barry Humphries developed his popular characters Dame Edna Everage and Sandy Stone in the late 1950s as quintessential suburban dwellers. As Healy (1994) says of these characters:

> they are clever, they are savage, they mark a sense of place and time, and the trace the scar tissue of suburban family memory. Everage and Stone embody and provoke both nostalgia and disdain for the suburb and suburban life. In their early incarnations, they were modern. They

drove cars, watched telly and consumed the world in movies. They lived in discreet houses on discreet blocks of land. He worked, she kept house. Yet they were also archaic . . . theirs was an existence of very peculiar passions and desires.

(Healy 1994: xv)

At the same time as being brutal representations of the suburb dweller, Humphries's characters, according to Healy (1994: xvi), also demonstrate the ambivalence that is often at the heart of aesthetic critiques of suburbia 'conceived as a savage commentary on the suburb as a cultural and spiritual desert, Sandy and Edna are also deeply ambivalent . . . like suburbia itself perhaps [they] were always about memories which swung widely between nostalgia and hatred'. This ambivalence coalesced with a suspicion that started to gain currency in the late 1950s and 1960s that beneath its bland exteriors the suburbs harboured the same seething underbelly many suspected was also lurking in country towns. This underbelly of sex, violence and betrayal was graphically revealed in the 1950s' movie and subsequent highly popular television series, *Peyton Place*. Again it is possible to argue that these representations relied on the discursive ambiguity between the suburbs and the country town – a slippage between the imagined rural and the suburban. Just as it was difficult to separate positive representations of life in the small town from those of the suburbs, it was also the case with the negative and the ambiguous. Like *Leave it to Beaver*, *Peyton Place* was as much a comment on suburbia as it was on the country town. Wilson (2001) also argues that the 'discovery' that suburbs had a 'dark side' has contributed to the ambivalence with which they are viewed:

> There is a fascination in the discovery that about 90 per cent of punk bands came from the suburbs. The suburbs are no longer seen as anonymous, boring and conformist. In the new myth, suburban couples take part in wife-swapping parties. Bored suburban housewives become part-time sex workers. The suburb is the haunt of the paedophile, even the mass murderer. Terrorists hide out there.
>
> (Wilson 2001: 111)

In a spirited defence of the suburban way of life, urban historian Hugh Stretton ([1970] 1989: 13) argues that, in highly suburbanized countries like Australia, the suburbs actually 'nourish most of the best as well as the worst of . . . lives, including . . . many of the country's best painters and poets, editors and critics, scientists and other discoverers, politicians, public servants and professionals'. Similarly, the cultural critic Donald Horne (1964: 25) wryly observed that 'since most Australians live in the suburbs of cities this means that intellectuals hate almost the whole community'. Not only that but also the suburbs are where many of its critics (like Humphries) grew up – which undoubtedly contributed to their ambivalent dealings with this world.

As modernism imploded and came to be conceptualized as postmodernism, and calls emerged for the barriers between 'art' and 'popular culture' to be breached, artists began to explore the contradictions of the urban landscape, the fluidity of urban relationships and their connections with personal biographies. Perhaps not surprisingly, the suburbs assumed a place at the centre of this endeavour with there being an outpouring of creative works by people who grew up, or currently live, in the suburbs seeking to explore their suburban experiences and memories through their art. Ian Craven's (1995) explanation of the upsurge in films dealing with suburban life in Australia could, albeit with differing emphases, be applied elsewhere. Craven (1995: 65) argues that in such films, 'centre protagonists explicitly seek to revalue their pasts and settle at least some of the scores of suburban childhoods, engaging suburbia as a site of unresolved trauma which must be confronted and thought through before stability can be found and a capacity for development achieved'.

In both their positive and negative guises, discourses of community and Utopia have always been central to the imagining of suburbia. Suburbia is in essence regarded as a community with propinquity. In the last decades of the twentieth century, however, the ideals of community and Utopia were being mobilized in a very different spatial context. This new urban imagining is being done with regards to the emerging idea and phenomenon of cyberspace and the possibility that this space gives users the opportunity to detach from the 'real' world and actually join the imagined and the represented. These worlds take the form of 'communities' and 'cities' which supposedly exist outside space and time – free from the bounds (and bonds) of place.

Virtual *gemeinschaft*

Cyberspace is as much a set of ideas and imaginings, as it is a mode of communication via personal computers and telephone lines. Although the forerunner to the Internet was first developed in the 1950s in the United States as a Cold War military initiative, it was not for several decades that access to this technology became more generally available (Wertheim 1997), by which time, the idea of cyberspace had already developed considerable mythological force. At least one commentator identifies 1984 as a watershed year in the popularization, or mythologizing, of the notion of cyberspace because this was the year when the first virtual reality system was developed and when William Gibson's highly influential work of 'cyber fiction', *Neuromancer*, was published (Burrows 1997). As Burrows (1997: 237) explains, cyberspace was in many ways a word and an idea before it was a reality. Gibson's fiction not only popularized the idea of a global computer matrix but also gave the matrix its name – cyberspace. Burrows (1997: 238) explains how this fictionalized 'technological vision' then 'fed back into both computer and information systems design and theory' and influenced the development of the global complex of computer networks and interactions that exist as cyberspace today and the ways in which this network is imagined. By the mid-1990s not only were there something like 50 million people worldwide reportedly using the Internet (making it, according to Wertheim (1997: 296), 'the faster growing "territory" in world history'), but, perhaps more importantly, the idea of cyberspace and its language of metaphors and specialist jargon, had soundly entered popular culture in the west.

Cyberspace is frequently positioned as being somehow outside the sphere of the social and the geographical, as being a place of freedom and placelessness, a naive 'utopian vision for postmodern times' (Robins 1995: 135). For Wertheim (1997: 296) this space is analogous with the early Christian idea of 'heaven' in the sense of being 'an idealized realm beyond the chaos and decay of the material world'. Others, such as Greinacher (1997: 290), suggest that cyberspace can offer those disillusioned with the 'real' world, the opportunity to escape into the 'multiple points of view, multiple visions and stories' and identities that are available there. Greinacher (1997) summarizes its appeal and apparent potential as follows:

> Cyberspace can meet the needs of people by providing employment, amusement, services, and forums for public gatherings. Users can attend to business from home terminals; download the daily newspaper or magazines from servers; browse home pages for travel information, home shopping and product information; and teleconference with coworkers and clients rather than meeting face-to-face. Cyberspace also enlarges the possibilities for home entertainment, enabling users to program their own animation sequences whenever and wherever they desire. Sites on the World Wide Web offer images and information, ranging from international politics to local community billboards, from religion to alternative sex, and from corporate-sponsored discussions to the more or less private chat of virtual self-help groups.
> (Greinacher 1997: 289)

In the context of widely varying promises and expectations, cyberspace is frequently regarded as facilitating the development of new forms of community and social engagement, which are touted as being highly democratic and free of the limitations of physical space (Greinacher 1997). Beginning with the title of one of the most influential works in the cyber-utopian tradition, Howard Rheingold's *The Virtual Community*, the language and promise of 'community' permeates cyber rhetoric (Robins 1995; McBeath and Webb 1997). Cyberspace supposedly offers its denizens the opportunity to interact freely with like-minded people anywhere in the world, and to build the types of communities its protagonists believe existed in earlier (pre-urban) times (Robins 1995: 136). In this respect, cyberspace is often presented as being a virtual 'town-square' (Aurigi and Graham 2000). Indeed, William Mitchell goes so far as to predict that not only could cyberspace replace the physical space of the town square, but also it could render obsolete a host of other place-based urban facilities, including libraries, museums, schools and hospitals (Greinacher 1997: 292). In what is a reformulation of the dream of the utopian city (see Chapter 2), many of these so-called virtual communities and imagined meeting places have developed, if not to replace existing urban environments, then closely to resemble some idealized conception of what they should be (or may have been) like.

Interestingly, too, for a 'space' that boasts of its 'placelessness', images, metaphors and the language of place are integral to cyberspace; for instance, 'chats' happen in rooms, people have email addresses, they travel the superhighway, visit websites, surf the net and, of course, dwell and interact in virtual cities. Cyberspace is an exceedingly physical place. It is also very urban. McBeath and Webb (1997) argue that, along with the notion of community, the idea of the city is fundamental to the construction of cyberspace, Aurigi and Graham (2000: 489) talk of there being a 'complex *articulation*' between 'cities, urban life, and the Internet' (original emphasis), while Burrows (1997: 242) claims that the 'world of cyberspace is itself an urban environment'. The urbanization of cyberspace takes a number of forms. For instance, Aurigi and Graham (2000) distinguish between 'grounded' and 'non-grounded' virtual cities. Grounded virtual cities are 'real' cities which have a web presence usually, but not necessarily, in the form of at least one official site. Many of these sites have been developed as part of place-marketing strategies and are a type of electronic travel brochure. They provide detailed maps of 'real space', and information about a range of facilities and services available there, including accommodation, attractions, local history, transportation and entertainment. Through visiting these virtual cities, it is often possible to organize an entire visit to the real city (including booking accommodation, making dinner reservations and acquiring theatre tickets). Similarly, such sites can provide local residents with ways of communicating with each other and their political representatives and of participating in local governance. In addition, they can also be an impetus for local business development. Aurigi and Graham (2000) also point out the map-like qualities of many of these 'grounded virtual cities'.

In contrast to 'grounded virtual cities', 'non-grounded' ones are those that do not refer to a 'real' place at all but which use the metaphors, language and imagery of the city to construct what are, in effect, elaborate chat rooms and marketplaces. In these cybercities you can 'chat' by the pool, meet virtual friends in the plaza, or visit the library, it is also possible for you to shop online, own a pet and find a (virtual) job through the employment office. In many such places you can take a role in the governance of the city by electing officials and participating in making laws (more and more of which mirror those of the 'real world' – and make many of these 'cities' highly regulated). Intriguingly, it is said to be possible for both the casual visitor and the resident to be a 'cyber*flâneur*' and, in the mode of Baudelaire in nineteenth-century Paris, to wander freely through the spaces of the cybercity listening in to other people's conversations, perhaps choosing to participate, maybe opting simply to observe (Greinacher 1997; Aurigi and Graham 2000; Mitchell 2000). Not unlike the Garden City, cybercities supposedly exist parallel to the physical world, containing all that is deemed best about 'real' urban environments but eschewing their 'less desirable' elements (and residents). It is in terms of this debate that the discourses of the virtual city meet those of the idealized community. In contrast to the 'real' city, the cybercity is conceptualized as being more *gemeinschaft* than *gesellschaft* (see Chapter 2). Nevertheless, the conceptual juxtaposition of the urban with community means that the cities of cyberworld are implicitly constructed in terms of the contradictory discourses of the rural and the urban and thus harbour many of the fundamental tensions discussed above and in Chapter 2 (McBeath and Webb 1997). Underpinning much of the rhetoric is a strong theme of anti-urbanism and the desire to escape encounters with difference. Manuel Castells (quoted in Graham and Marvin 2000: 136) speculates on the consequences for urban life of this anti-urbanism, as follows: 'secluded individualistic homes across an endless suburban sprawl turn inward to preserve their own logic and values, closing their doors to the immediate surrounding environment and opening their antennas to the sounds and images of the entire galaxy'.

The suggestion that cyberspace is somehow separate from 'reality', and the utopian escapist rhetoric that frames these claims, are clearly unsustainable. Anthony King (1996: 4) has argued that the distinction between the 'real' city of social and political struggle, the 'symbolic' city, and the psychological is necessarily illusionary – they coexist. Similarly, Robins (1995) rejects as a fanciful illusion the idea that cyberspace is a parallel realm or an autonomous space of freedom and community. Rather, he points out that the denizens of cyberspace are embodied subjects who exist in the 'real' world of social, political and economic structures. As with films, magazines and other forms of urban imaginary, cyberspace and the technology that makes it possible are being created in the context of these structures. Robins (1995: 153) concludes that the cyber-utopian 'ideal' is thus 'banal and unpersuasive' and calls for the debate about cyberspace to focus on the potential of this technology to engage with issues of inequality and the very real problems of contemporary urban society, including the deterioration of the public sphere. Maybe through such an engagement the 'real' city might actually merge with the imagined to create places that are equitable, clean, democratic and safe.

Conclusion: words and pictures

A work such as this cannot deal in any comprehensive way with the complex relationship that exists between the real and the imagined city – between the city of surfaces and politics, and that of film, television and other forms of cultural expression. This chapter has identified a number of key themes evident in the imaging of the city and considers what these representations might reveal about social relations and dominant ideas of the urban. As maps are perhaps the most ancient of all ways of representing space, the chapter begins by exploring the tensions between these apparent objective renderings of space and the 'realities' they attempt to construct. As de Certeau (1988) explains, maps are 'concept cities', representations and orderings of 'real' space but they cannot deal with the lived and the experiential dimensions of city life. In addition, maps are always partial, they are selective representations of spaces, realities and spatial relationships and, thus, foster some interests and worldviews at the expense of others. One geographical space can be mapped in a range of ways, something which is also the case with other urban representations, such as film and literature.

Popular cultural forms have variously represented the city as it is, as it might be, or as it is imagined. For instance, the work of Dickens and other reformers of the period attempted graphically to depict the brutality of life and living conditions in the industrial city, while others have used their art as a way of revealing what is hidden beneath the surface of the urban landscape. In every case, a representation is also about the relationship between the creator and the space – a romantic image of a New York building is as much a celebration of the artist's attachment to that city than an attempt to provide a 'realistic' rendering of its form. Another artist's image of the same building might be a metaphor for the danger and menace that lurks perhaps in the form of the building, or in its shadows, or more obliquely in progress and rationality. Not only are images produced within the context of the artist's sensibility and relationship with space, but also they are products of social and political conditions and contribute to the formation of dominant ideas about cities and urban cultures. One of the major ways in which the relationship between the real and the imagined has been negotiated is through the opposition of the rural and the urban. Embedded in this dichotomy are a series of value judgements and power relationships.

The chapter then explored how these tensions have been played out in representations of the suburb, which although neither 'urban' nor 'rural' are also constructed through the same sets of discursive oppositions. For many artists the suburbs as 'non-urban' are intellectual and cultural wastelands. However, in the popular imagination this residential form connects with powerful ideologies of the family, security, love and home to form an ideal residential environment. These ideological underpinnings are most evident in newspaper and magazine images used to sell suburbia but they also underpin popular representations in film and television where there is often an intriguing slippage between the rural and the suburban. Finally, the realm of cyberspace was discussed as yet another represented space where the discourses of the rural and the urban have resonance. Cyberspace is both virtual city and virtual community – a merging of what is imagined to be the 'best' of both spaces – at its core, though, it is the antithesis of the city, a virtual *gemeinschaft* hiding behind the walls and gates of the imaginary.

Further reading

Robins, K. (1995) Cyberspace and the world we live in, in M. Featherstone and R. Burrows (eds) *Cyberspace, Cyberbodies, Cyberpunk: Cultures of Technological Embodiment.* London: Sage.

Shields, R. (1996) A guide to urban representation and what to do about it: alternative traditions of urban theory, in A. King (ed.) *Re-presenting the City: Ethnicity, Capital and Culture in the Twenty-First Century Metropolis.* London: Macmillan.

Short, J. (1991) *Imagined Country: Society, Culture and Environment.* London and New York: Routledge.

8 CONCLUSION: BEYOND URBANISM?

> According to Derrida we cannot be *Whole*, according to Baudrillard we cannot be *Real*, according to Virilio we cannot be *There*.
> (Koolhaas 2000: 327, original emphases)

The city and its cultures are fundamental to the experiences and imaginings of contemporary society. Indeed, in many respects the urban landscape has become the defining emblem of modernity. The reasons for this profound connection are many and complex, lying in the foundations of the modern city, the factors that prompted its development, and in the centrality of both to the emerging discourses and processes of modernity. The industrial revolution of the eighteenth and nineteenth centuries was a time of exponential change and nowhere was the scope of this change more evident than in the rapid urbanization that transformed predominantly agricultural societies into highly urbanized ones. Industrialism dramatically altered the nature of work as well as the organization of society and space. It was not that the urban form of settlement was new – cities, of course, had existed since the earliest days of civilization. But, as has been suggested in this book, the urban environments wrought by industrialism were fundamentally different from those of earlier times, in particular they were organized according to essentially different principles (Giddens 1990). They, thus, demanded new methods of interpretation and analysis. The modern city was also a place of great contradictions – being simultaneously the site and symbol of progress, creativity, democracy and wealth, as well as of poverty, inequality, exploitation and discontent. Many, including artists, novelists, poets, social reformers and philosophers, have long tried to reveal and make sense of the ambiguities of the urban. Indeed, it was largely in an effort to explain the contradictions of the modern city (and the scope and pace of the industrial changes that had produced it) that sociology emerged as an academic discipline in the nineteenth century.

Principally, sociologists were concerned with the development of industrial capitalism and the consequences, contradictions and experiences of modernity. The result, in the formative years of the discipline at least, was that the modern city, the nature of urbanism and the quality of urban life became the accidental objects of sociological analysis. For some the assumption was that in understanding urban culture the character of modernity and the nature of capitalism would be revealed. Georg Simmel, for instance, was keen to analyse the culture and lived experience of modernity and the money economy and this concern led him to consider life in the modern metropolis. It was in the city, he suggested, that both processes had found their most obvious expression. For others, though, the task was more revolutionary being underpinned, in part, by the notion that in the social conditions of the industrial city lay the seeds of the transformation of society. Friedrich Engels was one who wrote graphic accounts of urban poverty and the wretched living conditions of the poor in the emerging modern city as part of a larger project examining the fundamental inequities that had been created by industrial capitalism. More recently, cultural theorists, such as Raban (1974), Chambers (1986) and Morris (1988, 1992) have also been drawn to examine the city and urban life. In particular, such cultural theorists have sought to understand urban culture as it is lived and experienced, and cities as the sites of difference and resistance rather than as repositories of the negative effects of social, political and economic structures and processes. This task led them to eschew the metanarratives and the overarching concerns of modernity (in particular, the privileging of the effects of capitalism), to consider, instead, the 'micro', the contingent and the personal dimensions of urban culture. This focus did not necessarily mean rejecting notions of politics (although this has sometimes been the case), but concentrated on the ways in which power is negotiated in particular contexts (including the city) and the role of identity, difference and culture in framing these processes. The outcomes of these struggles, it is usually argued within cultural studies, are not predetermined by social structures but are contingent on the nature of the encounter and its discourses.

Although grounded in divergent assumptions about society and modernity, and bringing a range of theoretical and methodological tools to their enquiry, it is possible to identify a common concern for all those who are fascinated by the city and its cultures. Structural and poststructural approaches alike are interested in investigating the nature of the urban condition – variously examining the complex tapestry of the city, its constituent cultures and their underpinning 'logics'. This understanding informed the discussion of *Cities and Urban Cultures*. The book considered a number of significant and, seemingly, contradictory themes in the study of urbanism, including the structuralism of Marxism and early feminism, and the more cultural (sometimes individualistic and voluntaristic) approaches that have been informed variously by the works of Barthes, Benjamin and de Certeau (among others). The task has been to identify and explore the core assumptions underpinning these significant theoretical and methodological approaches and to highlight the strengths of each and what aspects of the urban and urban life they reveal.

A key guiding thread has been the view that the expectation that any one approach alone can supply a complete answer to the questions of urbanism cannot be sustained – mechanical or one-dimensional explanations of phenomena as complex as cities and urban cultures can never be satisfactory. For instance, the structuralism of Marxism can provide penetrating insights into the insidious ways in which capitalism (in all its guises) directs and shapes the urban landscape, but in focusing on the macro, this perspective misses the textured, dynamic nature of culture and life 'on the street'. On the other hand, micro approaches, if they ignore the significance of factors and influences beyond the local and the individual, risk slipping into a conservative and inward-looking relativism. What is patently clear, therefore, is that the most fruitful explanations of urbanism are those that are at least aware of the many contradictory and intersecting levels on which urbanism operates and the various factors which, separately and in combination, shape it. When culturally informed insights into the fabric of everyday urban life are combined with more structural understandings of the big processes that continue to build cities and construct environments of fear, inequality and disadvantage, the result must be a much richer understanding of the contemporary city and urban cultures. The task of a book such as this, therefore, is to provide a number of pathways through this interpretative maze.

In exploring the ways in which some of these theoretical and lived connections are played out 'on the ground', the book has also considered several of the most significant trends in urban development and the building of cities since the nineteenth century, discussing some of the competing and reinforcing ways in which these processes have been imagined and explained. Central here were considerations of the calculated uses being made of local cultures, lifestyles and the arts in city reimaging strategies (Chapter 6), the contributions of modernism and postmodernism to the built environment and the discourses of urbanism (including in architecture and urban design – Chapter 5), and the significant role of the globalization of culture and the economy in influencing many current urban processes. In addition, the book has stressed the part that representations play in framing the dominant ways in which the city is imagined both in popular discourse and in the blueprints of urban planning and design professionals. Words and images appearing in film, literature, art and an array of popular cultural forms are important in informing dominant ideas about what constitutes the city and urban culture, including the imagined form and function of city centres, urban waterfronts and so-called 'global' cities. As suggested in Chapter 6, one result has been the emergence of an international competition of image and place identity which has enmeshed even regional deindustrializing cities in its logic. The 'real' city of physicality and struggle and the 'imagined' city of representations and symbols are thus entwined in the construction of urbanism.

An important theme of the book has been the significance to the imagining of the city of the contrast between the rural and the urban. Within urban studies this contrast has informed the real and the imagined, the lived and the structural. As was explored in Chapter 2, the rural–urban dichotomy is underpinned by an implicit comparison between the modern (city) and the pre-modern (rural) – between what is regarded as the *gesellschaft* of urbanism and the *gemeinschaft* of the rural. This dichotomy has become so entrenched in the popular imagination that it has informed, implicitly and explicitly, all urban thought since the nineteenth century, with any discussion of the urban necessarily pointing to its 'opposite' (the rural) if only as a silence. In particular, there continues to be an inherent assumption underpinning all studies of urbanism that the ways of life associated with the city are fundamentally different from those of the country, and exploring the contours of these differences has been the concern of scholars, planners, artists and architects. There is a tacit acceptance that a particular way of life was lost/destroyed with the development of the modern city. The question that recurs is: was this change for better or for worse?

Traditionally, the rural–urban dichotomy has supported the view that the quality of life in (pre-modern) rural environments and the nature of the personal relationships that flourish there were fundamentally better than those of the city. The supposition is that not only are urban environments unpleasant places to be, but also in the city it is just not possible to experience the depth of friendship and community that is found in the country. This view was held very strongly by the urban sociologists associated with the influential Chicago School, being expressed in the work of Louis Wirth ([1938] 1995), in particular. More 'cultural' approaches to the questions of urbanism, however, have sought to focus on what they regard as the positive aspects of urban life, arguing that diversity and anonymity can free people from the stifling bonds of ruralism. In other words, 'community' is not necessarily 'good', as it often involves close surveillance and social control. Some have suggested that community relationships and close bonds between neighbours can be as much a part of life in the city as in the country (Young and Wilmott [1957] 1962). It is apparent, though, that like all dichotomies, the rural versus the urban cannot withstand sustained examination and that both (as concepts and ways of life) are shot through with contradictions which many commentators and creative artists have attempted to explore. For instance, Marshall Berman (1988) explains that writers and social analysts of the nineteenth century were deeply ambivalent about life in the modern city, seeking to celebrate the urban and its possibilities at the same time as recognizing its limitations. For many, such as the Parisian poet Baudelaire, the streets and arcades of the nineteenth-century city were places of spectacle and stimulation as well as of tragedy.

The comparison with the pastoral remains implicit but the value judgements are rendered problematic. This contradictory view of the rural and the urban was sometimes even evident in the utopianism of early urban reformers, such as Ebenezer Howard and his vision for the ideal city. Although fundamentally a celebration of the rural idyll, Howard's model city sought to retain those elements of urban life he deemed to be positive (in particular, jobs, innovation and creativity). His utopian city, however, was hardly a city at all, stripped as it was of its diversity and spontaneity and located in a (highly regulated) quasi-rural environment of parks and gardens. More recently, the rural–urban dichotomy has assumed new and subtle complexions in a number of contemporary visions of urban utopias. The rural–urban dichotomy implicitly informs a range of urban discourses, including the nostalgic invocations of the pre-modern city that underpin the rhetoric of cultural planning (Chapter 6), the contradictory discourses of suburbia and suburban life apparent in art, literature and popular culture in particular (Chapter 7), and in the many discourses of globalization, especially those which celebrate the 'local' (Chapter 3). Even popular city reimaging blueprints (and the use of such terms as 'new' urbanism and the 'urban village') implicitly reference an imagined (lost but rebuildable) *gemeinschaft*. Arguably, too, the emerging discourses of cyberspace, with their recurring themes of the 'virtual city' and the 'cyber-community', are reworkings of the rural–urban dichotomy (Chapter 7).

The relationship between the city and contemporary culture is indivisible. As Iain Chambers (1986) argues it is in the city that popular culture is both produced and consumed – the city permeates its rhythms and informs its themes. Popular culture is a fundamentally urban phenomenon. The city is also where the cultural industries complex is located. As a result it is impossible to disentangle the influences of the urban landscape, economy, ways of life and aesthetic sensibility from popular forms of cultural expression. This indivisibility means, too, that the discourses of the urban and the rural –

gemeinschaft and *gesellschaft* (and the tensions between them) – are continually being played out in a variety of ways in contemporary cultural texts. These include the ways in which representations of space are coded rural and urban. Consider the city (and its silent 'other', the rural) implicit in television programmes, such as the American *Law and Order* and *ER*. Or the assumptions about both the rural and the urban embedded in *Ballykissangel* (from the UK) and *Northern Exposure* (from the United States). Similarly, the current fashion for television plots that pivot on the theme of escape to the country from the city is of significance also. Popular television series, such as *SeaChange* (Australia), *2000 Acres of Sky* and *Heartbeat* (both from the UK), all play on stereotypical notions of the urban and the rural in their locations, which are peopled by quirky characters and by constructing the city dweller as different. Other television programmes, such as the American *Friends* and *Seinfeld*, and *Coronation Street* and *EastEnders* from the UK are tales of life in the 'urban village'. Here is an urbanism of close friendship networks where *gemeinschaft* is experienced in local hotels, bars, restaurants and shops. In *Sex and the City* (US), 'the city' becomes a place of sexual liberation (for professional women, at least) and a site of unlimited possibilities and unconstrained choices. *The Simpsons* (US) comments on suburban life in an industrial (in fact, nuclear) city, while *Neighbours* (Australia) is a positive rendering of neighbouring and community in suburban 'Ramsay Street'. *Home and Away* (Australia) is an idyllic beachside township where troubled urban teenagers are given refuge and learn a set of 'old-fashioned' rural values.

Chambers (1986) also draws attention to the 'sound(s)' of the city, and both popular and more oppositional music forms (including 'rock', 'punk', 'rap' and 'new wave') are creations of the city and part of the urban soundtrack. Even music that emerges within more rural contexts, such as some folk music traditions, is filtered (by the cultural industries) through the city and its cultures before reaching a wider audience. In fact, it is not uncommon for the names of particular cities to fuse with the idea of a certain 'sound' or form of music – 'grunge' (Seattle), 'Merseybeat' (Liverpool), 'jazz' (New Orleans) – even 'country music' is linked with the city of Nashville. All contemporary music forms are framed in some way in terms of the discursive tensions between the rural and the urban. In the late 1970s the club scene in London and New York was where the rethinking of rock and roll took shape (Rowe 1995). 'Punk' and 'new wave' bands, such as the Sex Pistols and Blondie, emerged from within these urban environments to comment on contemporary urban culture. In the mid-1980s 'rap' music developed on 'the streets' of the city as the oppositional sound of black, working-class (male) struggle and of gang warfare. It is also an expression of New York (east-side) versus Los Angeles (west-side) rivalry, with both cities being constructed through the graphic lyrics of the songs of bands, such as NWA and Tupac (west-side) and Public Enemy and Notorious B.I.G. (east-side).

The concerns of this book, therefore, are central to the contemporary cultural experience. Over and over again the city is imagined and reimagined in cultural texts. Its spaces are important markers of identity and the sites of political and economic struggle. Cities are also where creativity and the cultural industries flourish, and where tradition and conservatism can be undermined. For some, the city, like Babylon, is a place from which to escape either through retreat to the country or behind the walls of fear, for others it is a place to be rehabilitated and rebuilt. Ideal cities are variously imagined in gardens, cyberspace, behind real and virtual walls, and in the oppositional spaces of representation. At their core, many urban imaginings are deeply nostalgic – fundamental rejections of the ambiguities and realities of the city, and of the messiness and unpredictability of urban culture. Frequently, it is a romanticized 'lost' rural existence of tranquility, homogeneity and significant personal relations that is being sought; even the celebration of difference can be predicated on notions of predictability.

The conflicting emotions of apprehension and exhilaration are at the heart of the urban experience. The city, in its various 'real' and 'imagined' forms, therefore, is at once damned, tolerated, manipulated and celebrated. Engaging with these contradictions is the challenge embedded in the question 'beyond urbanism' that forms the title of this chapter. Such a challenge can be met only by considering (but not necessarily resolving) the incongruities of urban difference, inequality and utopianism and by engaging with the complementary and inconsistent insights of a range of urban, social and cultural imaginings. It is only then that we might begin to understand the complexity and fluidity of the city, its cultures and possible futures.

GLOSSARY

Americanization: festival marketplace. A formula for redeveloping derelict waterfront sites which pivots on consumption, entertainment and spectacle. It was devised originally in the United States in the 1950s with the redevelopment of the Boston waterfront but since then has been adopted by cities around the world, including London, Sydney, San Francisco, New York and Barcelona. Americanization is a top-down approach to redevelopment and usually involves some kind of partnership between private developers and government.

Chicago School: a group of researchers associated with the University of Chicago who established urban sociology as a specific subdiscipline of sociology. They were interested in the structure of the urban environment and in identifying the rules governing urban life. Louis Wirth, a member of the Chicago School, was the first to develop a systematic definition of **urbanism**.

City Beautiful: emerged during the nineteenth century with the reconstruction of central Paris. City Beautiful endorses the building of grand boulevards, monumental neo-classical public architecture, parks and ceremonial spaces. The spaces of the City Beautiful are those of the civic or public realm. See also **public realm**.

City cultures: see **urbanism**.

Collective consumption: associated with the Marxist urban sociology of Manuel Castells, who argued that collective consumption, such as education, health service provision, town planning and transport which takes place within cities, is implicated in the reproduction of labour and the capitalist mode of production. See also **political economy**.

Cultural planning: see **Europeanization**.

Europeanization: cultural planning. The key objective of Europeanization is to nurture and promote local cultural activity in the city. This means first identifying what the cultural strengths of the city or region are (for example, in

Seattle, it was grunge, in Sheffield music and film) and then devising strategies to encourage this activity. See also **public realm**.

Festival marketplace: see **Americanization**.

Flâneur: a term popularized by the Marxist cultural critic Walter Benjamin. The *flâneur* was a literary construction of the nineteenth century who, according to Benjamin, passed his time strolling the arcades of Paris unearthing the myths and collective dreams of modernity. *Flânerie* is a way of reading **urban texts**, a methodology for uncovering social meanings embedded in the fabric of the city.

Garden City: an urban reform movement of the late nineteenth and early twentieth centuries associated with Ebenezer Howard. The objective of the Garden City movement was to build cities in the image of the country. In Howard's vision these were to be decentralized urban villages ringed by farmlands and gardens.

Gemeinschaft: community. Ferdinand Tonnies's term for social relationships that are intimate and enduring and exist between homogeneous people with kinship and friendship ties. The term has been used in urban sociology to categorize relationships in rural communities. See also *gesellschaft* and **rural–urban dichotomy**.

Gesellschaft: association. Ferdinand Tonnies used this term to describe social relations that are contractual and secondary. Within urban sociology, this term has been used to describe relationships in large industrial cities. See also *gemeinshaft* and **rural–urban dichotomy**.

Globalization: refers to two forces in particular. First, changes in technology that have compressed distances and made rapid travel and communication around the globe possible. Second, changes in technology and communications that have combined with the development of transnational corporations and the rapid movement of money and capital around the world.

Modernism: an aesthetic or cultural movement associated with modernity and the values of the Enlightenment, in particular a belief in rationality, truth and the control of nature. In architecture and urban design, modernism saw the fusing of the rational and technical to inform the construction of skyscrapers, top-down planning practices and massive slum clearances. See also **postmodernism**.

Political economy: the name by which Marxist urban sociology came to be known in the 1970s. Also called the 'new urban sociology'. Research within this tradition focused initially on collective consumption as being unique to cities and the role they play in fostering class-based inequalities. See also **collective consumption**.

Postmodernism: an aesthetic movement that rejects notions of rationality in favour of eclecticism and an engagement with local vernaculars and histories. Postmodern architecture makes playful use of symbolism and ornamentation while in urban design the emphasis is on community priorities and the specificity of place. See also **modernism**.

Public realm: an area of urban social life comprised of people from different backgrounds. The development of the public realm is often seen as depending on the existence of **public spaces** such as cultural precincts, town squares and public parks. Associated with cultural planning and using city cultures as a way of developing local citizenship. See also **City Beautiful**, **cultural planning** and **Europeanization**.

Public space: traditionally refers to those places (usually in the city centre) that are owned and used collectively by residents. Such places include main streets, public parks and gardens, town squares, cultural precincts, and public buildings such as libraries and civic centres. See also **public realm**.

Rural–urban dichotomy: the implicit and explicit comparison between the city and the country. Most theories of the city are underpinned by the idea of the rural as 'other'. In early urban sociology the rural was regarded as the site of clean environments and positive social relations while the city was seen as dirty and anonymous. Some argued that settlements could be ranked on a continuum with folk societies at one end and complex urban environments at the other. Many contemporary theories of urban cultures, however, see cities as cosmopolitan and exciting and the country as boring and inward looking. See also *gemeinschaft* and *gesellschaft*.

Urbanism: Louis Wirth's basic premise was that urbanism was the way of life of people who live in cities (the result of size, density and heterogeneity). However, it is now generally accepted that there is no single way of life that constitutes 'urbanism', nor are urban cultures the direct result of factors like size and density. Rather, urban life is a range of connecting, intersecting, reinforcing and undermining *urbanisms*. Urbanism is a dynamic process that refers to people's use of and identification with the places of the city. This process occurs within the context of a range of cultural, social and political influences. The terms urbanism and city cultures can be used interchangeably. See also **Chicago School**.

Urbanization: the process of urban expansion that changes the relationship between the proportion of the population living in the country and the proportion living in the city.

Urban text: associated with semiotics. Any aspect of the urban landscape or representation of the urban that can be 'read' or 'deconstructed' to reveal underpinning power relations and cultural values. For instance, an urban text could be a map, a planning document, a building or a streetscape.

REFERENCES

Alonso, W. (1963) Cities and city planners, *Daedalus*, 92: 824–39.
Anderson, N. (1923) *The Hobo*. Chicago: University of Chicago Press.
Appleby, S. (1990) Crawley: a space mythology, *New Formations*, 11: 19–44.
Ashworth, G. and Voogd, H. (1990) *Selling the City: Marketing Approaches in Public Sector Urban Planning*. London: Belhaven.
Atwood, M. (1999) *Cat's Eyes*. London: Virago.
Augustine, J. (1991) Character and poetry in the city, in M. Caws (ed.) *City Images: Perspectives from Literature, Philosophy, and Film*. New York: Gordon and Breach.
Aurigi, A. and Graham, S. (2000) Cyberspace and the city: the 'virtual city' in Europe, in G. Bridge and S. Watson (eds) *A Companion to the City*. Oxford: Blackwell.
Bachelard, G. (1969) *The Poetics of Space*. Boston, MA: Beacon.
Badcock, B. (1984) *Unfairly Structured Cities*. Oxford: Basil Blackwell.
Bagguley, P., Mark-Lawson, J., Shapiro, D. et al. (1990) *Restructuring: Place, Class and Gender*. London: Sage.
Barthes, R. (1968) *Elements of Semiology*. New York: Hill and Wang.
Barthes, R. ([1957] 1972) *Mythologies*. London: Cape.
Barthes, R. ([1970–71] 1986) Semiology and the urban, in M. Gottdiener and A. Lagopoulos (eds) *The City and the Sign: An Introduction to Urban Semiotics*. New York: Columbia University Press.
Bell, C. and Newby, H. (1974) *The Sociology of Community: A Selection of Readings*. London: Frank Cass.
Bell, C. and Newby, H. (1982) *Community Studies*. London: Allen and Unwin.
Bellamy, E. (1888) *Looking Backwards*. New York: Ticknor.
Benjamin, W. (1973) *Charles Baudelaire: A Lyric Poet in the Era of High Capitalism*, translated by H. Zohn. London: New Left Books.

Benjamin, W. ([1928] 1979) *One Way Street and Other Writings*, translated by E. Jephcott and K. Shorter. London: New Left Books.
Benjamin, W. ([1935] 1995) Paris: capital of the nineteenth century, in P. Kasinitz (ed.) *Metropolis: Centre and Symbol of our Times*. London: Macmillan.
Bennett, T. (2001) *Differing Diversities: Cultural Policy and Cultural Diversity*. Strasbourg: Cultural of Europe Publishing.
Berman, M. (1988) *All that is Solid Melts into Air: The Experience of Modernity*. New York: Penguin.
Berry, M. and Huxley, M. (1992) Big build: property, capital, the state and urban change in Australia, *International Journal of Urban and Regional Research*, 16: 35–60.
Bianchini, F. (1991) Cultural policies and planning in west European cities, in EIT Pty Ltd, *The Cultural Planning Conference*. Mornington, Vic.: Engineering Publications.
Bianchini, F. and Bloomfield, J. (1996) Urban cultural policies and the development of citizenship: reflections on contemporary European experience, *Culture and Policy*, 7(1): 85–113.
Bianchini, F. and Schwengel, H. (1991) Re-imagining the city, in J. Corner and S. Harvey (eds) *Enterprise and Heritage: Crosscurrents in National Culture*. London: Routledge.
Bianchini, F., Fisher, M., Montgomery, J. and Worpole, K. (1988) *City Centres City Cultures: The Role of the Arts in the Revitalisation of Town and Cities*. Manchester: Centre for Local Economic Strategies.
Blake, W. (1970) *Jerusalem, Selected Poems, and Prose*, edited with introduction, notes and commentary by Hazard Adams. New York: Holt, Rinehart and Winston.
Blakely, E. and Snyder, M. (1997) Divided we fall: gated and walled communities in the United States, in N. Ellin (ed.) *Architecture of Fear*. New York: Princeton Architectural Press.
Blanchard, J. (1872) *London: A Pilgrimage*. Illustrations by Gustave Doré. London: Grant.
Bondi, L. (1993) Locating identity politics, in M. Keith and S. Pile (eds) *Place and the Politics of Identity*. London: Routledge.
Bondi, L. and Christie, H. (2000) Working out the urban: gender relations and the city, in G. Bridge and S. Watson (eds) *A Companion to the City*. London: Blackwell.
Boyd, R. (1963) *Australian Ugliness*. Melbourne: Penguin.
Boyd, R. (1968) *Australia's Home: Its Origins, Builders and Occupiers*. Ringwood, Vic.: Pelican.
Boyer, M. (1990) The return of aesthetics to city planning, in D. Crow (ed.) *Philosophical Streets*. Washington, DC: Maisonneuve Press.
Boyer, M. (1992) Cities for sale: merchandising history at South Street Seaport, in M. Sorkin (ed.) *Variations on a Theme Park: The New American City and the End of Public Space*. New York: Hill and Wong.

Bridge, G. and Watson, S. (2000) City economies, in G. Bridge and S. Watson (eds) *A Companion to the City*. Oxford: Blackwell.

Bruce, S. (1996) Introduction, in S. Bruce (ed.) *Three Early Modern Utopias*. Oxford: Oxford University Press.

Buck-Morss, S. (1995) *The Dialectics of Seeing: Walter Benjamin and the Arcades Project*. Cambridge, MA and London: MIT Press.

Burrows, R. (1997) Cyberpunk as social theory: William Gibson and the sociological imagination, in S. Westwood and J. Williams (eds) *Imagining Cities: Scripts, Signs, Memory*. London and New York: Routledge.

Carter, P. (1987) *The Road to Botany Bay*. London: Faber and Faber.

Castells, M. (1972) *The Urban Question*. London: Edward Arnold.

Castells, M. (1976a) Is there an urban sociology?, in C. Pickvance (ed.) *Urban Sociology: Critical Essays*. London: Methuen.

Castells, M. (1976b) Theory and ideology in urban sociology, in C. Pickvance (ed.) *Urban Sociology: Critical Essays*. London: Methuen.

Castells, M. (1991) *The Informational City: Information Technology, Economic Restructuring and the Urban–Regional Process*. Oxford: Basil Blackwell.

Chambers, I. (1986) *Popular Culture: The Metropolitan Experience*. London: Methuen.

Chambers, I. (1993) Cities without maps, in J. Bird, B. Curtis, T. Putnam, G. Robertson and L. Tickner (eds) *Mapping the Futures: Local Cultures, Global Change*. London: Routledge.

Church, A. (1988) Urban regeneration in London docklands: a five year policy review, *Environment and Planning C: Government and Policy*, 6: 187–208.

Connell, R. (1977) *Ruling Class, Ruling Culture: Studies of Conflict, Power and Hegemony in Australian Life*. London: Cambridge University Press.

Cooke, P. (ed.) (1989) *Localities: The Changing Face of Urban Britain*. London: Unwin Hyman.

Craven, I. (1995) Cinema, postcolonialism and Australian suburbia, *Australian Studies*, 9: 43–70.

Crook, S., Pakulski, J. and Waters, M. (1992) *Postmodernization: Change in Advance Society*. London: Sage.

Daniels, S. (1992) The implications of industry: Turner and Leeds, in T. Barnes and J. Duncan (eds) *Writing Worlds: Discourse, Text and Metaphor in the Representation of Landscape*. London and New York: Routledge.

Davis, K. ([1965] 2000) The urbanization of the human population, in R. LeGates and F. Stout (eds) *The City Reader*. London and New York: Routledge.

Davis, M. (1990) *City of Quartz: Excavating the Future in Los Angeles*. London: Vintage.

Davison, G. (1983) The city as a natural system: theories of urban society in early nineteenth century Britain, in D. Fraser and A. Sutcliffe (eds) *The Pursuit of Urban History*. London: Edward Arnold.

Davison, G. (1994) The past and the future of the Australian suburb, in L. Johnson (ed.) *Suburban Dreaming: An Interdisciplinary Approach to Australian Cities*. Geelong, Vic.: Deakin University Press.

in M. Gottdiener and A. Lagopoulos (eds) *The City and the Sign: An Introduction to Urban Semiotics*. New York: Columbia University Press.
Gottdiener, M. and Lagopoulos, A. (1986a) Introduction, in M. Gottdiener and A. Lagopoulos (eds) *The City and the Sign: An Introduction to Urban Semiotics*. New York: Columbia University Press.
Gottdiener, M. and Lagopoulos, A. (1986b) Editors' introduction to R. Barthes 'semiology of the urban', in M. Gottdiener and A. Lagopoulos (eds) *The City and the Sign: An Introduction to Urban Semiotics*. New York: Columbia University Press.
Graham, A. (1999) City of Sydney sculpture walk – Martin Place, in D. Malor and H. Johnson (eds) *Proceedings of the Watch this Space Conference*. Newcastle, NSW: Art Associations of NSW and the University of Newcastle.
Graham, J. (1988) Post-modernism and Marxism, *Antipode*, 29: 60–6.
Graham, S. and Marvin, S. (2000) The social and cultural life of the city, in M. Miles, T. Hall and I. Borden (eds) *The City Cultures Reader*. London and New York: Routledge.
Greenhalgh, L. (1998) From arts policy to creative economy, *Media International Australia*, 85(May): 84–95.
Greinacher, U. (1997) Fear and dreaming in the American city: from open space to cyberspace, in N. Ellin (ed.) *Architecture of Fear*. New York: Princeton Architectural Press.
Griffiths, R. (1993) The politics of cultural planning in urban regeneration strategies, *Policy and Politics*, 21(1): 39–46.
Grogan, D. and Mercer, C. with Engwicht, D. (1995) *The Cultural Planning Handbook: An Essential Australian Guide*. Sydney: Allen and Unwin.
Habermas, J. (1991) *The Structural Transformation of the Public Sphere*. Cambridge, MA: MIT Press.
Hague, C. (1990) Scotland: back to the future for planning?, in J. Montgomery and A. Thornley (eds) *Radical Planning Initiatives: New Directions for Urban Planning in the 1990's*. Aldershot: Gower.
Hall, P. (1989) The turbulent eighth decade, *Journal of the American Planning Association*, 55(summer): 277–82.
Hall, P. (1992) *Cities of Tomorrow: An Intellectual History of Urban Planning and Design in the Twentieth Century*. Oxford: Basil Blackwell.
Hall, S. and Jefferson, T. (eds) (1976) *Resistance through Rituals: Youth Subcultures in Post-War Britain*. London: Hutchinson.
Halligan, J. and Paris, C. (1984) The politics of local government, in J. Halligan and C. Paris (eds) *Australian Urban Politics*. Melbourne: Longman Cheshire.
Hanff, H. (1984) *Apple of My Eye*. London: Futura.
Hannigan, J. (1998) *Fantasy City: Pleasure and Profit in the Postmodern Metropolis*. London: Routledge.
Harley, J. (1992) Deconstructing the map, in T. Barnes and J. Duncan (eds) *Writing Worlds: Discourse, Text and Metaphor in the Representation of Landscape*. London and New York: Routledge.

Harloe, M. (ed.) (1977) *Captive Cities*. London: Wiley.
Harloe, M., Pickvance, C. and Urry, J. (eds) (1990) *Place, Policy and Politics: Do Localities Matter?* London: Unwin Hyman.
Harvey, D. (1987) Three myths in search of a reality in urban studies, *Environment and Planning D: Society and Space*, 5: 367–76.
Harvey, D. (1989) *The Condition of Postmodernity: An Enquiry into the Origins of Cultural Change*. Oxford: Basil Blackwell.
Harvey, D. (1991) Afterword, in H. Lefebvre, *The Production of Space*. Oxford: Basil Blackwell.
Harvey, D. (1992) Social justice, postmodernism, and the city, *International Journal of Urban and Regional Research*, 16(4): 588–602.
Harvey, D. (2000) *Spaces of Hope*. Edinburgh: Edinburgh University Press.
Hayden, D. (1980) What would a non-sexist city be like? Speculations on housing, urban design, and human work, *Signs: Journal of Women in Culture and Society*, 5: S170–S188.
Healy, C. (1994) Introduction, in S. Ferber, C. Healy and C. McAuliffe (eds) *Beasts of Suburbia: Reinterpreting Cultures in Australian Suburbs*. Melbourne: Melbourne University Press.
Held, D. (1989) The decline of the nation state, in S. Hall and M. Jacques (eds) *New Times: The Changing Face of Politics in the 1990s*. London: Lawrence and Wishart.
Holcomb, B. (1993) Revisioning place: de- and re-constructing the image of the industrial city, in G. Kearns and C. Philo (eds) *Selling Places: The City as Cultural Capital, Past and Present*. Oxford: Pergamon.
Horne, D. (1964) *The Lucky Country*. Ringwood, Vic.: Penguin.
Howard, E. ([1902] 1965) *Garden Cities of Tomorrow*. London: Faber and Faber.
Hoyle, B. (1988) Development dynamics at the port-city interface, in B. Hoyle, D. Pinder and M. Hussain (eds) *Revitalizing the Waterfront: International Dimensions of Dockland Redevelopment*. London: Belhaven.
Hughes, R. (1997) *American Visions: The Epic History of Art in America*. London: Harvill.
Jacobs, J. (1961) *The Death and Life of Great American Cities*. London: Jonathan Cape.
Jacobs, J. and Fincher, R. (1998) Introduction, in R. Fincher and J. Jacobs (eds) *Cities of Difference*. New York: Guilford.
Jameson, F. (1991) *Postmodernism, or, the Cultural Logic of Late Capitalism*. London: Verso.
Jencks, C. (1984) *The Language of Post-Modern Architecture*. London: Academy Editions.
Jencks, C. (1996) *What was Post-Modernism?* London: Academy Editions.
Jopson, D. (2002) The savvy sliver of Sydney that puts it among the world's heavyweights . . ., *Sydney Morning Herald*, 4 March.
Jordan, E. (1999) *The Women's Movement and Women's Employment in Nineteenth Century Britain*. London: Routledge.

Kasinitz, P. (1995) Modernity and the urban ethos: introduction, in P. Kasinitz (ed.) *Metropolis: Centre and Symbol of our Times*. London: Macmillan.

Kazin, A. (1991) The New York writer and his landscape, in M. Caws (ed.) *City Images: Perspectives from Literature, Philosophy, and Film*. New York: Gordon and Breach.

Kearns, G. and Philo, C. (eds) (1993) *Selling Places: The City as Cultural Capital, Past and Present*. Oxford: Pergamon.

Keith, M. (2000) Walter Benjamin, urban studies and the narratives of city life, in G. Bridge and S. Watson (eds) *A Companion to the City*. Oxford: Blackwell.

Keith, M. and Pile, S. (eds) (1993) *Place and the Politics of Identity*. London: Routledge.

King, A. (1990) Architecture, capital and the globalization of culture, in M. Featherstone (ed.) *Global Culture: Nationalism, Globalization and Modernity*. London: Sage.

King, A. (1993) Identity and difference: the internationalization of capital and the globalization of culture, in P. Knox (ed.) *The Restless Urban Landscape*. Englewood Cliffs, NJ: Prentice Hall.

King, A. (1996) Introduction: cities, texts and paradigms, in A. King (ed.) *Re-Presenting the City: Ethnicity, Capital and Culture in the Twenty-First Century Metropolis*. London: Macmillan.

Kirby, A. (1983) On society without space: a critique of Saunders's nonspatial urban sociology, *Environment and Planning D: Society and Space*, 1: 226–34.

Koolhaas, R. (2000) Whatever happened to urbanism?, in M. Miles, T. Hall and I. Borden (eds) *The City Cultures Reader*. London: Routledge.

Landry, C. and Bianchini, F. (1995) *The Creative City*. London: Demos.

Landry, C., Greene, L., Matarasso, F. and Bianchini, F. (1996) *The Art of Regeneration: Urban Renewal through Cultural Activity*. Stroud: Comedia.

Lash, S. (1993) Berlin's second Modernity, in P. Knox (ed.) *The Restless Urban Landscape*. Englewood Cliffs, NJ: Prentice Hall.

Lash, S. and Urry, J. (1994) *Economies of Signs and Space*. London: Sage.

Law, C. (1992) Urban tourism and its contribution to economic regeneration, *Urban Studies*, 29: 599–618.

Law, C. (1994) *Urban Tourism*. London: Mansell.

Le Corbusier (Charles-Edouard Jeanneret) (1933) *The Radiant City*. London: Faber and Faber.

Le Corbusier (Charles-Edouard Jeanneret) ([1929] 1947) *The City of To-morrow and its Planning*. London: Architectural Press.

Le Corbusier (Charles-Edouard Jeanneret) ([1929] 2000) A contemporary city, in R. LeGates and F. Stout (eds) *The City Reader*. London and New York: Routledge.

Lefebvre, H. ([1974] 1991) *The Production of Space*. Oxford: Basil Blackwell.

Lévi-Strauss, C. (1955) *Triestes Tropiques*. Paris: Plon.

Lyotard, J-F. (1984) *The Postmodern Condition*. Manchester: Manchester University Press.

McAuliffe, C. (1994) Don't fence me in: artists and suburbia in the 1960s, in S.

Ferber, C. Healy and C. McAuliffe (eds) *Beasts of Suburbia: Reinterpreting Cultures in Australian Suburbs*. Melbourne: Melbourne University Press.

McBeath, G. and Webb, S. (1997) Cities, subjectivity and cyberspace, in S. Westwood and J. Williams (eds) *Imagining Cities: Scripts, Signs, Memory*. London and New York: Routledge.

McDowell, L. (1983) Towards an understanding of the gender division of urban space, *Environment and Planning D: Society and Space*, 1: 59–72.

McGuigan, J. (1999) *Modernity and Postmodern Culture*. Buckingham: Open University Press.

McNulty, R. (1988) What are the arts worth?, *Town and Country Planning*, 57: 266–8.

McNulty, R. (1991) Cultural planning: a movement for civic progress, in EIT Pty Ltd, *The Cultural Planning Conference*. Mornington, Vic.: Engineering Publications.

McNulty, R., Penne, R., Jacobson, D. and Partners for Livable Places (1986) *The Return of the Livable City*. Washington, DC: Acropolis.

Madsen, H. (1992) Place-marketing in Liverpool: a review, *International Journal of Urban and Regional Research*, 16: 633–40.

Marcuse, P. (2000) Cities in quarters, in G. Bridges and S. Watson (eds) *Companion to the City*. Oxford: Blackwell.

Markusen, A. (1980) City spatial structure, women's household work, and national urban policy, *Signs: Journal of Women in Culture and Society*, 5: S23–S45.

Marx, K. and Engels, F. ([1848] 1972) *The Communist Manifesto*. Harmondsworth: Penguin.

Massey, D. (1984) *Spatial Division of Labour: Social Structures and the Geography of Production*. London: Macmillan.

Massey, D. (1991) The political place of locality studies, *Environment and Planning A*, 23: 267–81.

Massey, D. (1992) A place called home?, *New Formations*, 17: 3–16.

Matrix (1984) *Making Space: Women and the Man-Made Environment*. London: Pluto.

Mercer, C. (1991a) Brisbane's cultural development strategy: the process, the politics and the product, in EIT Pty Ltd., *The Cultural Planning Conference*. Mornington, Vic.: Engineering Publications.

Mercer, C. (1991b) *Urbs et civitas*: cultural planning as city planning. Paper presented to the Urban Environments seminar series, The Economics of Place and People, Penrith, August.

Mercer, C. (1991c) 'Little supplements of life': cultural policy and the management of urban populations. Paper presented at the Institute for Cultural Policy Studies, Brisbane, March.

Metcalf, A. (1993) Mud and steel, *Labour History*, 64: 1–16.

Metcalf, A. and Bern, J. (1994) Stories of crisis: restructuring Australian industry and rewriting the past, *International Journal of Urban and Regional Research*, 18(4): 658–73.

Miles, M. (1997) *Art, Space and the City: Public Art and Urban Futures*. London and New York: Routledge.
Millett, K. (1970) *Sexual Politics*. New York: Avon.
Mingione, E. (1977) Theoretical elements for a Marxist analysis of urban development, in M. Harloe (ed.) *Captive Cities*. London: Wiley.
Mitchell, J. (1971) *Women's Estate*. Harmondsworth: Penguin.
Mitchell, W. (2000) Soft cities, in M. Miles, T. Hall and I. Borden (eds) *The City Cultures Reader*. London and New York: Routledge.
Monk, J. (1992) Gender in the landscape: expressions of power and meaning, in K. Anderson and F. Gale (eds) *Inventing Places: Studies in Cultural Geography*. Melbourne: Longman.
Montgomery, J. (1990) Counter revolution: out-of-town shopping and the future of town centres, in J. Montgomery and A. Thornley (eds) *Radical Planning Initiatives: New Directions for Urban Planning in the 1990s*. Aldershot: Gower.
Morawski, S. (1994) The hopeless game of *flânerie*, in K. Tester (ed.) *The Flâneur*. London: Routledge.
More, T. ([1516] 1996) Utopia, in. S. Bruce (ed.) *Three Early Modern Utopias*. Oxford: Oxford University Press.
Morgan, G. (1994) Acts of enclosure: crime and defensible space in contemporary cities, in K. Gibson and S. Watson (eds) *Metropolis Now: Planning and the Urban in Contemporary Australia*. Leichhardt: Pluto.
Morris, M. (1988) Things to do with shopping centres, in. S. Sheridan (ed.) *Grafts: Feminist Cultural Criticism*. London: Verso.
Morris, M. (1992) The man in the mirror: David Harvey's 'Condition of Postmodernity', *Theory, Culture and Society*, 9: 253–79.
Morris, M. (1993) Future fear, in J. Bird, B. Curtis, T. Putnam, G. Robertson and L. Tickner (eds) *Mapping the Futures: Local Cultures, Global Change*. London: Routledge.
Mulgan, G. (1989) The changing shape of the city, in S. Hall and M. Jacques (eds) *New Times: The Changing Face of Politics in the 1990s*. London: Lawrence and Wishart.
Mulgan, G. and Worpole, K. (1986) *Saturday Night or Sunday Morning? From Arts to Industry: New Forms of Cultural Policy*. London: Comedia.
Mumford, L. ([1938] 1958) *The Culture of Cities*. New York: Harcourt Brace.
Mumford, L. (1961) *The City in History: Its Origins, its Transformations and its Prospects*. London: Secker and Warburg.
New South Wales Property Services Group (1991) *A Partnership for the Future*. Promotional video.
Pahl, R. (1970) *Patterns of Urban Life*. London: Longman.
Pahl, R. (1975) *Whose City?* Harmondsworth: Penguin.
Pahl, R. (1978) Castells and collective consumption, *Sociology*, 12: 309–15.
Paris, C. (1983) Whatever happened to urban sociology? Critical reflections on social theory and the urban question, *Environment and Planning D: Society and Space*, 1: 217–26.

Park, E. (1936) Human ecology, *American Journal of Sociology*, 42: 1–15.
Park, R. (1952) *Human Conditions: The City and Human Ecology.* New York: Free Press.
Park, R. ([1925] 1967) The city: suggestions for the investigation of human behaviour in the urban environment, in R. Park, E. Burgess and R. McKenzie (eds) *The City.* Chicago: University of Chicago Press.
Park, R., Burgess, E. and McKenzie, R. (eds) ([1925] 1967) *The City.* Chicago: University of Chicago Press.
Patton, P. (1995) Imaginary cities: images of postmodernity, in S. Watson and K. Gibson (eds) *Postmodern Cities and Spaces.* Cambridge, MA and Oxford: Basil Blackwell.
Pickles, J. (1992) Texts, hermeneutics and propaganda maps, in T. Barnes and J. Duncan (eds) *Writing Worlds: Discourse, Text and Metaphor in the Representation of the Landscape.* London: Routledge.
Pickvance, C. (ed.) (1976) *Urban Sociology: Critical Essays.* London: Methuen.
Pickvance, C. (1984) The structuralist critique in urban studies, Urban Affairs Annual Review, *Cities in Transformation*, 26: 31–50.
Raban, J. (1974) *Soft City.* London: Hamish Hamilton.
Ravlich, R. (1988) City limits, *Meanjin*, 27: 468–82.
Redfield, R. (1965) *Little Community and Peasant Society and Culture.* Chicago: University of Chicago Press.
Rex, J. and Moore, R. (1967) *Race, Community and Conflict: A Study of Sparkbrook.* Oxford: Oxford University Press.
Richards, L. (1994) Suburbia: domestic dreaming, in L. Johnson (ed.) *Suburban Dreaming: An Interdisciplinary Approach to Australian Suburbs.* Geelong, Vic.: Deakin University Press.
Robins, K. (1995) Cyberspace and the world we live in, in M. Featherstone and R. Burrows (eds) *Cyberspace, Cyberbodies, Cyberpunk: Cultures of Technological Embodiment.* London: Sage.
Roche, M. (2000) *Mega-Events and Modernity: Olympics and Expos in the Growth of Global Culture.* London: Routledge.
Rodgers, J. (1985) On the degeneration of the public sphere, *Political Studies*, 33: 203–17.
Rowe, D. (1995) *Popular Cultures: Rock Music, Sport and the Politics of Pleasure.* London: Sage.
Rowe, D. (ed.) (1996) *Imaging Newcastle.* Newcastle: The University of Newcastle.
Rowe, D. and Stevenson, D. (1994) 'Provincial Paradise': urban tourism and city imaging outside the metropolis, *Australian and New Zealand Journal of Sociology*, 30(2): 178–94.
Rowse, T. (1978) Heaven and a hills hoist: Australian critics of suburbia, *Meanjin*, 37: 3–13.
Saegert, S. (1980) Masculine cities and feminine suburbs: polarised ideas, contradictory realities, *Signs* 5(3) (supplement): S93–S108.
Sandercock, L. and Forsyth, R. (1992) A gender agenda: new directions for planning theory', *Journal of the American Planning Association*, 58: 49–60.

Sassen, S. (1993) *The Global City*. Princeton, NJ: Princeton University Press.
Sassen, S. (1994) *Cities in a World Economy*. Thousand Oaks, CA: Pine Forge Press.
Sassen, S. (1996) Rebuilding the global city: economy, ethnicity and space, in A. King (ed.) *Re-Presenting the City: Ethnicity, Capital and Culture in the Twenty-First Century Metropolis*. London: Macmillan.
Saunders, P. (1981) *Social Theory and the Urban Question*. London: Hutchinson.
Saunders, P. (1983) Social theory and the urban question: a response to Paris and Kirby, *Environment and Planning D: Society and Space*, 1: 234–41.
Saunders, P. (1985) Space, the city and urban sociology, in D. Gregory and J. Urry (eds) *Social Relations and Spatial Structures*. London: Macmillan.
Savage, M. and Warde, A. (1993) *Urban Sociology, Capitalism and Modernity*. London: Macmillan.
Savage, M., Barlow, J., Duncan, S. and Saunders, P. (1987) 'Locality research': the Sussex programme on economic restructuring, social change and the locality, *Quarterly Journal of Social Affairs*, 3: 27–51.
Selby, S. (1984) *Dark City: The Film Noir*. Chicago and London: St James Press.
Semmler, C. (1988) Introduction, in K. Slessor (ed.) *Kenneth Slessor: Selected Poems*. Sydney and London: Angus and Robertson.
Sennett, R. (1977) *The Fall of the Public Man*. Cambridge: Cambridge University Press.
Sennett, R. (1990) *The Conscience of the Eye*. New York: Alfred A. Knopf.
Shields, R. (1994) Fancy footwork: Walter Benjamin's notes on *flânerie*, in K. Tester (ed.) *The Flâneur*. London: Routledge.
Shields, R. (1996) A guide to urban representation and what to do about it: alternative traditions of urban theory, in A. King (ed.) *Re-presenting the City: Ethnicity, Capital and Culture in the Twenty-First Century Metropolis*. London: Macmillan.
Short, J. (1991) *Imagined Country: Society, Culture and Environment*. London and New York: Routledge.
Signs: Journal of Women in Culture and Society (1980) Women and the American city, *Signs*, 5(3) (supplement).
Simmel, G. ([1903] 1995) The metropolis and mental life, in P. Kasinitz (ed.) *Metropolis: Centre and Symbol of our Times*. London: Macmillan.
Sjoberg, G. (1960) *The Preindustrial City, Past and Present*. New York: Free Press of Glencoe.
Slessor, K. (1988) Last Trams, in *Kenneth Slessor: Selected Poems*. Sydney and London: Angus and Robertson.
Smith, N. and Katz, C. (1993) Grounding metaphor: towards a spatialized politics, in M. Keith and S. Pile (eds) *Place and the Politics of Identity*. London: Routledge.
Sontag, S. (1979) Introduction, in W. Benjamin (ed.) *One Way Street and Other Writings*, translated by E. Jephcott and K. Shorter. London: New Left Books.
Sorkin, M. (1992) See you in Disneyland, in M. Sorkin (ed.) *Variations on a Theme Park: The New American City and the End of Public Space*. New York: Hill and Wong.
Sowden, T. (1994) Streets of discontent: artists and suburbia in the 1950s, in S.

Ferber, C. Healy and C. McAuliffe (eds) *Beasts of Suburbia: Reinterpreting Cultures in Australian Suburbs*. Melbourne: Melbourne University Press.

Spring, I. (1990) *Phantom Village: The Myth of the New Glasgow*. Edinburgh: Polygon.

Squier, S. (1991) Virginia Woolf's London and the feminist revision of modernism, in M. Caws (ed.) *City Images: Perspectives from Literature, Philosophy, and Film*. New York: Gordon and Breach.

Stern, R., Gilmartin, G. and Mellins, T. (assisted by D. Fishman and R. Gastil) (1987) *New York 1930: Architecture and Urbanism between the Two World Wars*. New York: Rizzoli.

Stevenson, D. (1992) Urban re-enchantment and the magic of cultural planning, *Culture and Policy*, 4: 3–18.

Stevenson, D. (1998) *Agendas in Place: Urban and Cultural Planning for Cities and Regions*. Rockhampton, Qld: Institute for Regional Sustainable Development, Central Queensland University Press.

Stevenson, D. (1999a) Community views: women and the politics of neighbourhood in an Australian suburb, *Journal of Sociology*, 35(2): 214–27.

Stevenson, D. (1999b) Reflections of a 'great port city': the case of Newcastle, Australia, *Environment and Planning D: Society and Space*, 17(1): 105–19.

Stevenson, D. (2000) *Art and Organisation: Making Australian Cultural Policy*. Brisbane: University of Queensland Press.

Stevenson, D. (2003) *Planning the 'Creative' City*. New York: Peter Lang.

Stevenson, D. and Paton, G. (2001) Representing decline: the role of the arts in framing discourses of deindustrialisation, *Media International Australia (Culture and Policy)*, 100: 129–47.

Stout, F. (2000) Visions of a new reality: the city and the emergence of modern visual culture, in R. LeGates and F. Stout (eds) *The City Reader*. London and New York: Routledge.

Stretton, H. ([1970] 1989) *Ideas for Australian Cities*. Sydney: Transit Australia Publishing.

Taylor, R. (translation editor) (1980) *Aesthetics and Politics: Debates between Bloch, Luacs, Brecht, Benjamin, Adorno*. London: Verso.

Tester, K. (ed.) (1994) *The Flâneur*. London: Routledge.

Thompson, S. (1994) Suburbs of opportunity: the power of home for migrant women, in K. Gibson and S. Watson (eds) *Metropolis Now: Planning and the Urban in Contemporary Australia*. Leichhardt: Pluto.

Thrasher, F. (1927) *The Gang*. Chicago: University of Chicago Press.

Tonnies, F. ([1887] 1957) *Community and Association*. London: Routledge and Kegan Paul.

Tunbridge, J. (1988) Policy convergence on the waterfront? A comparative assessment of North American revitalisation strategies, in B. Hoyle, D. Pinder and M. Hussain (eds) *Revitalizing the Waterfront: International Dimensions of Dockland Redevelopment*. London: Belhaven.

Tweedale, I. (1988) Waterfront redevelopment, economic restructuring and social impact, in B. Hoyle, D. Pinder and M. Hussain (eds) *Revitalizing the*

Waterfront: International Dimensions of Dockland Redevelopment. London: Belhaven.
Urry, J. (1985) Social relations, space and time, in D. Gregory and J. Urry (eds) *Social Relations and Spatial Structures*. London: Macmillan.
Urry, J. (1989) The end of organised capitalism, in S. Hall and M. Jacques (1989) *New Times: The Changing Face of Politics in the 1990s*. London: Lawrence and Wishart.
Wallerstein, I. (1987) World-systems analysis, in A. Giddens and J. Turner (eds) *Social Theory Today*. Oxford: Polity.
Watson, S. (1988) *Accommodating Inequality*. Sydney: Allen and Unwin.
Watson, S. (1992) Urban a/genders, *Refractory Girl*, 42: 2–3.
Weihsmann, H. (1997) The city in twilight: charting the genre of the 'city film' 1900–1930, in F. Penz and M. Thomas (eds) *Cinema and Architecture: Méliès, Mallet-Stevens, Multimedia*. London: British Film Institute.
Wenner, L. (1996) One more 'ism' for the road: dirt, globalism, and institutional analysis, *Journal of Sport and Social Issues*, 20(3): 235–9.
Wertheim, M. (1997) The pearly gates of cyberspace, in N. Ellin (ed.) *Architecture of Fear*. New York: Princeton Architectural Press.
Wexler, P. (1991) Citizenship in the semiotic society, in B. Turner (ed.) *Theories of Modernity and Postmodernity*. London: Sage.
Wild, R. (1981) *Australian Community Studies and Beyond*. Sydney: Allen and Unwin.
Williams, P. (1983) Introduction: theory and practice in urban studies, in P. Williams (ed.) *Social Processes and the City*. Sydney: Allen and Unwin.
Williams, R. (1973a) *The Country and the City*. London: Chatto and Windus.
Williams, R. (1973b) The city and the world, *Royal Institute of British Archietcts Journal*, August: 426–31.
Willis, A. (1993) *Illusions of Identity: The Art of Nation*. Sydney: Hale and Iremonger.
Willis, P. (1977) *Learning to Labour*. Farnborough: Saxon House.
Wilson, E. (1991) *The Sphinx in the City: Urban Life, the Control of Disorder and Women*. Berkeley, CA: University of California Press.
Wilson, E. (1995) The invisible *flâneur*, in S. Watson and K. Gibson (eds) *Postmodern Cities and Spaces*. Oxford: Basil Blackwell.
Wilson, E. (2001) *The Contradictions of Culture: Cities, Culture, Women*. London: Sage.
Winchester, H. (1992) The construction and deconstruction of women's roles in the urban landscape, in K. Anderson and F. Gale (eds) *Inventing Places: Studies in Cultural Geography*. Melbourne: Longman.
Wirth, L. ([1938] 1995) Urbanism as a way of life, in P. Kasinitz (ed.) *Metropolis: Centre and Symbol of our Times*. London: Macmillan.
Wolff, J. (1985) The invisible *flâneuse*: women and the literature of modernity, *Theory, Culture and Society*, 2(3): 37–46.
Worpole, K. (1991) The age of leisure, in J. Corner and S. Harvey (eds) *Enterprise and Heritage: Crosscurrents of National Culture*. London: Routledge.

Worpole, K. (1992) *Towns for People*. Buckingham: Open University Press.
Young, I. (1990) *Justice and the Politics of Difference*. Princeton, NJ: Princeton University Press.
Young, I. (1995) City life and difference, in P. Kasinitz (ed.) *Metropolis: Centre and Symbol of our Times*. London: Macmillan.
Young, M. and Willmott, P. ([1957] 1962) *Family and Kinship in East London*. Harmondsworth: Penguin.
Zorbaugh, H. (1926) The natural areas of the city, in E. Burgess (ed.) *The Urban Community*. Chicago: University of Chicago Press.
Zorbaugh, H. (1929) *The Gold Coast and the Slum*. Chicago: University of Chicago Press.
Zukin, S. (1980) A decade of the new urban sociology, *Theory and Society*, 9: 575–601.
Zukin, S. (1988) The postmodern debate over urban form, *Theory, Culture and Society*, 5: 431–46.
Zukin, S. (1989) *Loft Living: Culture and Capital in Urban Change*. New Brunswick, NJ: Rutgers University Press.
Zukin, S. (1992) Doing postmodernism: a forum, *Theory and Society*, 21(4): 463–5.
Zukin, S. (1997) *The Culture of Cities*. Oxford: Blackwell.
Zukin, S. (1998) Urban lifestyles: diversity and standardisation in spaces of consumption, *Urban Studies*, 35(5–6): 825–39.

INDEX

advertising, 125
Althusser, Louis, 35
Americanization, 100
architecture, architects, 1, 4, 5, 45, 46,
　　54, 56, 59, 62, 63, 64, 65, 68,
　　69, 73, 74, 75, 76, 77, 78, 79,
　　81, 82–3, 84, 86, 87, 89, 90, 94,
　　100, 101, 102, 103, 117, 122,
　　126
arts, 4, 5, 17, 55, 58, 66, 79, 80, 85,
　　–94, 97, 104, 105, 106, 114, 118,
　　121, 122, 123, 124, 126, 128,
　　134, 136, 138

Baltimore, 101, 102, 106
Barthes, Roland, 55, 58–61, 68, 118,
　　136
Baudelaire, Charles, 63, 75, 79–80,
　　121, 131, 138
Bellamy, Edward, 22
Benjamin, Walter, 26, 55, 62, 63–6, 68,
　　118, 136
Berlin, 80
Berman, Marshall, 43, 75, 79, 80, 138
body, the, 60, 89
　　city as, 16–17
Bonaventure Hotel, 89–90

Bondi, Liz, 40–1
Boston, 101, 103, 106
boulevards, 73, 75, 76, 80
British Labour Party, 107–8
Bronx, the, 81
built environment, 33, 66, 73–4, 75,
　　82–3, 93, 96, 100, 102, 104,
　　105, 136
Burnham, Daniel, 76–7

Canberra, 77, 86
capitalism, 33, 34, 35, 36, 37, 39, 50,
　　51, 62, 63, 64, 67, 88–9, 93, 95,
　　96, 98, 122, 135, 136
cartography, see maps/mapping
Castells, Manuel, 33, 34–5, 36
central business districts (CBDs), 27, 88
Chambers, Iain, 135, 138
Chicago, 77, 82
Chicago School, 20, 26–9, 32, 34, 57,
　　58, 81, 116, 137
citizenship, 107–8
City Beautiful, the, 74–8, 82, 86
city–country comparison, 12, 13, 14,
　　19, 20, 23, 24, 25, 26, 29, 81
　　see urban–rural dichotomy
city cultures, see urban, culture

city–suburbs dichotomy, 123
class, 16, 17–18, 29, 34, 37, 38, 42, 44, 45, 47, 50, 51, 62, 65, 66, 81, 82, 84, 85, 89, 97, 115, 140
collective consumption, 35
community, 13, 20, 21, 26, 29, 42, 43, 47, 48, 74, 81, 85, 86, 90, 94, 107, 120, 124, 125, 126, 128, 130, 131, 132, 137, 139
community studies, 29
consumption, 50, 51, 64, 65, 85, 93, 94, 96, 97, 98, 100, 138
crime, 23, 32, 45, 46, 47
cultural citizenship, 107–10
cultural development, 104
cultural identity, 48, 67
cultural planning, 39, 44, 90, 94, 100, 103, 104–7, 116, 138
cultural studies, 5, 33, 36, 37, 40, 54, 55, 56, 58, 62, 66–7, 115, 118, 135
cultural theory/approach, 5, 33, 42, 49, 51, 54, 55, 81, 135
cyberspace, 109, 128–32, 138

Davis, Kingsley, 13, 14
Davis, Mike, 45–6, 47
De Certeau, Michel, 1, 3, 41–2, 67, 68–70, 80, 88, 116, 118, 136
De Saussure, Ferdinand, 58
deconstruction, 118
democracy, 107, 134
demography, 13, 14–15, 27, 32, 54, 80, 84, 93
department stores, 65
Derrida, Jacques, 55, 118, 134
Deutsche, Rosalyn, 5
deviancy, 28, 45
difference and diversity, 5, 33, 40, 41, 42, 43–4, 47, 48–9, 51, 55, 81, 87, 102, 104, 126, 131, 135, 140
discourse, discourses, 22, 43, 48, 59, 61, 63, 66, 70, 81, 94, 104, 106, 107, 109, 117, 123, 124, 127, 128, 131, 134, 135, 136, 138, 139
Donald, James, 16
Dunleavy, Patrick, 36
Durkheim, Emile, 19, 20

Eco, Umberto, 61
ecological mapping, 28
Eiffel Tower, 3, 60
Empire State building, 2
Engels, Friedrich, 4, 12, 16, 19, 135, 138
epistemology, 49, 50, 57
Epstein, Dora, 39
ethnicity, 27, 32, 44, 47, 62, 107
ethnography, 26–9, 58, 81, 116
Europeanization, 90, 100, 103, 104–7

families, 13, 16, 28, 29, 126
Fascism, 77
feminism, 32–3, 37, 41, 62, 136
Ferriss, Hugh, 4
festival marketplaces, 100–4
film, 1, 114–15, 119–20, 122, 123, 125
Fiske, John, 67
Flâneur, the, 55, 62–5, 66, 79, 80, 131
Flâneuse, 66
Flusty, Steven, 46–7
fortress cities, 46
Foucault, Michel, 42, 55, 79
freeways, 74

Garden City, 22, 23, 76, 84, 86, 131
gated or walled estates, 46
gemeinschaft, 20–1, 22, 23, 81, 110, 114, 128, 131, 137, 138, 139
gender, 32, 36–40, 41, 42, 51, 62, 65–6, 75, 107, 110
gentrification, 47, 82, 97
gesellschaft, 20–1, 114, 131, 137, 139
ghettoization, 109
Giddens, Anthony, 4, 14
Girouard, Mark, 21

Glasgow, 106
global cities, 95–7, 137
globalization, 2, 33, 47, 48–9, 51, 93, 94, 95–7, 98, 102, 136, 138
Graham, Anne, 66
Graham, Julie, 56

Habermas, Jürgen, 109
Hall, Peter, 77, 78, 84
Harloe, Michael, 36
Harvey, David, 21, 36, 47, 50, 51, 56, 58, 87, 88, 99, 101, 102
Haussmann, Georges, 65, 74, 75, 76, 77, 79, 80
Hayden, Delores, 39
heterogeneity, 21, 24, 28, 32, 44, 47, 81
home security, 46
homelessness, 45, 47, 99
homogeneity, 23, 29, 43, 44, 47, 48, 125, 126, 140
housing, 16, 17, 18, 22, 23, 34, 35, 37, 38, 74, 86, 87, 88, 90, 105, 106, 125, 126
Howard, Ebenezer, 22–3, 84, 138
Hughes, Robert, 2, 3, 83, 121
health and hygiene, 18–19 *see also* sanitation

identity, 32, 33, 40, 41, 42, 43, 44, 49, 50, 55, 56, 57, 58, 59, 66, 67–8, 69, 73, 75, 93, 107, 116, 121, 135, 140
ideology, 33, 38, 42, 59, 61, 67, 82, 83, 86, 90, 108, 115, 116, 117
image/imaging, 94, 98, 99, 100, 102, 131, 137
indigenous identity, 48, 49
industrial cities, 96, 99, 100, 132
industrial revolution, 13, 14, 15, 20, 22, 29–30, 120, 134
industrialism, 12, 14, 15, 16–18, 24, 96, 134
industrialization, 4, 12, 13, 15, 63, 103, 122

inequality, 5, 15, 16, 17–18, 32, 34, 36–7, 38, 40, 41, 43, 44, 45, 47, 48, 50, 51, 66, 97, 106, 132, 134, 135, 136, 140

Jacobs, Jane, 81, 82, 85, 86
Jameson, Frederic, 88, 89
Jencks, Charles, 78, 87, 88, 89
Jordan, Furneaux, 82, 83

Kasinitz, Philip, 3
Krier, Leon, 90

labour, 36, 38, 50, 89, 95, 97
Lacan, Jacques, 60
language, 61, 70, 78, 118, 130, 131
Lash, Scott, 50
law and order, 46, 76
Le Corbusier (Charles-Edouard Jeanneret), 78, 82, 83, 84–6, 87
Lefebvre, Henri, 35, 36
leisure and recreation, 17, 38, 45, 100, 101, 108, 129
Lévi-Strauss, Claude, 58
lifestyle, 32, 44, 47, 50, 81, 85, 93, 97, 125, 126, 136
literature, 114, 118, 119, 120, 121–2, 123, 124, 126, 138
living conditions, 17–18
'local', the, 50, 51, 74, 86, 87, 90–1, 136, 138
local identity/culture, 33, 48, 49, 50, 86, 90, 94, 102, 104, 106, 107, 136
locality studies, 49–50, 51, 96
London, 17, 25, 29, 56, 57, 69, 74, 80, 81, 95, 101, 102, 103, 121, 139
Los Angeles, 46, 89, 95, 114–15, 139

Manchester, 16, 96
Manhattan, 1, 3, 4, 84, 97
maps/mapping, 69, 115–18, 130, 131
Marcuse, Peter, 44, 45, 47, 122

marginalization, 28, 29, 32, 33, 38, 45, 48
Marx, Karl, 4, 12, 19, 34, 138
Marxism, 32–3, 35–6, 41, 47, 50, 57, 62, 63, 86, 136
Massey, Doreen, 50, 69
media, 1, 99, 103, 114, 119, 120, 126
Metropolis, 115, 120
metropolises, 2, 16, 23, 24, 25, 26, 57, 64, 79, 80, 135
migration and migrants, 13, 14–15, 42
Mingione, Enzo, 36
modernism, 1, 62, 63, 74, 78, 79, 80, 81, 82–6, 87, 88, 89, 126
modernity, 2, 4, 12, 24, 26, 55, 63, 78–9, 121, 134, 135
modernization, 78, 80
Moore, Robert, 34
More, Thomas, 21, 22, 23, 84
Morris, Meagan, 51, 135
Moses, Robert, 81, 82, 86
Mumford, Lewis, 16, 18, 22, 76
music, 139
myths and mythologies, 58, 59, 60, 68, 69, 98, 102, 121, 123, 124, 125, 127, 128

naming, 70
narrative, 69, 70
neighbourhoods, 17, 23, 27, 28, 29, 37, 38, 42, 47, 58, 59, 65, 69, 73, 74, 81, 82, 96, 116, 139
New Brutalism, 83
New towns movement, 22, *see* Garden City
New York City, 1–2, 3, 47, 70, 74, 78, 80, 81, 83, 95, 101, 114, 120, 121, 122, 139, 140
Newcastle (Australia), 102–3

Olympic Games, 99
other, the and otherness, 43, 44, 49, 69, 125, 139

Pahl, Ray, 34
Paris, 3, 35, 55, 60, 63, 64–6, 74, 75, 76, 77, 79, 80, 85, 121
Park, Robert, 26, 28
pastiche, 73, 74, 90
photography, 17, 58, 66, 121, 122
Pickvance, Chris, 36
place, 50, 54, 65, 78, 87, 89, 91, 96, 98, 102, 116, 123, 125, 128, 129, 130
place-marketing/identity, 98, 100–2, 137
place-names, 70, 125
Plato, 22
policing and security, 39, 45, 46, 67
political economy, 34, 36, 57
political struggle/resistance, 35, 43, 67–8, 86, 121, 131, 135, 140
politics of place, 5
popular culture, 17, 58, 67–8, 70, 114, 124, 126–7, 128, 129, 137, 138
postcolonialism, 40, 74
postmodernism, 49, 55, 56, 57, 58, 61, 74, 86, 87–91, 101, 120, 128, 129
postmodernity, 55–6
poststructuralism, 40, 54, 55, 61, 135
poverty, 16, 17, 45, 49, 76, 82, 97, 134, 135
power, 4, 34, 42–3, 44, 47, 48, 54, 58, 59, 61, 62, 67, 74–5, 76, 77, 88, 116, 118, 122, 134
progress, 4, 122, 134
psychoanalysis, 40, 60
public realm, 75, 107, 110
public space, 37, 39, 65, 66, 110, 132

Raban, Jonathan, 56, 57, 58, 61, 69, 87, 135
race, 27, 32, 44, 47
Radiant City, the, 78, 84, 86
regional cities, 96, 102

INDEX

reimaging campaigns, 98, 100, 101–4, 106, 107, 110, 136
religion, 49, 75
representation, 17, 20, 35, 55, 59, 62, 68–9, 97, 113–33, 137, 139, 140
residential suburbs/environments, 15, 45, 124
Rex, John, 34
roads, 80, 81, 105
Rohe, Mies van der, 83
Rouse, James, 101
rural idyll, 22, 38, 99, 114, 125, 127, 130, 138
ruralism, 20, 21, 122, 123, 137
rural–urban dichotomy, 20–1, 23, 29, 30, 38, 114, 118, 121, 122–3, 124, 125, 126, 131, 137–9
rustbelt zones, 48

San Francisco, 101
sanitation, 16, 17, 18, 76
semiotics/semiology, 55, 58–62, 118
Sennett, Richard, 108, 109, 110
September 11, 1, 4
service economy, 93
shopping, 45, 94, 129, 131
shopping centres/malls, 45, 61, 126
sidewalks, 81, 85
Simmel, Georg, 23–4, 25–6, 41, 57, 63, 135
skyscrapers, 2, 3–4, 73, 78, 79, 82, 83, 84, 85, 114
Slessor, Kenneth, x, 121
slums, 17, 18, 19, 28, 29, 74, 75, 76, 77, 80, 81, 86, 97
social justice, 33, 38, 43, 105
social theory, 40
social welfare, 16
socialism, 35
sociology, 4, 5, 19, 26, 27, 29, 33, 34, 35, 36, 50, 54, 55, 57, 61–2, 97, 116, 134, 135, 137
spectacles and festivals, 93, 99, 100, 101, 138

street, the, 80, 90, 136
streets, 18–19, 22, 24, 45, 68, 75, 76, 80, 81, 85, 119, 120, 125, 138
structuralism, 35, 58, 60, 135–6
subjectivity, 40, 41–2, 55, 56, 89, *see* identity
suburbanization, 17–18, 38, 39, 80
suburbia, 123–8, 138, 139
suburbs, 15, 17, 18, 38, 42, 69, 70, 80, 85, 90, 97, 114, 121, 138
surveillance, 26, 45, 46, 67, 137
Sydney, 66, 99, 101

technological revolution, 96
technology, 4, 15, 97, 122, 123, 128–9, 132
Third World, 14
Tonnies, Ferdinand, 20
tourism, 93, 94, 99, 100, 103, 105, 115, 116
transport, 15, 78, 80, 81, 105

urban
  blight, 81
  culture, 6, 19, 24–5, 26, 28, 41, 50, 54, 63, 65, 66, 73, 74, 75, 79, 81, 93, 94, 107, 110, 120, 135, 136, 139, 140
  decay, 27, 45, 97, 100
  decline, 45, 94–7, 98, 104, 106–7
  democracy, 44, 49
  design, 45, 46, 56, 62, 68, 73, 74–5, 76, 77, 78, 82, 83, 84, 87, 102, 105, 109, 110, 122, 137
  division, 44–7, 97
  fear, 3, 4, 39, 46, 57, 69, 109, 110, 119, 120, 122, 124, 136, 140
  governance, 16, 105, 108, 131
  growth, 13–14
  ideals, 23, 47, 84, 138, 140
  imaginary, 21, 23, 40, 56, 62, 68, 69, 70, 73, 75, 98, 102, 110, 113–33, 140

urban–*cont'd*
  landscape, 5, 15, 32, 33, 36, 37, 55, 60, 61, 62, 63, 64, 74, 79, 80, 84, 90, 93, 97, 101, 106, 117, 128, 134, 136, 138
  managerialism, 34, 36
  planning, 5, 17, 23, 27, 34, 39, 41, 42, 47, 57, 59, 66, 68, 76, 77, 80, 81, 82, 83, 86, 88, 90, 100, 105, 117, 126, 137
  processes, 27, 34, 35
  quartier, 90
  (re)development, 5, 27, 45, 62, 75, 77, 80, 81, 82, 85–6, 88, 90, 98, 99, 100, 101, 102–3, 106, 117, 136
  reform movements, 17, 23, 76, 81
  renewal/rejuvenation, 78, 80, 81, 82, 86, 100, 101, 104, 106, 107
  safety, 39
  space, 27, 35, 37, 38, 39, 40, 41, 43, 44, 45, 46, 47, 56, 57, 60, 63, 64, 66, 68, 69, 73, 75, 77, 79, 80, 89, 93, 94, 96, 97, 98, 108, 109, 110, 117, 119
    as text, 51, 56, 58, 59–61, 63, 68
    in text, 63, 113–33
  studies/research, 4, 5, 6, 26, 27, 33, 34, 35, 36, 37, 38, 39, 47, 49, 50, 51, 54, 55, 56, 57, 61, 62, 66, 79, 118, 137
    theory and methods of, 5, 28–9, 40, 42, 54, 56, 136
  symbolism, 61, 65, 77, 98, 102, 103
  texts, 54–72, *see* urban, space, as text
  /human geography, 5, 50, 62, 116
urbanism, 4, 5, 6, 13, 14–15, 15, 19, 20–1, 22, 23, 29, 33, 40, 56, 69, 80, 81, 85, 87, 94, 100, 101, 107, 109, 110, 120, 121, 122, 123, 135–7, 139, 140
urbanization, 13–14, 15–19, 20, 30, 122, 130, 134
Urry, John, 50, 95
utopias, utopianism, 4, 15, 19–23, 24, 35, 39, 55, 64, 83, 84, 86, 119, 124, 128, 129, 130, 131, 132, 138, 140

Vancouver, 103
Vienna, 74, 77

walking, 19, 24, 67–9, 70
Washington, DC, 76
Watson, Sophie, 38
Weber, Max, 4, 19, 33, 34, 36
Williams, Raymond, 20
Wirth, Louis, 20, 26, 29, 32, 81, 137
Wolff, Janet, 66
work, 38, 47, *see* labour
World Trade Center, 1, 2, 4

Young and Willmott, 81
Young, Iris Marion, 43–4, 109

Zukin, Sharon, 36, 49, 109

Debord, G. (1977) *Society of the Spectacle.* Detroit, MI: Red and Black.
De Certeau, M. (1988) *The Practice of Everyday Life.* Berkeley, CA: University of California Press.
Derrida, J. (1976) *Of Grammatology.* Baltimore, MD: Johns Hopkins University Press.
De Saussure, F. (1960) *Course in General Linguistics.* London: Peter Owen.
Deutsche, R. (1996) *Evictions: Art and Spatial Politics.* Cambridge, MA and London: MIT Press.
Devereux, A. (1925) New York as seen by an Australian, *Literary Digest,* 84 (21 February): 52.
Dickens, C. (1966) *Oliver Twist.* Harmondsworth: Penguin.
Dickens, C. (1978) *Nicholas Nickleby.* Harmondsworth: Penguin.
Dickens, C. (1985) *Hard Times.* Harmondsworth: Penguin.
Donald, J. (1992) Metropolis: the city as text, in R. Bocock and K. Thompson (eds) *Social and Cultural Forms of Modernity.* Cambridge: Polity.
Duncan, J. and Duncan, N. (1992) Ideology and bliss: Roland Barthes and the secret histories of landscape, in T. Barnes and J. Duncan (eds) *Writing Worlds: Discourse, Text and Metaphor in the Representation of Landscape.* London and New York: Routledge.
Dunleavy, P. (1980) *Urban Political Analysis: The Politics of Collective Consumption.* London: Macmillan.
Durkheim, E. ([1893] 1960) *The Division of Labour in Society.* New York: Free Press of Glencoe.
Eco, U. (1976) *A Theory of Semiotics.* Bloomington, IN: Indiana Press.
Ellin, N. (1999) *Postmodern Urbanism.* New York: Princeton Architectural Press.
Engels, F. ([1872] 1942) *The Housing Question.* London: Lawrence and Wishart.
Engels, F. ([1892] 1969) *The Condition of the Working Class in England.* Frogmore, St Albans: Panther.
Environment and Planning A (1989) Spatial divisions of labour in practice, *Environment and Planning A,* 21: 655–700.
Environment and Planning A (1991) New perspectives on the locality debate, *Environment and Planning A,* 23 (special issue).
Epstein, D. (1997) Abject terror: a story of fear, sex, and architecture, in N. Ellin (ed.) *Architecture of Fear.* New York: Princeton Architectural Press.
Evans, G. (2001) *Cultural Planning: An Urban Renaissance.* London: Routledge.
Featherstone, M. (1990) Global culture: an introduction, in M. Featherstone (ed.) *Global Culture: Nationalism, Globalization and Modernity.* London: Sage.
Featherstone, M. (1998) The *flâneur,* the city and virtual public life, *Urban Studies,* 35(5–6): 909–25.
Ferriss, H. (1929) *The Metropolis of Tomorrow.* New York: Columbia University Press.
Ferriss, H. (1953) *Power in Building: An Artist's View of Contemporary Architecture.* New York: Columbia University Press.
Fincher, R. and Jacobs, J. (eds) (1998) *Cities of Difference.* New York: Guilford.
Firestone, S. (1970) *The Dialectic of Sex: The Case for Feminist Revolution.* New York: Bantam.

Fiske, J. (1989a) *Understanding Popular Culture*. London: Unwin Hyman.
Fiske, J. (1989b) *Reading the Popular*. London: Unwin Hyman.
Fiske, J., Hodge, B. and Turner, G. (1988) *Myths of Oz: Reading Australian Popular Culture*. Sydney: Allen and Unwin.
Flusty, S. (1997) Building paranoia, in N. Ellin (ed.) *Architecture of Fear*. New York: Princeton Architectural Press.
Ford, L. (1994) Sunshine and shadow: lighting and colour in the depiction of cities on film, in A. Aitken and L. Zonn (eds) *Place, Power, Situation and Spectacle: A Geography of Film*. Lanham, MD: Rowman and Littlefield.
Foucault, M. (1972) *The Archaeology of Knowledge*. New York: Pantheon.
Foucault, M. (1980) *Power/Knowledge: Selected Interviews and Other Writings 1972–1977*. New York: Pantheon.
Foucault, M. (1986) What is Enlightenment?, in P. Rabinow (ed.) *The Foucault Reader*. Harmondsworth: Penguin.
Frankenberg, R. (1965) *Communities in Britain: Social Life in Town and Country*. Harmondsworth: Penguin.
Frisby, D. (1986) *Fragments of Modernity: Theories of Modernity in the Work of Simmel, Kracauer and Benjamin*. Cambridge, MA: MIT Press.
Frost, L. (1991) *The New Urban Frontier*. Kensington, NSW: University of New South Wales Press.
Furneaux Jordan, R. (1988) *Western Architecture: A Concise History*. London: Thames and Hudson.
Gans, H. (1962a) *The Urban Villagers*. New York: Free Press.
Gans, H. (1962b) Urbanism and suburbanism as ways of life, in M. Rose (ed.) *Human Behaviour and Social Process*. London: Routledge and Kegan Paul.
Ghilardi, L. (2001) Cultural planning and cultural diversity, in *Differing Diversities: Cultural Policy and Cultural Diversity*, research position paper no. 4. Strasbourg: Council of Europe Publishing.
Giddens, A. (1985) Time, space and regionalisation, in D. Gregory and J. Urry (eds) *Social Relations and Spatial Structures*. London: Macmillan.
Giddens, A. (1990) *The Consequences of Modernity*. Cambridge: Polity.
Girouard, M. (1986) *Cities and People: A Social and Architectural History*. New Haven, CT and London: Yale University Press.
Girouard, M. (1990) *The English Town*. New Haven, CT and London: Yale University Press.
Glass, F. (1994) Mythologising spaces: representing the city in Australian literature, in L.C. Johnson (ed.) *Suburban Dreaming: An Interdisciplinary Approach to Australian Cities*. Geelong, Vic.: Deakin University Press.
Goodwin, M. (1993) The city as commodity: the contested spaces of urban development, in G. Kearns and C. Philo (eds) *Selling Places: The City as Cultural Capital, Past and Present*, Oxford: Pergamon.
Gottdiener, M. (1984) Debate on the theory of space: towards an urban praxis. Urban affairs annual review, *Cities in Transformation*, 26: 199–218.
Gottdiener, M. (1986) Recapturing the centre: a semiotic analysis of shopping malls,